SOCIOLOGICAL
SELF-IMAGES

SOCIOLOGICAL SELF-IMAGES

A Collective Portrait

Edited by
IRVING LOUIS HOROWITZ
RUTGERS UNIVERSITY

SAGE PUBLICATIONS / BEVERLY HILLS, CALIFORNIA

For information address:

SAGE PUBLICATIONS, INC.
275 South Beverly Drive
Beverly Hills, California 90212

FIRST PRINTING

Standard Book Number 8039-0057-0 (C)
                     8039-0058-9 (P)

Library of Congress Catalog Card No. 76-92355

Contents

To the undergraduate students of social science

1

INTRODUCTION

IRVING LOUIS HOROWITZ

THIS SET OF PAPERS on sociological self-images has had a considerable impact on me. Little did I know that in requesting a set of answers to a battery of biographical questions, the results would be as close to an informal methodological guidebook as anything currently extant in the social science literature.

To those who scan this introduction prior to reading the papers, my opening remarks may seem flamboyant or exaggerated. In fact, my response to the work of colleagues close to me over the past decade is one that I believe will be shared by many readers.

Perhaps self-reflection is a mark of maturity, or maybe it is a mark of senility—not the decadence of a person but of a science. This is a risk each commentator must run—whether privately or publicly. I choose to think that those who have contributed to this symposium, risking as they do the disapproval of colleagues who prefer to think that personal reflections are better kept out of print, or at least out of the scientific purview of the young, have made a fundamental contribution to the subjective processes by which a science gets done. One is often tempted to assume that the rationality of the final sociological product is a consequence of the rationality of the method for realizing that product. These papers are an emphatic refutation of such mythological notions of sociological effort. But if they point up the frailty of the method, they also celebrate the complexity of the results. For sociology is not only a series of findings, but also a set of styles—often as incompatible and indigestible as the findings.

Given the nature of the contributions, my editing was necessarily (and I am sure from the viewpoint of each author, gratefully) held to an absolute minimum. In this way, the distinctive style, as well as the substantive issues, surface without the usual distillation process called editorial work. It is perhaps appropriate to add in this connection that my own contribution was written and submitted to the *American Behavioral Scientist* (in which a selection of the papers in this volume originally appeared) prior to the receipt of the others. In this way, I guaranteed that I would have no advantage in viewing other papers before the submission of my own. As a matter of fact, this is the first time that any of the contributors will see the essays as a whole.

Each of the contributors was asked to comment on the following questions:

(1) What do you consider to be the most uniquely defining characteristics of your way of doing sociology?

(2) What is your view of the current relationship of sociological theory and social application?

(3) Who are the sociologists whom you are either influenced by or most respect? Are they the same now as in your formative years?

(4) Which of your own writings do you like best and why?

(5) What impact would you say your sociological efforts have had on reshaping the field?

The contributors answered these questions at their own discretion, and at whatever length they felt appropriate.

It is interesting to note how each of the contributors differentially responded to the above questions. Some spent a great deal of time on one question and very little on the other four. Others tried to even out their responses to each of the five questions. Those whose writing was an individual effort tended to spend considerable time discussing the process of creation. Those who wrote with collaborators spent much more time on the socialization process involved in the act of producing a manuscript rather than on the creative processes involved in the writing of it.

[10]

A brief comment is in order concerning how the contributors were selected. Obviously, the first criterion was personal acquaintance with the men involved. This is not the kind of symposium convened for settling an outstanding problem. Indeed, there was no convocation and no financial considerations at all, just a shared belief that biography and sociology are deeply connected. Second, was my wish to seek representation from different types of sociological approaches: neo-dialectical sociology, social naturalism, mathematical model construction, exchange and balance theory, economic and political sociology, sociologies built upon ethnography and others constructed in terms of empirical models. Third, and perhaps the main consideration, is the intrinsic interest these men possess for a sizable body of social scientists—myself very definitely included. This does not mean that each scholar represents the vanguard of his field or even the pinnacle of success. The sociologists included here are of different ages, affiliations, and varied career stages. They nonetheless have in common hard work in the world and even harder self-reflection about such work.

What is so genuinely interesting is the wide consensus that there is in fact a subjective side to methodology, that the simple egalitarianism of the training process cannot in and of itself either describe or define the limits of intellectual endeavor and creation. Thus what becomes clear is the existence of a set of factors rarely talked about and still less frequently examined, having to do with the behavior of unusual people, and it is these parameters, these factors, that begin to close the gap between the information we have about the world and the knowledge we have about the producers of that information.

In this sense I consider the following set of papers a continuation of my longstanding interest in the sociology of knowledge, especially in the sociology of sociology. For what we have is a great deal of information about the impact of macro-institutions and large-scale ideological factors which weigh upon the production of social scientific information. But we have thus far done very little in the area of the intimate factors and the micro-institutions, such as university training, collegial relationships and cohort formations that obviously have a great bearing on the way work gets done. And if these papers cannot possibly present a synthetic view of the connection and interpenetration of intimacies and institutions, then at least they have the merit of posing this relationship as a problem in the sociology of knowledge that requires urgent examination.

The process of the person becoming a sociologist is intimately linked to the sociologist becoming a person. Perhaps this simple, yet elusive, truth is what most characterizes these papers. It is this dialectical outcome which most impresses me about the symposium as a whole. Hopefully, this volume will do at least as much for the reader.

− I. L. H.

Rutgers University
New Brunswick, N.J.

May, 1969

2

A LIFE OF SYNTHESIS

GEORGE CASPAR HOMANS

MY GREAT INTEREST and pleasure in life is bringing order out of chaos. What sort of chaos makes little odds so long as it looks as if order could be brought out of it, so the more obvious the chaos the more apt it is to attract my notice. I see this trait in the long weekends I have spent on my fifty-four acres of land at Medfield, Massachusetts, sometimes called the snake ranch. For years I have tried to organize this abandoned farm, now grown up to blueberry pasture and second-growth trees, on soil thin and full of rocks at best, into what I call a walking woods, clear enough of dead branches and fallen timber so that I can stroll about with pleasure to view the micro-scenery. From time to time the New England hurricanes reduce the snake ranch to chaos again; and indeed in the long run nature is gaining on me, as it must on all of us, but I observe that the compulsion to reduce to some order survives every defeat. I must be getting intermittent reinforcement.

My compulsion is not just to bring order out of chaos. It is to bring order not in detail but in gross, not just to chaotic parts but to some chaotic whole, however the whole be defined. Thus I want to organize all my land, however crudely, though it means I must forego perfection in some single glade.

This effort has been characteristic of my work in sociology from the beginning. *An Introduction to Pareto* (1934), which I wrote with Charles P. Curtis, was an attempt to organize the main ideas of the fairly chaotic *Sociologie Générale* so that the argument would stand out clearly for the benefit of the intelligent reader. This book is still the best exposition of, rather than commentary on, Pareto's sociology in English and, I suspect, in any language.

I am asked to say which sociologists have most influenced me. Pareto is certainly one of them—not that I think his particular apparatus is one that we can build on. He never faced up to the problem of social structure. One would never learn from him that institutions made any difference. And though his treatment of equilibrium is admirable in the abstract, because he really knew what he was talking about, there is great doubt in my mind that a notion of equilibrium can, for the time being, be usefully employed in the explanation of social phenomena. What one gets from Pareto instead are important *aperçus*—the system perishes, the *aperçus* remain—such as his comments on the use of force in human affairs and above all a cast of mind that finds guff at once intolerable and delightful. Many sociologists could still benefit from him—though I fear that some of my colleagues can no more forego guff than I can tobacco. Let me illustrate what we can learn from Pareto. It is said that whenever he was depressed he would open a volume of Hegel at random and never fail to get a laugh. There are many Hegels still among us. The supply is not getting shorter, and so, gloriously, the laughter remains.

The same effort at gross synthesis marked my *English Villagers of the Thirteenth Century* (1941). The work was undertaken partly for reasons that had nothing to do with sociology. I was just another WASP looking for his ancestors. It was also undertaken under the influence of the functional anthropology of the time—not its theoretical program but its empirical one, which called for showing how all the aspects of a society are somehow interrelated. I do not now believe that they *are* interrelated all that closely, certainly not in the sense that a change in any one institution must necessarily produce a change in all the others. But my effort in *English Villagers* was in this direction, an attempt to describe many aspects, so far as they were reconstructible from the records, and to show at least a few relationships.

English Villagers is my favorite among my books. I got very few facts wrong—one point especially about an institution called the "curtesy" of England, the rights of a widower in land held by his wife. But even this mistake, which I corrected in the second edition, produced its own compensation. The mistake was pointed

[14]

out to me in a letter from an English solicitor, Hugh Reynolds. The letter led to a correspondence, and Reynolds became one of my good friends. What I like about the book is all its lovely facts, arranged in reasonable order, and with no nonsense about theory except for the last chapter, which could well be dropped. Not that I am against theory—that is, explanation—but it is easier to get the facts straight than to explain them.

Synthesis, Parasitism, and Approximation

There are two realities that any writer of a work of synthesis must must face. First, unless he is an anthropologist describing a society for the first time, he will have to rely on the work of others on secondary sources. He will not be able to produce wholly new findings. His originality will at best lie in the synthesis itself. That is, he will necessarily be an intellectual parasite, and he had better be ready to tolerate the ambiguity of that role. In *English Villagers* I produced only one generalization wholly new to medieval scholarship, but that one was of some importance. It related different rules of inheritance to different types of field system, that is, to different types of agricultural organization. The relationship has never been adequately explained. I tried to bring out one element in the explanation in a paper of mine on "The Frisians in East Anglia" (1957). It is my favorite among my papers, as *English Villagers* is among my books—all those lovely facts again. But I fear that its charm can only be appreciated by a few specialists— and they are apt to disagree with its conclusions.

The other reality that the writer of a work of synthesis must face derives from his purpose: to give the reader some intellectual control of a whole system. For this purpose it is much more important to state initially, generalizations that are largely true rather than to try from the first to enter all their qualifications in detail. For instance, the open-field areas of England were not all submitted to open-field systems of agriculture. But to emphasize this point at the beginning would distract attention from the fact that, in the main, the open-field areas differed in institutions from the nonopen field, and differed in institutions other than agricultural. If one were attracted too soon by the details, one would be led aside into narrowly technological types of explanation and fail to cope with the big picture. This is just a complicated way of saying that a synthesis must avoid not seeing the woods for the trees.

Face the set of gross generalizations first, before going back to qualify individual findings.. This rule holds even better for theoretical generalizations than it does for merely descriptive ones, such as those put forward in *English Villagers*. If the empirical findings are themselves pretty crude, don't make the general propositions used to explain them less crude. Indeed, don't worry, if the general propositions fail to explain all of the findings. If they can be used to explain some of the more obvious ones they will have done pretty well. Once one has gotten some intellectual control of the whole, one's faith is that one will be better able to understand the problems presented by deviant details and perhaps even to fit them in. Above all, never hesitate to state a generalization for whose truth a prima facie case can be made, just because one suspects it has limitations. Come out with it. Act as if it were universal truth. A proposition unstated is one that cannot be criticized. Since there are always plenty of scholars eager to show one is wrong, give them the opportunity and pleasure of doing so, and incidentally leave them the labor of finding the limitations of one's propositions. Science is supposed to be a collaborative venture. Why do all the work oneself?

The doctrine of the first approximation I got from my mentor, Lawrence J. Henderson, professor of biological chemistry, philosopher of science, and apologist for the work of Pareto. He used to say: "After all, the first approximation to a curve is a straight line." He also freed me from the tyranny of other conventional wisdom in science, such as the doctrine that the only legitimate method must be the experiment employing either physical or statistical controls.

English Villagers was a static study: it investigated the inter-relations of English rural institutions during a limited period of time, the end of the thirteenth century, in abstraction from the changes that were necessarily in progress. But it led me into more dynamic work. In the middle fifties Harvard ran short of historians of medieval England, and the history department asked me to under-take teaching in this field. Since then I have offered a course every other year on the social and economic history of England up to the English colonization in America. I tell my students that the course runs "from the Anglo-Saxon invasions to the founding of Harvard College"—the latter being, of course, the dim, far-off, divine event towards which the whole of English history moved. To prepare for this course I have had to keep up with the literature in the field. In the last fifty years, and without anyone's ever sanctimoniously mouthing the word "theory," enormous prog-ress has been made. I believe that we can really understand in a way we never did before some of the main trends in English history. In the course of this development the distinctions between historical, economic, and sociological "approaches" have largely disappeared. The problem, not the approach, is in control. When they deal with the same problems in English history, men in different disciplines will behave in much the same ways and take the same sorts of factors into account. A good example of the result is Lawrence Stone's book *The Crisis of the Aristocracy, 1558-1641* (1965). I also came to doubt that any general proposi-tions held good of the historical process as such, as distinguished from propositions about the behavior of the men who took part in the process; to doubt, accordingly, that there was any general subject called "social change": there was only a multitude of social changes.

Since this has been my experience, I think it a little silly that we continue to ask students—as we do at least at Harvard—to study those historical sociologists Marx and Weber. Max Weber, we are told (Parsons, 1937), based his great study of the origins of modern capitalism on the question: Why did capitalism develop in northwest Europe rather than in China, India, or ancient Israel, in spite of the fact that the material and technical conditions in these other civilizations were at least as advanced as they were in the West? Weber's answer to the question was that the West differed from the others only in possessing a religion with the qualities of radical Protestantism, and that therefore radical Protestantism must have made the difference. The trouble with this argument is that the other things that Weber assumed were equal were not in fact equal. The West possessed, and the East did not, the long-range sailing ship armed with a broadside battery of relatively cheap iron cannon (see Cipolla, 1965). With such ships the Portuguese—who were not Protestants—could dominate the trade of the Indian Ocean almost as soon as they arrived in India. It was seaborne trade that made the fortunes of the West, and the first great, modern capitalist organizations were the joint-stock, overseas trading companies of England and Holland. The West was also superior to the East by the end of the middle ages in such mechanical arts as the harnessing and transmission of power—gearing, belting, shafting, clockwork, wind- and water-mills—all crucial experiences for the industrial revolution (see White, 1962). We do not know why the West was superior in these skills, but it was not Protestantism that did the trick, since the superiority in ships, guns, and machinery antedates Protestantism. Weber was one of the great historians of his time, but, not surprisingly, we now know a great deal more history than he did. If we really want our students to understand the rise of modern capitalism, we had better send them to the modern research, though it will mean a great deal more work for them than a single reading of *The Protestant Ethic.*

Karl Marx, too, was obviously a great man, and never more so than in his emphasis on material conditions and interests and on the organization of production, an emphasis some of our modern sociologists have succeeded in blacking out. But his point, though crucial, is a pretty general one. Marx is of much less use in accounting for the specifics of any historical process. Take the transition from feudalism to capitalism. All the stuff about contradictions and the dialectic helps us not at all. What, for that matter, *is* feudalism? If it means any regime based on rural landlordism, then any regime in western Europe between the Dark Ages and the eighteenth century was feudal. But we medieval historians know that there was a world of difference between eleventh-century and eighteenth-century France or England. Indeed, feudalism in the strict sense as a military and governmental system was dead by the thirteenth century. If we want to understand the actual social transitions, the last person we should go to is Marx—once we have gotten his overall guidance. We must really do the hard work of studying the modern research.

But it is time for me to leave history. My next main book was *The Human Group* (1950). This again was a work of synthesis, but one of a very different kind from *English Villagers,* and one that made me even more of a parasite, as I contributed no empirical work of my own whatsoever. I was familiar with a number of field studies of fairly small groups, studies that had fascinated me with their wealth of carefully observed detail and the many sides of group life they had examined. My mentor, Lawrence Henderson, had impressed me with the importance of constructing a conceptual scheme: the division of the observables into classes to be designated by specific names, that is, specific concepts. If the data could not be divided into classes, the relations between the classes could, rather obviously, not be established. *The Human Group* was a work of synthesis in attempting to set up a conceptual scheme for the study of social organization as revealed in all these field studies. My choice of classes—interaction, sentiment, and activity— was partly dictated by my reaction against the work of my friends Eliot Chapple and Conrad Arensberg (1940). If their emphasis on interaction rates and the origination of interaction, as the crucial independent variables in social behavior, was exaggerated, as I believe it was, what sorts of things needed to be added?

In considering the relations between the classes of data, I set up a further distinction between the internal system of a group and the external. The latter consists simply of the given conditions, given in the sense that one does not choose to account for them further, within which the relations between members of a group develop and upon which the development sometimes reacts. An obvious example is the geographical layout of a room within which a group works. I now wish I had spoken simply of the given (or boundary) conditions and not of the external system. The latter phrase sounds pompous, and pomposity is one of the besetting sins of theoretical writing in sociology. More important, the given conditions rarely form a system in the sense that they are related to one another.

The Human Group has been by far the most popular of my books. It is readable; it provides exercise but not exhausting exercise for a student's mind, and the material from the original field studies cannot but entertain him. Better still, it will sharpen his own perceptions. The student who will follow the example of the analyses performed in the book will himself be able to carry out a pretty satisfactory analysis of any group he studies on his own hook. Mind you, it will be analysis and nothing more. But analysis is something. I think the book is, in its limited way, really useful, and I am not at all ashamed of it.

Of all the writers in English on scientific subjects the one I most admire, both for style and for tenor of mind, is that fascinating man, Sir Francis Bacon, Baron Verulam, Viscount St. Albans, Lord Chancellor of England. Especially his *Novum Organum* contains, in elegant English, aphorisms that a sociologist will still do well to meditate upon. I know that it is now fashionable to decry Bacon's method of induction, which, as he says, "derives axioms from the senses and particulars, rising by a gradual and unbroken ascent, so that it arrives at the most general axioms last of all" (Aphorism XIX). Today we are more apt to follow another great man, Claude Bernard, and argue that, instead of merely scanning the data, we should start with "a preconceived idea," an hypothesis. But remember that Bernard was talking of the experimenter. In speaking (1927:58) of the observer, he wrote: "One must observe without preconceived ideas; the spirit of the observer ought to be passive; that is to say, to keep silent; he listens to nature and writes under her dictation."

I have always been far more the observer than the experimenter. No doubt one never looks at nature with a wholly vacant mind. For that matter, certain frameworks of thought are built into the very structure of our language. But I am still a Baconian in that I love to idly scan large bodies of half-organized data, such as field reports. Whatever may be going on in my unconscious, my conscious mind feels like a blank. I do not start with hypotheses, yet hypotheses will keep popping out at me, as if by their own energy, not mine. It is a lazy man's, the parasite's, method of doing science. Naturally I now believe that good science is done by some of the damnedest methods.

At any rate, after I had set up the conceptual scheme of *The Human Group*, I began, almost as an afterthought, to write up hypotheses, propositions, about the relations between the variables subsumed under the different concepts, especially propositions that seemed to hold good of more than one of the empirical studies I had examined. In stating the propositions it did not disturb me in the least that they were crude first approximations, nor that I had failed to establish the conditions within which they held good. Bob Merton is apt to say that one should establish these conditions before one states the proposition. In a pig's eye! If one waits to establish all the conditions, one may never get around to stating the proposition, and to have a proposition that sums up even a part of the data is the most precious thing one can have in science. Nor did it disturb me that what I was doing was *"post factum interpretation,"* of which, again, Bob Merton disapproved (1957:93-95). In *post factum* interpretation I was in the company of Newton and Darwin. Oh! The silly doctrines that have been thrown up at me in social science! A work of synthesis must consist largely of *post factum* interpretation, if only because the material must first exist before one can synthesize it.

The final emphasis in *The Human Group* on propositions led me eventually into attempting a different kind of synthesis. Following the publication of that book, I began teaching a course, which I still teach, called "An Introduction to the Study of Small Groups," and later I prepared with Henry Riecken a review of research in this field for *The Handbook of Social Psychology* (1954). In this work I had to review a large number of the findings about social behavior not only from field, but also from experimental and survey research.

My efforts at synthesis in this field were not so much directed at setting up an adequate conceptual scheme, as at reducing the number of really independent findings by showing that many of them followed under particular conditions from still more general propositions. Indeed I now think it is idle to set up a conceptual scheme in advance of the propositions to be stated in terms of the scheme. The generalization of the propositions and the refinement of the concepts must go together. Certainly the new work required modification of the scheme developed in *The Human Group*. If *English Villagers* was a synthesis of data, and *The Human Group* a synthesis through concepts, the new work was an attempt at theoretical synthesis or, as I prefer to call it now, a synthesis through explanation.

The metaphor I had long used for the state of sociology was the hollow frontier. Brazil has had a hollow frontier for centuries. Successive waves of adventurers have swept through the backlands, trying to get rich quick on gold, diamonds, coffee, and rubber, but leaving behind them no area of continuous settlement consolidated for civilization. In the same way in sociology, scholars had exploited a series of new and "exciting" ideas at what was called the "growing" or sometimes the "cutting" edge of the subject. But what was the edge growing *from?* The fact was that the center was hollow. There was no central area of agreed-upon intellectual organization of the massively important but obvious and unexciting findings. In its absence, consolidated growth could hardly be maintained. The usual complaint was that growth was not cumulative. My diagnosis was that the man who would consolidate must at least forego "excitement," at whatever cost to his capacity to titillate his students and colleagues.

Something of the same sort was true of social psychology, which shared with sociology the field of small group research. Even the best texts, such as Roger Brown's (1965), presented a series of topics, not very obviously related to one another in subject matter and certainly not related by a few general principles. Braithwaite (1953:307) described the situation well: "The aesthetic defect of psychological theory as a scientific deductive system is that it has a vast number of separate highest-level hypotheses; up to the present it has succeeded hardly at all in unifying itself by the use of colligating concepts, as physical science did in the seventeenth century."

The impulse to synthesis is indeed an esthetic impulse. If the advanced sciences had been made esthetically satisfying when their multifarious empirical findings could be shown to follow from a few general propositions, the same, I felt sure, could be done for the less advanced science of human behavior. I felt sure as a matter of faith: there is no a priori reason to believe that, if one province of nature can be made to yield to intellectual organization, all can. Should at least the obvious and massive common findings be made to yield, I need not worry greatly about the rest. They would eventually come in like stragglers from a surrendered army: they would have nowhere else to go.

SOCIOLOGICAL AXIOMS AND PSYCHOLOGICAL PROPOSITIONS

I was strengthened in my faith by the growing conviction that I knew what some of the general, unifying propositions of the social sciences were. Though, following Bacon's rule, I arrived at the most general axioms last of all, I did not have to discover them. In some vulgar form they had undoubtedly been known to mankind for millenia. In their modern, experimentally tested form I called them the propositions of behavioral psychology. I myself preferred the way they were formulated by my friend Fred Skinner (1953),

[23]

since he brought in the fewest unnecessary assumptions, but several psychologists had stated, in language different from his, propositions of the same substance.

The fact that they were already known need not prevent my using them. My reputation as a parasite was already well established; I could not fall any lower. In any case they had not been effectively used to explain social phenomena. Fred Skinner himself, though a great psychologist, was not a great social psychologist. One could confidently predict from Skinner's own propositions, when applied to the social condition, that his planned utopian community, Walden Two, would not in fact work out, if it were ever tried, in the way he sincerely believed it was going to work.

True, if one wanted one's book to be popular among social psychologists, it was a mistake to hitch up with Skinner in any way. One reason, it sometimes seemed, why the social psychologists had failed to unify their field was their subconscious feeling that they could do so only by adopting a mechanistic psychology they could not bring themselves emotionally to accept. But a mechanistic philosophy did not bother me. A mechanistic philosophy is simply a deterministic one. I knew that my own behavior was determined in many ways. If the behavior of others was not determined, we could not successfully predict their behavior, as we often could do. By an indefensible but common philosophical principle I assumed that, if human behavior were deterministic in any respect, it was deterministic in all, even if we did not yet know and probably would never know all the details. I could not see that this belief made the slightest emotional or practical difference to me as a man, though no doubt in the eyes of some others it made me a coarse bastard. Nor did it make any difference to me as a scientist—but then a scientist is necessarily a determinist.

The results of my efforts at showing that many of the findings of the more social parts of social psychology follow from the propositions of behavioral psychology appeared first in my paper, "Social Behavior as Exchange" (1958), and then in my third main book, *Social Behavior: Its Elementary Forms* (1961). As before, I

[24]

did not worry greatly about qualifications. Unconsciously, I adopted the strategy Braithwaite recommended for the use of tendency statements in explanatory systems. A tendency statement is one that holds good within unspecified or unknown conditions. Most of the propositions of the social sciences are tendency statements. Braithwaite's (1953:365-66) recommendation is: "What is frequently profitable is to put forward a quasi-deductive system of tendency statements all subject to the same, though unknown, condition. Observations which are prima facie contrary to the lowest-level tendency statements in such a system can then be used to give information about the unknown condition to which the whole system is subject." Let me put the advice in a cruder form: if one does not even try to show that empirical findings follow logically from a few more general ones, one can never discover why the system has gone wrong, as it is almost bound to do in some degree. But if one does, maybe with luck one can. More crudely still: no action, no feedback.

Though *Social Behavior* goes farther than other social psychologies in attempting to unify its field by tying phenomena down to basic principles, I am still not satisfied with it. What worries me is not that there are phenomena we can explain only rather sketchily through behavioral principles. As I have said, I believe without justification that, if we can explain any social phenomena in this way, we shall eventually be able to explain them all. What worries me rather is the sheer exposition. The main points get into the book somewhere, but in putting forward a controversial thesis, the utmost in clarity is needed, and certain topics, notably such important ones as status and power, I handled rather clumsily. If I live long enough, I shall get out an improved second edition. In the meantime, my chapter on "Elementary Social Processes" (1967a) in *Sociology,* edited by Neil Smelser, is an improvement, brief as it is.

There is another kind of synthesis, which is still to be performed, but which I shall never undertake. In *Social Behavior* I undertook to explain the character of some of the basic social

[25]

processes. It is much more difficult to explain how these processes combine, under different boundary conditions, to produce the detailed structures of particular human groups and their changes over time—especially when, as I suspect, small differences in the conditions may produce disproportionately large differences in the structures or their development. To do this job will require men far better trained in mathematics and computer technology than I am or ever shall be. But I have great faith in the generation of sociologists next below my own, men like Ted Blalock, Jim Coleman, Jim Davis, Bob Hamblin, Arthur Stinchcombe, Harrison White, and Hans Zetterberg, men who are inoculated against the nonsense about theory that bemused my generation and who are much better trained technically. I am especially encouraged by Jim Coleman's (1964) recognition of the power of a simple rationality assumption to account for the development of certain norms. He has taken the crucial step towards realizing that the general propositions explaining social behavior are psychological. Peter Blau, a man whom otherwise I greatly admire, cannot quite bring himself to take it. I see his toes getting into the cold water but no more.

My conviction that the general propositions to be used in explaining social behavior are psychological put me right up against one of the great names in the sociological tradition, Emile Durkheim—not the Durkheim of a great empirical study like *Suicide* (1951) but the Durkheim of *The Rules of Sociological Method* (1927), with its discussion of *social facts:* "Since their essential characteristic consists in the power they possess of exercising, from outside, a pressure on individual consciousness, it must be that they do not derive from individual consciousness and that accordingly sociology is not a corollary of psychology" (1927:124-5). I had been bothered by Durkheim ever since I had been told by Elton Mayo to read him, and as time went on I had become more and more assured that his statement was absurd. Not only absurd, but obviously absurd. Not only absurd now, but absurd when Durkheim wrote it, even though what he meant by psychology was not what we mean by it now: he thought in terms of psychological

[26]

traits and not of psychological propositions. I even doubt whether Durkheim always believed it himself. Certainly there were social facts, but from these facts his conclusion did not follow. Why had we over the years surrendered our critical judgments to Durkheim and his successors, the functionalists? Many of their empirical pieces of work were excellent, but whenever they got up—and they often did—on their theoretical high horses, they maundered. I have no answer to the question except that Durkheim provided sociology with an identity, which as an insecure newcomer to the sciences it badly needed: he provided sociology with a theory it could feel was really its own.

If I am right, sociology must give up this kind of identity. But it need not feel too badly; it will have companions in misery, if misery it be. All the other social sciences will have to give up their identities at the same time: the general propositions of all the social sciences are the same, and all are psychological. This does not mean that each science will not retain its own special tasks. Much of sociology has rightly concentrated on social structures. Its most interesting theoretical task will remain that of showing how structures, relative enduring relationships between men, are created and maintained by individual human choices, choices constrained by the choices of others, but still choices.

I know that by attacking Durkheim here by epithet alone I have not heeded Emerson's advice to Justice Holmes when the latter turned in a term paper attacking Plato: "When you strike at a king you must kill him!" My excuse is that I have done my best to kill Durkheim with argument at all-too-great lengths elsewhere (1964a, 1967b, and forthcoming).

If I were to name a figure of the past whom I admire more than Durkheim, I would name Malinowski first. He has a far better "feel" for what I believe human society to be really like, even though the society he studied was a primitive one. Above all, I admire *Crime and Custom in Savage Society*, especially remarks like: "The true problem is not to study how human life submits to rules—it simply does not; the real problem is how the rules become adapted to life" (1961:127). How oracular! Yet how wise it seems when meditated on! And how un-Durkheimian! One could argue that Malinowski was a functionalist. He even called himself one. But if he was a functionalist, he was one of a very different stripe from Durkheim or Radcliffe-Brown. While they tried to explain institutions by showing how they contributed to the survival of a society, Malinowski did so by showing how they met the needs of men. The former (societal functionalism) is a very different theory from the latter (psychological functionalism) which did not prevent Bob Merton's lumping the two together in his functionalist paradigm (1957:52). But then, what is a paradigm without a proposition? The fact is that psychological functionalism, but not societal, readily becomes a behavioral psychology.

Logic Versus Explanation

The synthesis that *Social Behavior* intended to effect was theoretical. It tried to show that a variety of empirical findings followed from a small number of general propositions. If nothing else had done so earlier, this work alone would have discouraged me with "grand theory" in sociology. Theorists continually harped on the vital importance of theory, that is, the importance of what they themselves did, and by dint of impressive iteration they had made the idea stick. Graduate students dreamed of becoming pure theorists, as if theory did not have to be about anything in particular. Yet what *was* a theory? If I judged from what grand theorists like Talcott Parsons said, and even more from what they did in the name of theory, their notion of theory was not mine. For them a theory was a conceptual scheme, often a set of categories. For me a conceptual scheme—and I myself had developed one in *The Human Group*—was not enough. "A conceptual scheme is not a theory!" I used to shout to myself. For them, the categories, the concepts, were supposed to be "logically" related to one another. For me, the concepts were to be empirically related.

[28]

Nature, not logic, made a relationship what it was. Logic was a matter of the relationship between propositions, not between concepts. For me, the heart of any theory, as indeed of all success in science, was a set of propositions, each of the general form: x varies as y. The trouble with grand theory was not that it failed to make contact with data. Data could always be subsumed under one or another of the categories. The trouble was rather that it lacked propositions. That is, it was not a theory at all.

Following up my originally rather inchoate dissatisfaction with grand theory, I took the trouble to read what the philosophers had been recently writing about the nature of scientific theory. Perhaps I only read the ones that would confirm me in my views, but at least I found myself confirmed by some philosophers generally accepted as able, such as Braithwaite (1953), Nagel (1961), and Hempel (1965). A theory of a phenomenon is an explanation of it. An explanation consists of at least three propositions, each, including the proposition to be explained (*explicandum*), stating a relationship between properties of nature. The propositions form a deductive system, such that the *explicandum* follows as a conclusion in logic from the others in the set: this is where logic comes in. At least one of the propositions has to be more general than the others: hence this is known as the "covering law" view of explanation. Finally, a theory is described as powerful when a large number of individual deductive systems share a small number of the same general propositions, so that a few principles account, when applied to different given conditions, for a wide variety of empirical findings. Plenty of tricky issues remain unresolved in the study of scientific explanation, such as the status of so-called theoretical terms, but on the main lines of doctrine there was substantial agreement among some philosophers.

If this was theory, it was not what the grand theorists produced. My instinctive distrust of their work received intellectual justification. I could not claim that I had myself succeeded in *Social Behavior* in meeting the standards of theoretical work, but at least I had come closer than the grand theorists had done, and I

[29]

hoped to do still better in later work. In several articles and in a little book with a big title, *The Nature of Social Science,* I set forth my views on the problem of explanation in social science (also see 1962 and 1964b).

The chief stumbling block I meet in my efforts to explain explanation is the notion that one has explained an event when one has found its causes, or when one has found the independent variables that determine changes in a dependent one. It is splendid to find the causes of things, but it is not strictly explanation. For example, the cause of a high tide is the passage of the moon across the local meridian. In one of the everyday meanings of explanation, the moon's movement explains the tide's, but not in the scientific meaning. The reason is that, according to the latter, what is to be explained is always a relationship—in this case the very relationship between cause and effect, between the moon's movement and the tide's. This relationship, this proposition, is explained by showing that it follows from the gravitation law under specific, given conditions. The cause of the tides was known for ages before the explanation was known.

I am asked what impact my sociological efforts have had in reshaping the field. It is hard to tell whether they have effected any change, especially any that would not have occurred in due course without my intervention. This does not bother me, for a successful revolutionary is stuck with his success. He has to take responsibility for its results, and the joys of responsibility are few. I have tried to reduce the incidence of guff in sociology, but the species responds to the antibiotic by breeding more virulent strains. Did we kill Marx to get Marcuse? What folly if we did! At times I suspect that both sense and nonsense have increased in sociology at the expense of some middle ground. As for more specific issues, the battle for what is inaccurately called "psychological reductionism" is still far from won. Only in persuading sociologists to take a more sensible view of theory do I find tangible evidence of success, and mighty little of that. In the early editions of his *Social Theory and Social Structure,* Bob Merton wrote: "The term *socio-*

logical theory refers to logically interconnected conceptions which are limited and modest in scope, rather than all-embracing and grandiose." In his new revision he writes: "The term *sociological theory* refers to logically interconnected sets of propositions from which empirical uniformities can be derived."[1] Some progress has been made, but I dare say it was not my fault. As President Lowell of Harvard used to say, one cannot both accomplish something and get the credit for it. If our view of theory has changed for the better, I do not fear for "psychological reductionism." A man who will construct real theories, that is, explanations, cannot help realizing that the general propositions used in explaining social behavior are psychological.

I am asked, finally, to state my view on the current relationship between sociological theory and social application. I have little to say. I have been concerned with the intellectual organization of the fundamentals of my subject, and I have no personal experience with application. In any event, what theory are we talking about? Since most formal sociological theory is inadequate as theory, application may not suffer if it is guided only by empirical knowledge and a sense of the possible. Theory may have more to learn from application than application from theory. What I am sure of is that sociologists have contributed greatly to the empirical understanding of the major problems of the society. In so doing they have also made clear how difficult effective action on some of the problems is apt to be. On both counts they have served their country well. I should now like to see us bring out demands for "action *now*" into some proportion with our conviction—or lack of it—that we know what action would actually work.

NOTES

1. Compare page 5 of Merton's *Social Theory and Social Structure* (1957) with page 39 of his *On Theoretical Sociology* (1967).

REFERENCES

BERNARD, C. (1927) Introduction á l'Etude de la Médicine Expérimentale. Paris: Flammation.

BRAITHWAITE, R. B. (1953) Scientific Explanation. Cambridge: Cambridge University Press.

BROWN, R. (1965) Social Psychology. New York: Free Press.

CHAPPLE, E. and C. M. ARENSBERG (1940) "Measuring human relations." Genetic Psychology Mongraphs 22: 3-147.

CIPOLLA, C. M. (1965) Guns, Sails, and Empires. New York: Pantheon Books.

COLEMAN, J. S. (1964) "Collective decisions." Sociological Inquiry 34: 166-81.

DURKHEIM, E. (1951) Suicide. New York: Macmillan.

––– (1927) Les Règles de la Méthode Sociologique. Paris: Alcan.

HEMPEL, C. G. (1965) Aspects of Scientific Explanation. New York: Free Press.

HOMANS, G. C. (forthcoming) "The sociological relevance of behaviorism," in R. L. Burgess and D. Bushnell, Jr. (eds.) Behavioral Sociology.

––– (1967a) "Elementary social processes." Pp. 30-78 in N. Smelser (ed.) Sociology: An Introduction. New York: John Wiley.

––– (1967b) The Nature of Social Science. New York: Harcourt, Brace & World.

––– (1964a) "Contemporary theory in sociology." Pp. 951-77 in R. E. L. Farris (ed.) Handbook of Modern Sociology. Chicago: Rand McNally.

––– (1964b) "Bringing men back in." American Sociological Review 29: 809-18.

––– (1962) Sentiments and Activities. New York: Free Press.

––– (1961) Social Behavior: Its Elementary Forms. New York: Harcourt, Brace & World.

––– (1958) "Social behavior as exchange." American Journal of Sociology 63: 597-606.

––– (1957) "The Frisians in East Anglia." Economic Historical Review, 2d ser. 10: 189-106.

––– (1950) The Human Group. New York: Harcourt, Brace.

––– (1941) English Villagers of the Thirteenth Century. Cambridge, Mass.: Harvard University Press [Second ed. (1960) New York: Russell & Russell].

––– and C. P. CURTIS (1934) An Introduction to Pareto. New York: Alfred A. Knopf.

[32]

MALINOWSKI, B. (1961) Crime and Custom in Savage Society. London: Routledge.

MERTON, R. K. (1967) On Theoretical Sociology. New York: Free Press.

——— (1957) Social Theory and Social Structure. Glencoe, Ill.: Free Press.

NAGEL, E. (1961) The Structure of Science. New York: Harcourt, Brace & World.

PARSONS, T. (1937) The Structure of Social Action. New York: McGraw-Hill.

RIECKEN, H. W. and G. C. HOMANS (1954) "Psychological aspects of social structure." Pp. 786-832 in G. Lindzey (ed.) Handbook of Social Psychology. Cambridge, Mass.: Addison-Wesley.

SKINNER, B. F. (1953) Science and Human Behavior. New York: Macmillan.

STONE, L. (1965) The Crisis of the Aristocracy, 1558-1641. Oxford: Oxford University Press.

WHITE, L., JR. (1962) Medieval Technology and Social Change. Oxford: Oxford University Press.

3

REFLECTIONS ON MY WORK

WILLIAM FOOTE WHYTE

I WOULD CHARACTERIZE my style of research in the following ways:

(1) *Immersion in field work.* I began my research experience as a participant observer on the street corners and remained very deeply involved for three and a half years. I have never had such full immersion since that time: but from 1942 until 1954 I maintained a heavy personal involvement in field work; getting into the field myself for long periods on at least a two-day-a-week basis. When, after my first study in industry, I found myself supervising the research of graduate students, I felt an urge to be involved in the field myself. It seemed to me that I could only make my best contribution if I was out there, observing some of the same phenomena that students were observing, interviewing some of the same people or people like them. I feel that whatever theorizing I have been able to do has grown as much out of the personal experience of confronting the phenomena in the field as it has out of intellectual processes in the office.

(2) *Utilization of administrative experience as participant observer.* Since 1955 I have no longer been in a position to spend substantial time myself in field work, but I have sought to maintain the excitement of personal involvement by regarding myself as a participant observer in administrative activities. First came my experience (1956 to 1961) as director of the Social Science Research Center at Cornell University and then (since 1962) with Lawrence K. Williams of Cornell and José Matos Mar of San Marcos University in Peru. I have been involved in a rather large-

[35]

scale comparative and longitudinal study of rural communities, along with research in high schools and business organizations.

As director of the Social Science Research Center, my entire staff consisted of a part-time assistant director and a secretary. I had no authority over any of the professors in the social sciences and a very limited budget to use as bait for promoting activities that I found interesting. I recognized that I could make a useful contribution to Cornell only insofar as I was able to stimulate voluntary cooperation across departmental and college lines. To do the job, I had to think about what would work and what would not work, and since some activities I promoted seemed to succeed where others made little headway, I was naturally led to reflection about the underlying social process.

My participant-observer-as-research-administrator role grew out of an attempt to resolve the problems of role conflict in research administration: personal involvement in research versus project administration.

My Social Science Research Center experience pointed the way toward an attempted resolution of this conflict. If it were possible to structure the research activities so that they would provide payoffs for all concerned, then the organization would operate primarily in terms of voluntary cooperation, and those with the chief administrative responsibilities would be relieved to a large extent from the tasks of detailed supervision, inspection, and policing of activities.

Furthermore, it occurred to me that if we did prove successful in reconciling the apparently irreconcilable, the conclusions to be drawn from our experience should have some scientific as well as practical value. To the extent that I could treat myself as a participant observer in the process of developing this new form of organization, I would be gathering data for analysis and report-writing in the process of administration. One published article (1967) has already come largely out of this experience, and others are in process. I am finding this experience not only productive in data but in the stimulus it provides toward building new and better theories of organizational behavior and interorganizational relations. In fact, I am now in the process of developing a new theoretical framework for the analysis of organizational behavior, and this is evolving directly out of my research-administration experience.

(3) *Combination of research methods.* For almost the first twenty years, I was completely committed to the field methods of interviewing and observation. I had little use for questionnaires and no experience with them. While I did occasionally have responsibility for a student thesis in which a questionnaire was used, my first direct experience with the survey method came in my 1954-55 year of research on industrial relations with Creole Petroleum Corporation in Venezuela. While some of the problems I was studying seemed to lend themselves well to my usual interviewing-observational approach, the problem of worker attitudes and values regarding living in a company home versus owning one's own home clearly called for a survey approach, and so I began in this direction somewhat tentatively in Venezuela. In the course of my fourteen months in Peru (1961-62) while I continued research through interviewing and observation, I encountered further problems that seemed to demand the survey approach, or a combination of the two approaches. Here I was fortunate in being able to collaborate with Lawrence K. Williams, who had come to Cornell after extensive experience in the Survey Research Center at the University of Michigan. Since that time he and I have been collaborating on a series of studies in organizations and communities, utilizing survey methods combined with interviewing and observation. I have come to recognize that the two approaches are not competitive. As I have argued elsewhere (1965), each of the two has its own strengths and weaknesses, and to a high degree the strengths of one method complement the weaknesses of the other.

Beginning in late 1966 or early 1967, particularly through involvement in the Chancay Valley study directed by Dr. Matos, I have been discovering how economic and historical data can be integrated with survey data and also with data from anthropological-type interviewing and observation.

(4) *Flexibility.* While anyone likes to think that he himself is flexible while other people are rigid, I think I can show evidence of flexibility in the development of my research career. I began with an urban community study. Then for many years I carried out studies in industrial sociology. Now, while I have continued industrial organizational studies (in Peru), I have also focused attention on Peruvian high school students, and I am concentrating particularly upon development and change in rural communities in Peru. As I attempt to put it all together in Peru, I hope one day to be able to write a book about that nation, based as much as possible upon the fruits of research (my own and that of others) extending across a range from urban to rural, from organizations to communities.

I began in an Italian-American slum district, learning enough Italian to be able to communicate with the older people. I am now deeply involved in Latin American studies, having developed enough Spanish to handle field work, teaching, or research supervision.

(5) *Collaboration with key informants.* The man I called "Doc" in *Street Corner Society* (1943d) was far more to me than an informant in the usual sense of the term. Beginning as my chief guide into the intricacies of Cornerville, he came to be also a collaborator in the research. We spent many hours discussing what he and I were observing. Piece by piece, he read through the first draft of the book and gave me his detailed criticisms. With Ralph Orlandella, then a leader of another corner gang, I also established a collaborative relationship that contributed to the book and that we have been able to revive from time to time in the intervening years.

In my first union-management case study, I found international representative Sidney Garfield providing me with my most valuable data and interpretations on the change from conflict to cooperation. As I became fascinated with his accounts of his experiences in other union-management situations that I was not studying, I proposed that we collaborate on a series of articles on "The Collective Bargaining Process" (1950-51). While I did all the writing, I could not really say that this series was more mine than his, for he provided nearly all of the case material and a large part of the analysis also. These materials and the ideas they generated for me helped later to shape the section on bargaining in my textbook, *Men at Work* (1961). Richard Walton and Robert McKersie (1965) have made liberal use of these cases in their impressive effort to place bargaining in a behavioral science framework.

Early in my work in Peru I encountered Robert R. Braun, who was then serving as interim director of IPAE, the Peruvian management association, and developing his own business as a management consultant. A Peruvian citizen who had emigrated from Vienna twenty-six years earlier, Braun was tri-lingual (German, Spanish, and English). As accountant, factory manager, or consultant, Braun had worked with Peruvian, English, and United States management people, fitting in and yet always maintaining the detachment that produces insights.

Braun asked me a series of questions about the factory studies I hoped to carry out, then invited me to his home so that we could talk further. With few preliminaries, he then made me his offer, in something like these words:

> I am very much interested in what you are doing. Now, while I am making a comfortable living with my consulting, it doesn't take up all my time. I wish you would feel free to call on me at any time for anything you think I can do for you.

I was then five thousand miles and twenty-five years away from my beginnings in Cornerville, but Braun's words projected me momentarily into that settlement house, where Doc had made precisely the same offer. I accepted without hesitation. For the rest of my fourteen months in Peru, I consulted Braun on every major move I made and on all the ideas that were emerging from the study. He became not only my chief cultural consultant but also my most valued critic of Bill Whyte in action. When I was to present something before a management group or to seek entree for a plant study, I would discuss my approach with Braun beforehand and then, if he had been present for the occasion, I would later get his feedback impressions of why the others had reacted to me as they did.

After I returned from Peru and Braun went to Geneva to become Secretary General of CIOS (the international organization of scientific management), our collaboration continued by correspondence. It has so far led to two joint publications (1966 and 1968) with more in process.

From these and other similar experiences, I am induced to generalize in this way. The researcher who treats all of those he meets in a field study as passive informants is missing some of the major values that can come out of field experience. Now, whenever I get involved in a new field study, I go in with the following assumption: I will soon encounter one or more people who are at least as smart as I am, who know far more about their organization than I do, who already have considerable insight into what is going on, who can be encouraged to develop further their analytical talents and observational skills, and who will enjoy working with me.

(6) *Efficiency in Production.* I am not troubled by the well-known professional "writing block." When I have some idea of what I want to say, I can get it said in a hurry. Even when my ideas are confused, I find the exercise of writing an essential step toward clarification.

I started writing, beyond required school exercises, at about the age of eleven. When still in grade school, I wrote an endless continued story. As a senior in high school I was responsible for writing the weekly school page for the *Bronxville Press,* which meant delivering about twenty pages of typed copy to my editor every Sunday night.

Through the Cornerville period, I typed both field notes and drafts of the book. On my next study, I began dictating field notes. In 1948 I dictated the first draft of *Pattern for Industrial Peace* (1949). Since that time I have dictated nearly everything I have written, working from a detailed outline.

While I am a fairly fast (if somewhat erratic) touch typist, I estimate that I can dictate a first draft two and one-half to three times as fast as I can type it. Revision of the dictated draft does indeed take more time than I need for a typed draft, but the difference is not great, so the net gain is enormous.

(7) *Concern with application.* From the beginning I have been concerned with the application of research knowledge to human problems. I attended the first meeting of the Society for Applied Anthropology in 1941 and have been active in that society ever since, serving as editor of *Human Organization* for six years. I am a charter member and also one-time president of another association with a strong orientation toward the practical application of research knowledge: the Industrial Relations Research Association.

On Applied Research

I have never accepted the presumed dichotomy between basic or "pure" research and applied research. It seems to me that whether research makes a basic contribution to knowledge depends not upon the motivation of the researcher but upon the potential generalizability of the research findings. Chester I. Barnard (1957) expressed this very well when he criticized a National Science Foundation report which sought to separate basic from applied projects.

> As one example, we have Karl Jansky's discovery of radio signals from outer space. Jansky, according to the report, was not engaged in

basic research; he merely made a basic discovery. Here the confusion arises from labeling research according to the motives for which it is carried on; there is an element of snobbery involved which ought not to be encouraged. After all, Louis Pasteur made his great contributions to the foundations of bacteriology in trying to find solutions to the practical problems of the French silk and wine industries. The whole discussion demonstrates that the dichotomy between basic and applied research can be overemphasized.

While I would agree that important advances in knowledge can arise whether or not a given project involves any attempt to apply its research findings, it seems to me likely that our field would progress more rapidly if more people were willing to do applied research. If a man has an obligation to try to apply his research findings, the effort he must make to come to terms with the realities of the field situation is likely to prevent him from indulging in ivory tower theorizing, which sounds impressive but leads nowhere. In short, I regard application as a necessary testing ground for the knowledge we think we have acquired.

I think there has been an unfortunate trend toward snobbism in sociology during the last twenty to thirty years. It seems to be assumed that the man who does "pure" research and has no concern whatsoever with application wins high prestige from his professional colleagues, whereas the man who is concerned with applied research may be looked upon as something of a hack. Where were we when "the Great Society" burst upon us (before its sidetracking by the Vietnam war) and seemed to promise government-guided transformations of the quality of American life? When government administrators, charged with the building of new and adventurous programs in the fields of housing, employment, training, and community development, called out for the guidance that they hoped behavioral scientists would be able to give them, we found that there were pitifully few among us who had anything practical to contribute.

I do not mean to give the impression that I have always been deeply involved in the application of research findings. Only once have I taken on a project where the application of research findings was the major objective (Whyte and Hamilton, 1965). Still, in nearly everything I have written I have had in the back of my mind the question: can this be put to some practical use? At least I have tried to make myself understandable to men of action, and I have always been interested in communicating with them. At this writing, as chairman of the Subcommittee on Research of the National Manpower Commission of the Department of Labor, I am now working to link research to some of the training and human development problems of our explosive urban areas.

What Sociologists Have Influenced Me?

In the early stages of my research career, sociological influences were notable for their absence. In the *Street Corner Society* study, I was particularly influenced by social anthropologists Conrad M. Arensberg and Eliot D. Chapple, who in turn had got their start in the direction I was then pursuing with W. Lloyd Warner. I learned my research methods from them and also the conception of my field of study. For the first decade of my professional career, the only sociologist whose influence I can now testify to was Everett C. Hughes. He seems to me then—as he still does now—a master at the sociological context.

I should also mention certain influences by reaction: the physiologist and the part-time sociologist, Lawrence J. Henderson and Louis Wirth. While I sat in on Henderson's famous seminar on Pareto, it was not that experience that influenced me. Henderson believed nearly all social scientists were soft-headed sentimentalists, and in the Monday evening dinners of the Society of Fellows at Harvard, he was always ready to pounce on any words of mine that tended to confirm this impression of me and my colleagues. For years, as I wrote up my research, I could feel Henderson peering over my shoulder, ready to attack any confusion of value judgment with scientific evidence.

[43]

In my period at the University of Chicago, students had to consider not only which professors they were working for but also which they were working *against*. If you took your main work with Warner and Hughes, as I did, you had to be prepared to fight off Wirth in your field and thesis examinations. Wirth began his thesis questioning (on *Street Corner Society*) by asking me to define a slum district. If I defined it in terms of "social disorganization," this would throw into question my interpretation of my slum. But since everybody else defined it that way, how could I avoid those terms? Through what seemed an endless grilling, I stuck to a definition in terms of geography, population density, housing conditions, and such objective factors. This did not satisfy Wirth, of course, and he kept after me with a skill that I found both impressive and infuriating. Still, he probably did me good because, in writing *Street Corner Society*, I had not bothered to orient myself to the literature. In preparing for the exam, I wrote a long introductory statement, examining the literature on slums, and pointing out what my distinctive contributions were. That exercise, plus the stimulus of the exam, led to the publication of several articles (1943a, 1943b, 1943c) that oriented me to the field and furnished the footnotes that *Street Corner Society* lacked.

As I pushed ahead with industrial studies after finishing graduate work at Chicago, the main personal intellectual influences upon me still came from outside of sociology. I think particularly of Muzafer Sherif, the social psychologist, whose experiments in intergroup relations seem to me classics in the field. My industrial studies were more directly influenced by Leonard Sayles and George Strauss, both of whom received their interdisciplinary doctorate at Massachusetts Institute of Technology.

It is only in the third decade of my professional career, beginning in approximately 1956, that sociologists have come to have a major impact upon my thinking. I am indebeted to George C. Homans, Peter Blau, and Alvin Gouldner for their development of exchange theory, which seems to me to set forth a main line of my future theoretical development. I consider Joan Woodward, the

British sociologist (whom I have never met) a major influence in showing me systematic ways to examine the impact of technology upon organization structure and upon the organization of work activities.

My Books

I suppose the favorite among my books has to be *Street Corner Society.* I lived that study, and it still brings back vivid memories.

I suppose the book is particularly popular with students, and with professors who want to introduce students to sociology, because it presents live characters and whole human situations. While I am not generally regarded as a theoretician, I like to think that certain aspects of *Street Corner Society* have stimulated generalizable research results in the works of other people. Muzafer Sherif and his students (i.e., Harvey, 1953) utilized the relationship I observed between bowling performance and rank in the informal group to develop their own line of social experiments. Scudder Mekeel (1943) claimed that my discussion of "The Social Role of the Settlement House" could be applied practically word for word to the relations between the Indian Bureau and the Indians.

In the field of industry, my favorite is *Money and Motivation* (1955). I did not live this book in the sense that I lived *Street Corner Society,* but it represents a milestone of quite a different sort. By the time I put together *Money and Motivation* I had done a number of case studies in industry and had become increasingly concerned about possibilities of generalization beyond a given case. From time to time over a ten-year period before publication of this book, I had been working on the problems of financial incentives and worker motivation. An earlier effort to put together a book in collaboration with Donald Roy, Melville Dalton, and Orvis Collins did not come off. Years later as I was reading another article by Roy dealing with incentives and motivation—in my bathtub—I suddenly saw how this new piece fitted into certain gaps, and the framework of the book quickly evolved in my mind. I certainly set forth there no grand scheme, but I feel that my collaborators and I were able to pull together apparently disparate fragments of data and put them into a coherent framework.

I have somewhat mixed feelings about *Street Corner Society*. It is not entirely pleasant for an author to have to admit that his best book was also his first book. Have I been going down hill since then? Perhaps, but I like to think that the book or books that I see now evolving out of my Peruvian studies will one day stand at least on a par with *Street Corner Society*.

My Impact on Sociology

Up to this point, I feel that I have had little impact upon the development of general theory in sociology. I have contributed more to methodology in writing about field methods and the role of the participant observer. Perhaps the publication of *Street Corner Society* helped to set off the boom in small group research. I have certainly played a role in shaping the field of industrial sociology or organizational behavior, through my writing and through the students who have worked with me.

Not so long ago I had the impression that many sociologists regarded my favorite research methods as obsolete—interesting things to do until you learn how to be more "scientific." Now I think I see the tide turning toward an appreciation of the distinctive values and limitations of various research methods.

It seems to me that the heyday of the questionnaire came in with the development of new data processing technology during World War II and the postwar years. The investigator could now process such enormous amounts of data in so many ways that many sociologists were overwhelmed with the wonder of it all. For years many sociologists seemed to assume that the only "hard" research was questionnaire research.

[46]

I feel that this heyday has now passed. As I review the research findings of several decades of questionnaire surveys on one of the most studied problems in industrial sociology, the man-boss relationship, I am oppressed and also depressed with how little has been learned by so many bright people and so many hard-working machines. Few correlations have held up from one study to the next. Why this should be the case is beyond the scope of this paper (see Whyte, 1963 and 1965), but I believe that sociologists are increasingly recognizing that the questionnaire is not an all-purpose instrument but has certain very serious limiations.

I now believe that the combination of research methods that is representative of my current work will come increasingly to be the pattern in our field. I think I can even see that almost forgotten figure, the participant observer, coming back into view. In my service on the Subcommittee on Research of the Department of Labor's National Manpower Commission, I have been arguing that before-and-after measures of the effects of a given governmental program are not good enough. We need to know what went on within the program that may be presumed to account for the differences, if any, in our before-and-after measures. In other words, we need data on social processes, and questionnaires do not provide such data. Who is to provide such data? Somebody who is out in the field observing what is going on, perhaps even a participant observer.

I have been gratified to learn that the agency has managed to encourage some young sociologists to get into the field as participant observers in connection with one or another of the poverty programs. While the scientific results are not yet in, I was struck by the practical implications of a comment from an executive of the agency:

> When the research men do a questionnaire study, we have to wait six months to a year after the data are all in before they can carry out their analysis and tell us what they have found out. With the participant observer, it is quite different. By the time he comes out of the field—if not before—he can tell us a great deal about the nature of the program

he is studying. He can point out to us problems of policies or procedures that we can do something about and that we never would have
discovered through a questionnaire survey.

I also see a new emphasis upon systematic quantitative measures
of observed behavior, from Eliot D. Chapple's interaction chrono-
graph to other methods which are less precise but more readily
usable in field studies.

I would like to think that the well-trained sociologist of the
near future will be well grounded in interviewing and observation,
experimental methods, and questionnaire surveys. Will it take
longer to train our students in this broad range of methods? Not if
we shift our emphasis from systematic coverage of the literature
(which in large measure simply documents our ignorance) toward
providing students the tools for finding things out for themselves.

NOTE

1. My relations with "Doc" are discussed in detail in the appendix to
Street Corner Society (1955 enlarged edition).

REFERENCES

BARNARD, C. I. (1957) "A national science policy." Scientific American 45
(November).
HARVEY, O. J. (1953) "An experimental approach to the study of status
relations in informal groups." American Sociological Review 18: 357-67.
MEKEEL, S. (1943) "Comparative notes on the social role of the Settlement
House as contrasted with that of the United States Indian Service."
Applied Anthropology 3 (December).
WALTON, R. and McKERSIE, R. (1965) A Behavioral Theory of Labor
Negotiations: An Analysis of a Social Interaction System. New York:
McGraw-Hill.

WHYTE, W. F. (1968) "On language and culture." In Howard S. Becker et al. (eds.) Institutions and the Person. Chicago: Aldine.

——— (1967) "Models for building and changing organizations." Human Organization 26, nos. 1-2 (Spring-Summer).

——— (1965) "A field in search of a focus." Industrial and Labor Relations Review 18, no. 3 (April).

——— (1963) "Toward an integrated approach to research in organizational behavior." The 1963 Presidential Address of the Industrial Relations Research Association, Reprint No. 155 in Proceedings of the IRRA. Ithaca: New York State School of Industrial and Labor Relations, Cornell University.

——— (1961) Men at Work. Homewood, Ill.: Irwin-Dorsey.

——— (1955) Money and Motivation. New York: Harper.

——— (1949) Pattern for Industrial Peace. New York: Harper.

——— (1943a) "Social organization in the slums." American Sociological Review 8 (February).

——— (1943b) "A slum sex code." American Journal of Sociology (July).

——— (1943c) "A challenge to political scientists." American Political Science Review 34 (August).

——— (1943d) Street Corner Society. Chicago: University of Chicago Press.

4

MIND, METHODOLOGY, AND MACROSOCIOLOGY

IRVING LOUIS HOROWITZ

What do you consider to be the most uniquely defining characteristics of your way of doing sociology?

A meaningful answer has to be broken down into three parts: since one does sociology *technically,* one side of it consists of what is sometimes gratuitously referred to as methodology; at another level, one operates *intellectually,* that is, at what is sometimes vaguely referred to as formulating theory; and *strategically,* there is what is sometimes pompously referred to as professional choice.

At the technical level, the main point in my work is the relationship between large-scale events and a relatively clear model for interpreting such events. It is absurd to make a priori assumptions that the scale of a relation or event necessarily determines the results or quality of the research. For example, from my own point of view, and in my own experience, it is often simpler to make predictions about the behavior of Soviet foreign policy than to make predictions about individuals—even those one knows with a good deal of intimacy. Aggregate data may therefore be more malleable, more susceptible of hard results than individual data. The old-fashioned assumption that a laboratory setting in which sociologists engaged in small group research can produce more certainty in accounting for interaction is largely a psychologistic myth. If small group studies had a high generalizing potency, the spin-off from laboratory results would be infinitely greater than, in fact, it is. We are now in a position to treat aggregates as conceptual units, and in so doing develop explanations and predictions about national behavior and even international behavior quite consonant with the most advanced methods in the social sciences. Such data is just as likely to be firm in its predictive value as small group research. Of all the group theorists, Homans alone sensed this point when he noted that group analysis is not a question of how many people are involved, but how much theory can be generated.

Intellectually, I aim to integrate in my work what is implied precisely by that word itself, namely, intellectuality. I work with the assumption that a fruitful mind empowered by a complex idea can get one further than uncultivated mindlessness, lacking in rich preconceptions. To use the current language of our field, conceptual variables are extremely important if one is to ultimately operationalize the results of sociology, or for that matter give it a level of credibility that data itself can never achieve. The notion that sociology is a tabula rasa, and that theory "gets generated" from the data bank, is highly questionable. Ask any computer-rich sociologist if the data "leads" to a certain set of inviolable conclusions, and you get a resounding negative. To start with no assumptions means to end with no theory.

I believe that the meaning and values of a leading assumption structures the mind, makes the world intelligible. I believe we need to use the available data whenever possible, rather than at the level of generating data for others to do the interpretation. This is clearly a pragmatic judgment of what is and is not important. On the other hand, it is a judgment that can have vast scientific implications. There are those who bask in the sunlight of information, and have nothing but contempt for those who do the interpretation. On the other hand, from my own point of view, while the two go together, one has to make a decision as to whether the largest payoff is found at the data-gathering or concept-formation end of the sociological continuum. Without information there can be no interpretation, and without empirical study there can be no rational goals, but that does not mean one must do all things at all times. Decisions about priorities—intellectual decisions—have to be made. These are often largely personal and dependent on one's sensitivities, not only to the state of the field, but more directly on the state of one's own professional and human ends. And this after all entails a level of self-awareness which, for lack of a better term, we call "mind."

From a strategic point of view, I place great store in publishing what is important or at least socially defined as important, even though all of the information may not be presently available. Given the professional emphasis on precision of data, this strategic decision may involve a superficial loss of prestige and even claims of catering to personal vanity. Indeed, it may even end up in the loss of high professional status ranking. But this risk must be taken if temporality in sociology is to be given any meaning, if the concept of "news" is seriously taken. The problem of significant research magnifies as one moves from issues of sociological fact to problems of sociological meaning. The strategic response to the sociological situation is to transform what is newsworthy, that is, what is relevant to large numbers of people, what is not esoteric, private, or finely specialized, into social science. And the analytic framework must in turn be of sufficient worth to generate further news, further significant interest.

The dialectic of my particular sociological strategy is to start with a problem deemed newsworthy, and transform the level at which the discourse about the problem has previously been raised by introducing variables at the level of social stratification and social psychology. This must be done effectively enough so that the news becomes not only transformed by the sociology, but ultimately yields a better conception of the news, as well as more attention to its rational behavior in the world because of an enriched awareness of its leading events at any given time.

What is your view of the current relationship of sociological theory and social application?

Having spent a considerable amount of time with this question and also having written a great deal on questions of theory and

[53]

applied research, I believe that what ought to be done now is to turn the problem around and ask: Is this distinction between general theory and specific application really as vital today as it may have been thirty or forty years ago? In a recent dissertation, J. Timothy Sprehe found that upwards of 90 percent of the sociologists believe in the worth of, if they do not advocate, some form of applied social research. As a corollary finding, very few are now willing to stake out their own career lines as general sociologists. The general sociologist, or rather the sociologist who believes in the generalizing nature of his enterprise, is like the general medical practitioner. He assumes a kind of modesty, but too often ends up in a futile imperialism, a touching faith that everything can be known by the sociological savant. He loses specificity in exchange for abstraction. In retaliation he runs the risk of focusing on the deficiencies of people, of his colleagues, rather than on the deficient models he still wants to cling to. But the bifurcation between theory and application is no longer real or vital because social science methods have been too well authenticated for that. Also, the trivia of sheer "findings" without a rich conceptual framework does less well than formerly. So the quality and ends of sociological research have become the more recent and important concern. Methods are less important than methods for what end. The issue is perhaps best framed as a competition between forms of application. That is to say, the notion of application is at this point in sociological history inextricably linked to the nature of the sociological discipline itself. The question has now shifted to: What kind of applications? Under whose auspices? Toward what goals?

It is not enough to speak in homiletics about bringing men back into sociology. These issues rear their heads because they involve bringing moral judgment back into sociology. Decisions must be made about the use of sociology in support of Vietnam pacification programs or ghetto rehabilitation programs. Sociology can scarcely avoid the problem of priorities, if not of choices. The kind of sociological techniques brought to the fore may in either case be roughly the same. But the background variables that go into this

[54]

decision are clearly not the same. One reason this, the choice between kinds of applied sociology, is such a serious problem is that in sponsored research (which so much applied research is), some kinds guarantee the researcher and the clientele, while other kinds of sociology guarantee the financial sponsor of the project. This is a problem which has been raised most sharply in relation to various federal overseas projects. My own position on this is well enough defined elsewhere so as not to require elaboration here. The relationship of social science to the government is on the rise, and shows no sign of slackening—despite federal pressure from radicals. The question becomes: What will be the form of this relationship? What are the guarantees that can be provided for the researchers no less than for those who are being researched?

We must maximize the amount of self-scrutiny and minimize the amount of external control over the behavior of scientists in general, and sociologists in particular. On the other hand, self-scrutiny does not mean a vicious, if subtle, policing of the field by would-be sociological *gauleiters*. It is important to allow the field to grow unfettered, without at the same time turning over the policy aspects of research to the federal government, or the scholarly aspects of research to a professional establishment. If the federal government is here for a long time to stay, sociology must be perfectly frank in declaring that it too is here for a long time to stay—as a tough-minded, critical co-worker, not as a peddler selling old wives' tales, or a service industry for the powerful.

Who are the sociologists whom you are either
influenced by or most respect? Are they the same now as in
your formative years?

American social scientists do not play this game of influence-hunting and name-dropping with quite the same vigor as do the Europeans. It seems to be a curse of grand theorists in particular, because their concerns are often egotistically enwrapped with "immorality" rather than with contemporaneity. Thus they often approach those by whom they have been influenced as mere predecessors to themselves rather than as figures with important contemporary value or even as voices recording a past. To enhance their own stature they are sure to be "influenced" only by the "best," by those who rank on a commercial scale of the "top ten."

When I refer to "influences," therefore, I want to make clear that I am referring to continuously relevant men whom I am not superseding, to very different kinds of men who have helped me to clarify things I already felt I wanted to say independently of them, and to men who have communicated something to me, irrespective of the responses of others to them. I would name C. Wright Mills and Samuel Stouffer as having this importance to me.

From my point of view Mills represented. imaginative sociology, not only as a specific way out of grand theory and shallow empiricism, but even more importantly, Mills understood that intellect stands for stripping away secrecy; and for replacing the effect of secrecy upon impressionable "masses" with rational understanding upon a public. He did this by a kind of blood-and-thunder empiricism where scientifically organized fact and rational sociology stand uniquely in judgment of ideology. Sociology stands over and above various ideologies like socialism, Marxism, fascism. In this, he was truer to the sociological tradition than were his colleagues who rode him so unmercifully.

Another great value of Mills is that in the face of sociology nothing was sacrilegious; no secret ritual of any organization, whether it be police, Puerto Ricans, prostitutes, the American power structure, or Soviet Politburo, had the right to stand above criticism. All doctrines which grant special rights based on authority, tradition, or any of the various Peircian categories of belief without knowledge, deserved and received contempt at his hand. I venture to say that when the shouting dies down, as it now largely has abated, Mills will be remembered as a man who uniquely stressed moral purpose in sociology. It was a moral purpose which somehow managed not to intrude on scientific canons but, rather, underscored the scientific enterprise. It did this by showing how sociology as science is a struggle no less than a tradition.

[56]

As for Stouffer, I realize that this will come as something of a surprise, since I am not particularly known as statistically oriented in the field; and in truth, he came to my deepest attention only five years ago. I think it was Stouffer's great value to combine macrosociological concerns with a survey research methodolgy that was both unique and successful. He had a way of working on the most significant problems, from the organizational life of the American soldier to problems of Communism and conformity in American life, which never drained the blood out of a problem in order to complicate the methodology. In Stouffer, unlike most contemporary methodologists, one never feels any contempt for real world problems, nor is there any merely frivolous playing with ideas which some survey researchers exhibit. Stouffer's work is as serious as it was accessible to those who care to look. Despite his own crude scientistic formulations, which made him his own worst intellectual adversary, I can always look at a Stouffer work and be deeply impressed with the theoretical insights therein expressed. Stouffer builds up empirically what many more abstract theorists do by rational design. And the impact of this empirical buildup is very great (as in the case of his showing how slight was the American concern for political problems even at the height of the McCarthy scare). He observed, through a given problem, like McCarthyism, how, in effect, the American public had become profoundly psychological and sociological in its fundamental concern and at the same time very much nonpolitical. In fact, he showed how political questions in America are transformed into a therapeutic, social or personal goal—and he did this by survey data.

As a matter of fact, the age of Stouffer ended with him because the need for this kind of survey research has passed on with the high-powered computer techniques that can now sample total populations in a total way. But he did represent sophistication in sociology for a generation that needed it. He represented it in a way that still left a good deal of room for what was important. Stouffer was uniquely gifted in linking qualitative to quantitative results—something at which most researchers remain inept.

[57]

It is not only fair but necessary to add a special word for my nonsociological mentor, Abraham Edel—a scholar whom I consider to be one of our most significant social theorists, one of the few authentic friends of social science in the philosophic blather called positivism. His extraordinary set of works on ethical judgment, not to mention the force of his personality, made a profound dent on my thinking. In fact, he moved me from philosophy to sociology more assuredly than any other single influence. Among the main lessons I derived from both the man and his work (although, obviously, not necessarily the way Edel considers his own most important statements) are the following: (a) Ethical statements do not have to be juxtaposed over and against empirical statements. Since every act is both empirical and ethical, every act requires an analysis of the structure of reality and also an evaluation process concerning the worth of that structure. (b) Once ethical judgment is seen in a contextually relevant decision-making framework, the tradition of philosophical Dualism joins the great chain of Being in the world of obsolete theory construction. (c) The way to handle any decision-making problem, or any social problem for that matter, is to adopt a nonrestrictive attitude of levels of reality. A soundly based science is a specific reflex of a relatively well-defined reality level. The analysis of issues, or of how people make choices, is one which entails a broad use of anthropology, sociology, political science, and economics—all of which are then put through a historical frame of reference. (d) Finally, by so doing, the mystification of the world is removed, not by a struggle between contending parties within the social sciences, but between social science (which is an expression not only of how men make ethical decisions, but is heuristic in helping them make more rational decisions) and the maze of madness through which our age is now passing. The end of mystification, not the end of ideology, becomes the true mission of the social sciences. These lessons I have learned from Edel. Others may have learned them too, from other sources; Wirth, Key, Boas, etc. But to have been taught them by so brilliant and persuasive a mentor made the whole educational bundle—with its gnarled fusion of irrelevance and incoherence—very much worth the price.

Among those who are living, many other people have influenced me. I will not embarrass them by claiming any ancestry or demanding any reciprocity. It might simply be best to mention them and then explain why in a general way they have influenced me directly as people, no less than as representative types. Five additional men influential upon my thinking are Herbert Blumer, Robert Lynd, Anatol Rapoport, David Riesman, and Howard S. Becker. I have listed them randomly—since frankly, I cannot rightly provide an order of priorities; that simply is not the way one behaves or responds in real life, and hence there is no reason to do so here.

I consider Howard Becker's work to be of extreme importance and profound meaning. It is from him that I have best understood the relationship between social deviance and political marginality. He made me appreciate how in the social world the two are much closer than one might imagine. And further, how in the social world the deviant may often have less protection and behavioral legitimation than the marginal man.

In all of these men, a strong note of scientific humanism: there is a sense of commitment, of purpose, a feeling that criticism has a proper place in sociology along with positive construction. In each case, there is a radical thrust that derives from an empirical look at big chunks of the world rather than from any conceptual preconditions or categories. In many ways these men represent sociology without tears. They have offered a humanism that does not rest on a theory of civilization as in the founding days of American sociology with men like Giddings, Ward, and Barnes—but rather on a theory of human survival in society. The basic modesty of this quest stands in marked contrast to an earlier generation of macrosociologists who had an ideology based on the prerequisites for doing important work, but realized so little. Too many early American sociologists had a rhetoric that surpassed their realities— or what they in fact were willing to *do* to change society. My own "favorites," my own sociological friends, have no such weakness—they have the courage of their convictions, and the convictions that promote courage. In some measure these early pioneers have been forgotten because a good deal of what they preached had to do with levels of abstraction that were not only nonsociological, but downright removed from an empirical world inhabited by people. When sociology becomes too categorical in the way it carves up the structure of the world, it loses a great deal of its freshness and vitality. This, along with the highly imitative, mimetic qualities of our early sociology did the primate in—and no amount of resurrection can restore the humpty-dumpties of the past to a contemporary tone. They belong to the history of sociology, not to sociological theory.

Just as at present, when sociology becomes too enamored of the models built, it runs the risk of shaping people to models, rather than the other way about. Perhaps the quickest, shorthand way of getting at why men as different as Becker and Riesman influence me, is that they best combine the concerns of social stratification with those of social psychology. In other words, the interaction between the structures of the world and the actions that men take to change or reinforce those structures is the measure of an authentic modern sociology.

These men managed to avoid the false dichotomization between personality "factors" and institutional "factors." Hence, they created a sociology that never became one-sided, dogmatic, and hopelessly irrelevant over time. The struggle between laboratory styles and ethnographic styles has increasingly been revealed as a polarization of futile opposites—between precision and significance, small range and large range, and structure and spontaneity—as if they were items one had to decide between. It is precisely because of such polemics that real world problems escaped attention; and in my less generous moments I have come to think that it was such debates that allowed the participants to use methodology as an escape hatch rather than instrumentally.

[60]

Which of your own writings do you like best, and why?

The two works I like best and in point of fact the only two works which I unreservedly like, are *Radicalism and the Revolt Against Reason* and *Three Worlds of Development.* They were done nearly a decade apart, and they were responses to different situations externally and emotionally, but in the long pull of time I think that they each will be seen to represent an authentic piece of work.

In the case of *Radicalism and the Revolt Against Reason* the technical question raised, and raised properly in my opinion, is: What happens to socialism between the death of Marx and Engels and the birth of Lenin and Stalin? Geographically, what happens to socialism in industrialized Western Europe when the predictions start failing and the prophets have passed away? Politically, what happens between the death of social democracy and the rise of Bolshevism? The answer given is that basically radicalism turns to irrationalism, to forms of disorganization and personal salvationism, to a kind of millenialism that was obviously distinct from and alien to the original, highly rationalistic socialistic vision. But more important than the empirical content of the study, or the specific center of focus which is, of course, Georges Sorel, is that the whole age of the 1960s, our present decade, exhibits a kind of radicalism remarkably similar to the *fin de siècle* I described in that earlier book. There was that same faith in conspiratorial theories, the same reliance on small revolutionary bands rather than large-scale mass mobilization; there was the same contempt for the values of industrialization and the same demands to create a radical man no matter how unradical the existing society might be.

In other words, what took place in the *fin de siècle* and what is taking place in the sixties in America is a shift from the society to the individual, from the re-creation of the social order to the salvation of the personal soul turned political. Further, radicalism gets redefined as voluntarism rather than as determinism. Marxism is both a theory of revolution and a theory of determination, of the inexorable movement from one state power to another, from one social system to another, from one economic framework to another. Radicalism, in its present "swinging sixties" form as at the *fin de siècle,* picks up the former option without the latter, eschews this kind of historical bridge to the future. They exhibit a shared demand for confrontation that pays scant attention to historical circumstances of limits. The struggle between social democracy and socialism, which I describe in *Radicalism and the Revolt Against Reason,* is perhaps being played out again in the struggle between so-called *radical* politics against so-called *progressive* or liberal politics. For these reasons I think this was an important book.

Three Worlds of Development is perhaps less important for any specific point it raises about the nature of the Third World than the fact that it offers a conceptual framework for dealing with three worlds in a developmental interaction. It gets beyond the nation-building imagery which abounds in sociology and political science, and into a triadic framework which is conceptually manageable and empirically verifiable—or disconfirmable as the case may be. If the net is cast so wide that many fish manage to squirm through it, so be it. In this book I went after the big whales who dominate the social ocean; and on this count, I still have not had a criticism that would deny me the catch.

What is wrong with most books on development is that they treat national development or community development or industrial development as fixed processes. There is little consideration given to the implausibilities of how 150-odd (count them!) nations develop; and how these developmental patterns intersect to form a meaningful world system. The task of specializing in so many nations, and Lord knows how many individual communities, is Herculean. There is an absence of conceptual unity or reliability in most developmental studies. I think *Three Worlds of Development* overcame this by seeing the universe as subdivided along lines of urbanization, immigration, industrialization, etc., as well as nationalization.

Like any net cast wide, important issues remain unresolved. *Three Worlds of Development* does not say much about Tanzania or Paraguay; it does not have that much to say about possible exceptions, either narrow or wide, to the general theory stated in the book. On the other hand, the structure of *Three Worlds of Development* encompasses a concept of the Third World without making a shabby celebrationist myth out of that concept; and without forgetting its relative instability with respect to the large powers of the world. For these reasons I think *Three Worlds of Development* is something I have written that remains worthwhile.

What impact would you say your sociological efforts have had on reshaping the field?

It is obviously presumptuous to place oneself in the sociological cosmos. However, the very notion of "impact" is an ephemeral thing, especially in a society which is geared to mass communications and which takes popular culture heroes much too seriously, and too briefly. Still, I suppose I ought to assess the effect I think my work has had in strengthening those tendencies within the field which never altogether passed away, although they came close to being extinguished in the functionalist celebration.

At the level of general theory the tendency most strengthened by my work has been the concept of conflict and conflict resolution as underlying social events based on a dynamic nature of things. The classical figures I have worked with in a serious way, such as Karl Marx, Georges Sorel, Georg Simmel, and Ludwig Gumplowicz, provided important source materials for the unfolding of my own theory of conflict, by stressing the dynamic, unstable character of social phenomena. Further, the area—Latin America— with which I am most familiar has reinforced precisely such theoretical tendencies.

I believe that the importance of the tendency in sociology to switch from consensus to conflict metaphors better describes how the world actually functions. The people who claim to examine society scientifically can ill afford to be less exact than those who offer descriptions of how the world gets written up in the daily press. The amount of conflict in the world, if it is not accounted for seriously, leads to a notion of consensus as a *goal* rather than as a model, to a vague celebration of the social order that is. Further, without a theory of conflict one can never get a more general theory of cooperation, of why men seek and value harmony.

The idea that society at any given time is a stable consensual arrangement, formulated by passage of conflict through an institutional apparatus, emerging as a thing of truth and beauty, may explain certain kinds of continuities. But these are unique to a given time and place and do not explain the long-run processes, more common and more universal, of change, of social dynamics. A consensual emphasis focuses on stability, and approaches irrational admiration of imaginary periods of stability, without adequately addressing the more basic processes which account for their temporariness. A theory of dynamics involves conflict and is more consistently well related to long-range events, to history, to past-present distinctions, to the fundamental fact that all things alter. Further, conflict orientations have the advantage of keeping the sociologist on the outlook for those things which are not well reported in society, those factors that are subject to breakdown. Sociology runs the risk, as long as it remains consensualist, of describing the obvious, of describing parts of a system that work. And this commonsensical charge will not dissolve with academic jargon. What is really interesting to most people, and I daresay even to most sociologists, is to understand why things *stop* working, or conditions under which the normal forms of anticipation and planning no longer provide the necessary cures. Only then do sociological doctors have something to offer the social patients.

At the level of specific application, more demanding than any single book, essay, or professional activity, is the work I do connected with *Trans-action* magazine. Institutions have a way of generating a life of their own, pushing aside pretensions of individuals to immortality, importance, or proprietary claims over organizational achievements. Sociology is itself an institutional fabric, sometimes torn and tattered, yet able to withstand the shocks of criticism (and unfortunately at times to resist the waves of change) precisely because institutions are "real," even if they are "man made."

From a personal viewpoint, *Trans-action* has delivered on the promissory note tendered to the profession in 1964 in my opening statement in *The New Sociology*. Then it could be properly asked: "Okay, this is the article of faith, where are the hard results?" The answer was not long in coming. In a social and educational milieu ripe for changes in sociological style as well as substance, the magazine found a ready acceptance. Over the years, and with the tremendous cooperation of many first-rate people, particularly Mary S. Strong and George Talbot, the founding spirit of the magazine (worked out collaboratively by such outstanding scholars as Alvin W. Gouldner, Lee Rainwater who joined us a bit later on, and by an equally fine series of editors such as Leonard Zweig, Warren Boroson, and currently Nelson W. Aldrich) became an accomplished fact.

Trans-action itself is not only a social science magazine disseminating information to a wider public; it has become a force for construction. It was, for example, a very early proponent of the war against poverty, and a voice consistently raised from the outset against the oppressive condition of Black Americans. It has become a force for criticism. It was the first major periodical to carry serious comment on the vile aspects of government sponsored social research, the first to document the conditions which make sexual assault and social deviance endemic to the American system, and in the forefront in drawing attention to the creation of a new American underclass, composed of white and Black, native and ethnic minorities, and quite distinct from the traditional factory working class.

The magazine is now six years old; five of those years have been spent as a university charge and one as an independent firm wholly owned and operated by the social science professionals. My pride in being connected with the publication of *Trans-action* from its origins is matched only by the sober recognition of the human travails involved in producing such a publication every month, and in the trepidations involved in charting its future. The only "glamour" in the business of publishing *Trans-action* is in the final product itself, which is as it should be. People don't want to read editorial aches and pains. But the plain truth is that for sheer excitement and enjoyment, my activities on the magazine cannot be matched. Whether or not it does in fact best measure my personal "impact" on the field of sociology is of far smaller consequence than the impact of the magazine on me. And for this I am extremely grateful.

At the other end of the "business" I would say that a really important development in sociology has to do with recognition that it is directly linked to a policy-making world in which the very content of the field gets defined by policy demands. The most obvious case of this is in the field of area studies which has opened up a vast new horizon of field experiences, not on the basis of autonomous history of sociology but rather on the basis of the extrinsic or political history of sociology. My own work in this area has been to develop a framework for understanding the interaction of autonomy and policy as it relates to sociology. Perhaps this is nothing more than the problem of individuality and collectivity writ large, or perhaps even larger, the question of virtue and its deviations. Perhaps in this way I am returning to early philosophic interests. In any event, my own personal impact in this area of policy research, for what it is worth, has been to measure the impact of values on a science in transition, or rather a sociology that now gratuitously takes its scientific claims for granted, and invites others to do likewise.

I believe that the task of sociology remains the stripping away of mystification. But now the question of mystique has become intrinsic to sociology itself, to possession of a set of jargon and symbols functioning to persuade a public of its primitive comprehension rather than to clarify the world. And it is to this issue that

I shall be addressing myself with increasing persistence in the forthcoming period. Meanwhile, all sociologists, and sociology itself as a science, must make up their minds whether the laboratory style of investigation is the world, or whether the world of investigation is their laboratory.

5

INTELLECTUAL JOURNEY

LLEWELLYN GROSS

FEW IDEAS ARE MORE PROSAIC than that the writer as scientist or scholar strives to order experience by creating symbolic configurations and systems or, as the case may be, by dismantling and renovating older ones. In this respect I have been like others in academia. However, the avenue through which I entered the mainstream of sociology was less than conventional. Adolescent interest in philosophy, together with an overly acute consciousness of man's pathos, led me to ponder the course of good and evil, of happiness and suffering, of the bizarre and the inexplicable in everyday affairs. The awesome and often destructive consequences of human inequality I found appalling and still do. How impossible, it seems, for most people to identify with those who differ from themselves, despite the manifest evidence that personal fortune is largely a matter of chance—the accidents of birth and the vagaries of circumstance. Our failure to identify with others can be taken to account for most of the world's ills—the brutality of political and ethnic servitude, the violence of war and crime, the absence of compassion for the needy, the common discourtesies by which our lives are diminished and depleted.

Methods: Logical and Sociological

If the secrets of this sometimes impossible world could be found, I would have to know more about people. Sociology and psychology could provide information; philosophy, the road to fuller understanding. But as matters turned out, my graduate work devolved around methods and methodology—statistical, metrical, experimental, and operational. Mathematics, logic, and philosophical analysis were encouraged on the assumption, I believe, that they could be used to simplify the thicket of complexities in which behavioral science thrives so well. Little official attention was given to the formation of systematic theories. Men like Durkheim and Weber were, or so I understood, somewhat outdated for the hard science that sociology was rapidly becoming. What we needed to know of the empirical world could be gotten from Lundberg with assists from Carnap, Dewey, and Feigl. Plato, Hume, and Kant were neglected then as they are today, probably because most sociologists have few doubts about the limits of observational errors. In due course I came to learn that the strong winds of operationalism did not blend well with philosophy. Dissatisfied with the deficiencies of two theses on scale construction, I attempted to find in logical positivism a basis for illuminating the conceptual problems of sociology. To understand something of its appeal I must trace a line of development which many will recognize as historically significant in Western thought.

A pervasive but sometimes obscure distinction separates the world of knowledge or truth into "rational" and "empirical" categories. Each of these has been defined in so many ways that their "synonyms" have provided widely disparate meanings. The first category has been variously identified with knowledge of truths (Descartes), knowledge of the truth of proposition (Hobbes), universal knowledge (Locke, Berkeley), truths of reason (Leibniz), knowledge of the relation of ideas (Hume), rational knowledge based on understanding and reason (Kant), deductive knowledge (Mill), etc. The second category has been variously identified with knowledge of things and their affections (Descartes), knowledge of fact or of sense (Hobbes), experimental knowledge (Locke), knowledge of particulars (Berkeley), truths of fact (Leibniz), matter-of-fact knowledge (Hume), empirical knowledge based on understanding and intuition (Kant), inductive knowledge (Mill), etc. "Rational knowledge" is generally associated with mathematical necessity, logical analysis, universal certainty, and validity. "Empirical knowledge" is generally associated with perceptual contingencies, historical observations, experimental probabilities, and scientific inferences. Philosophers differ on the completeness or finality of these distinctions, on their degrees of interdependence. Thus, a number of them, particularly Hobbes, Locke, Mill, and in a later period, Pierce, James, Schiller, Husserl, Mead, and Lewis found a place for *experience* in both realms of knowledge.

In the literature of sociology, the two categories have appeared in diverse guises as intellectual counters from the very beginning; this was especially evident among those who looked to social conditions for sources of knowledge. Durkheim's distinction between empiricism (contingent, variable, and unique) and a priorism (necessary and universal categories), Marx's separation of pure thought (abstract or false consciousness) and the real world (historical man and social existence), Scheler's division between essential knowledge and factual knowledge or ideal factors and real factors, Mannheim's relationship between the actual and the possible or the immanent and the extrinsic, Dilthey's two world views of naturalism and idealism of freedom, Schelting's assumptions about objective knowledge and cultural knowledge, Sorokin's separation of ideational cultures from sensate cultures, and Merton's queries on the relationship between mental productions and their existential bases, may be seen as dependent upon categories which are cognates of "rational" and "empirical." Again, variations in terminological usage are so great that differences outweigh similarities. Although sociologists view social structures and group processes as determinants in the choice of ideas, many deny the importance of "reason." Quite often, they introduce ancillary concepts which either exclude, reduce, or obliterate distinctions between the two categories. The fact remains, however, that any study of the social conditions of knowledge requires interpretations which presuppose or refract some version of the rational-empirical·spectrum. Veblen's stress on thought styles as dependent upon community organization, Mead's emphasis upon mind as a social product, Znaniecki's relationship between the thinker and his social circle, not to

[71]

mention special studies in the sociology of professions and occupations, can be restated in vocabularies which reflect these categories.

New aspects of this fundamental problem were pursued in fresh profusion by the logical positivists. They began by attempting to demonstrate that all reference to entities beyond the reach of observation or experience is meaningless (nonsense). In the "principle of verifiability" they affirmed that the meaning of a proposition lies in its method of verification. A host of difficulties followed. Does method of verification refer to the proof or test of truth, the establishment of an empirical generalization or a logical tautology? Some replied by asserting that words or sentences alone have meaning. On this assumption, verification could not be taken as identical with a sentence's meaning but only as a way of showing its meaning by passing directly to the properties of things. However, to talk about the properties of things, they must be defined and definition requires words. To make sure that such words are not arbitrary, logical rules must be stated to insure that a sentence will be used to refer to certain properties. In what sense then, if any, can it be said that logical rules are true rather than used? Do they not provide us with the possibility of logical order rather than with facts of observation or experience? It was evident, therefore, that the concepts of observation and experience needed further analysis. Schlick suggested that "verifiability by experience" meant verifiability by mental states which the individual alone can experience. Scientific knowledge is knowledge of structured relations in which others' experiences are identical with one's own. Observation or experience is, accordingly, the "content" which fills the form of scientific structure.

Almost concurrently Neurath claimed that sentences cannot be compared with an "inexpressible reality" but only with other sentences. Verification is not a relation between sentences and experiences; in place of experience are protocol sentences interpreted as acts of perception, behavioristic and biological. All empirical statements can be expressed in the language of physics; all sciences are equally "natural" and thus form a unity. Following

Neurath, Carnap suggested that all empirical statements can be expressed in a single language with a single method of translation. Since scientific statements must be tested by reference to experience, "structure" and "experience" must be expressible in a single language. Later he argued that all statements about "meaning" or "content" are pseudo-object statements. Thus, a lecture on Babylon does not tell us about a physical entity but about the appearance of the word Babylon in a certain set of sentences. In *The Logical Syntax of Language,* Carnap declares that we may choose to construct as many languages as we wish with whatever rules we find convenient for governing them. Syntax, pure and descriptive, is nothing more than the physics of language. Empiricists may admit as protocol statements "thing-language" predicates or "psychological" predicates (acts) as long as they are observable. In *Testability and Meaning,* he is confronted with the problem of such dispositional predicates as "soluble" and "visible"; to handle them he substituted reduction sentences for the thesis that all language is translatable into observables. In *Philosophy and Logical Syntax* he distinguishes between direct and indirect verification. Only protocol statements can be directly verified; singular and universal statements require indirect verification. Testability is preferred to indirect verification when experimental methods are available; when they are not available, the term "confirmation" is more appropriate. At this point, a proposition is meaningless only when it does not have empirical consequences.

Other contributors, England's ordinary language philosphers, Tarski in Poland and Quine in this country, served both to clarify and muddy these distinctions. Ogden and Richards, Stevenson, and then Morris introduced what might be called social psychological considerations. The former separated proper symbols, names of spatio-temporal events, from emotive signs which have no symbolic function. Stevenson separated emotive from descriptive statements and Morris used the term "pragmatics" to describe the relation between signs and their interpreters. It became increasingly apparent that there were no incorrigible statements. In principle, every statement might be rejected in the light of further experience. Moreover, certain logical (analytic) principles may have to be abandoned in the light of scientific changes (Quine).

Popper's views seemed to follow this dialectical trend. He attached little importance to problems of meaning, truth, and explanation as others understood these terms. The verifiability criteria of meaning rested on arbitrary stipulations. Methods for determining the scientific character of theories, of separating them from pseudoscience, are more significant than their truth. This he called "the problem of demarcation." A scientific hypothesis is not acceptable merely because it explains everything which can possibly happen; it cannot explain any observation unless it is incompatible with some possible observation. Since observations for supporting hypotheses are easily found, a more severe test is whether systematic attempts have been made to refute them. Only when a hypothesis has the capacity to produce consequences different from what is already known can it add to our knowledge. We are born with expectations of regularity; what we need is a critical attitude, a willingness to subject our generalizations to testing. Since there is no problem of finding observations to support theories there is no problem of induction. The problem is to eliminate false generalizations by showing that they lead to false conclusions. If the "truth content" but not the "falsity content" of a theory's logical consequences is greater than that of other theories, it has greater "verisimilitude."

Neodialectic Inquiry

The above account is an elementary version of the problems I faced in trying to understand the concepts and methods of social science. Admitting that conceptual order requires the exclusion of some viewpoints, are there any approaches sounder than the current practice of arriving at research decisions by "legislating" assumptions? Shouldn't sociologists reexamine the universe of

[74]

human understanding, the network of linguistic distinctions common to Western man? Could familiar perspectives be expanded by introducing dialectical modes of analysis inherited from civilizations as far removed as China and the early Greeks? I thought so, labeled the broader perspective "neodialectic," and regarded it as a metatheoretical framework. To avoid intellectual closure I suggested that we attempt to spell out, at one and the same time, significant issues and malleable criteria for evaluating them. The central premise of the perspective assumed that all words are joined in varying degrees of meaning with others, that they stand in relation to one another as opposites, complements, synonyms, analogies, etc. By graduating the pliable senses of properties and relations, the boundaries of linguistic communities could be more clearly understood. "The sense or direction of properties and relations is provided by their context: specified elements, qualities, occurrences, events, incidents, items, units, dimensions, factors, components, episodes, categories, conditions, or circumstances. Because of man's inability to isolate permanently any part or aspect of the things of experience, regard for the features through which they are known is always essential. This is what is meant by context. Each thing is itself a composition of contexts, and every context requires, in due course, an assessment of its context, and so on, through an endless regression, limited only by the successive deficiencies under which man labors." Above all, I wished to avoid fixed commitments to particular vocabularies, methods, situations, or modes of understanding. Since men live in different cognitive worlds consisting of nearly unique as well as universal qualities of experience, any subject, topic, text, of *leitmotiv* would be the proper object of neodialectic inquiry. On this assumption, the crucial role played by imagination, conjecture, serendipity, and nondemonstrative inference, could be brought to the forefront of attention.

After noting the pervasiveness of dialectical patterns of reasoning in the writings of Pareto, Simmel, Weber, Mead, Mannheim, Sorokin, Merton, Parsons, Lynd, Bendix and other sociologists, not

[75]

to mention their prevalence in literature, history, mathematics, and natural science, I had to conclude that dialectical thinking is an inescapable aspect of every scholarly endeavor. Can the neodialectic framework be taken to embrace all possible perspectives? Must it, like other frameworks, produce its own kinds of opposites—an antineodialectic framework? To this question I wrote, "No doubt, any particular phase of neodialectical inquiry can be viewed from the perspective of what it excludes; but at the terminal points of analysis, contrasting perspectives provide the resources for its subsequent enlargement. Through these resources neodialectic attempts to find a place for the views which oppose it: to account, in principle, for both truth and error, clarity and confusion, sense and nonsense. In striving to be inclusive it strives to explain the degree of partiality and adequacy of that which is directed against it, and if this can be shown as expressible within it, and not permanently set apart, then neodialectic may be regarded as an 'open system' with 'open textures' of meaning. For what appears to stand outside of it constitutes the essential conditions of its growth. Without successively expansible contexts, the affirmation of new structures and new unities, would be barren of significance. Beyond such unities, the advocate of 'antidialectics' as a self-contained realm of knowledge must claim that neodialectic offers not more than a partial view of the universe."

The Grammar of Sociology

I implied that the idea of a neodialectical approach to sociology grew out of my interest in philosophy, particularly logical positivism and the critiques advanced within it. It was inevitable, then, that I should continually assess the twin contributions of logical reconstruction and empirical observation to sociology. Any contention that the aims of logical reconstruction are not highly prized in sociology would be disputed by few professionals. For those whose prose styles have garnered recognition, analytic attempts to achieve clarity and preciseness are arid or artificial. To them, the elimina-

[76]

tion of vagueness through adherence to logical norms would exclude much that is currently intelligible. Perhaps, then, a grammar of relationships which admits the desirability of some kinds of vagueness while restricting others would be more acceptable. On this view, the most suitable language may not be logical reconstruction but the quasi-consistent rhetoric of appearance and metaphor, of possibilities, potentialities and plausibilities, of contingencies, conjectures and "creative" schema. Any term or statement could be regarded as generic whenever it had the power to produce others or when the variety of meanings imparted (or impacted) in its historical usage encompassed a sizeable portion of human experiences.

As much as I would like to believe that logic is the parent of social consensus, my experience is not sanguine. Most attempts to tailor our understanding to the texture of logical inference or to shape ordinary sentences into logical frames are not unlike trying to "carve cameos on the surface of a cheese souffle." The emotionally sensitized words by which we feel as animal faith the intentions of others seem to be most compelling. Our habits of thought rather than our rational judgments are usually decisive in the appraisals we make of social science. No wonder, then, that the language of daily affairs carries greater conviction than the logical reconstruction of scientific statements.

Reflections of this nature have aroused my interest in exploring the possibility of complementing scientific logic with a rational orthography of sociological and everyday discourse. If schemata for charting logistics, rhetoric, and logomancy (word-making games) can be detected and arbitrated, we may learn much about the mainsprings and vehicles of communication. In what fashion is logical comprehension prefigured in the deposits of public truisms and neighborhood gossip; the revelations and confabulations of deviant communities; the polemics and casuistry of political parties; the argot of voluntarism and dilettantism in youth groups; the sermonizings, chastisements, and redemptions of charismatic leaders; the intentionality and imagination of artistic utterances; the jargon of

[77]

"doxies" and "isms"? What is the mix of clarity and correctness in public commentaries and private recitals; in automated self-communing and indecision; in chronicles of personal vulnerability, melioration, and redress? Is it possible to sketch the "logical" contours of lunacy and folly?

By ordering linguistic signs in unfamiliar ways, by shifting the loci of particularity, generality, and collaterality, hidden chains or patterns of sociological relations may be brought to view. This should not be seen as an altogether contrived process. If our experiences move in every conceivable direction and are revealed in the amplitude and resonance of preferred phrases, the latter may serve as guides to social understanding. If, furthermore, the latent understandings of both highly literate and uneducated people can be decoded, the problems shared by sociology and everyday life will become translucent. To be sure, scientific gains have been made by forcing ill-formed data into well-formed formulae, but this is less than obvious to many able sociologists. For them, novel views of conceptual connectedness, presumably beyond the domain of logical reference, should be welcome.

Admittedly, some kind of rational process must be pursued if we are to grasp and assimilate one another's perspectives. However, the demonstration that certain propositions easily follow others, by step-wise necessities, may not provide an appropriate beginning. The student is best instructed by reminding him of what he already knows, by helping him delineate styles of thought to which he subscribes. From this prolepsis he may be persuaded to conclusions he can accept (or will compel himself to accept) by virtue of the bearing of *his* experiences upon *his* judgments. The arrangement of propositions in orderly schemes is a vantage point only for those prepared to listen. For those who lack the scaffold and thus the vista, there can be no vision of tidy progression from premises to conclusions. No matter how persuasive the argument, one may simply refuse to see, or to accept, and that is the end of the matter. Still, such barriers should not be overemphasized. Underlying every discovery, made without benefit of logic or mathematics, has been some pattern of regularity discernable within the lineaments of a rational rhetoric.

Problems with Empirical Research

I am less troubled by the shortcomings of logical analysis than I am by the image of "empirical research" that sways the profession. Perhaps I can illustrate the nature of my concern by offering a few vignettes, leaving for later discussion the problems which stem from reducing empirical research to observations in a field situation. It is commonly recognized that sentences consisting largely of the kinds of observational terms by which everyday things are described will not produce the unanimity of interpretation assumed by many empiricists. For this reason, we would more nearly agree on what a book looks like and what it means to see somebody tasting, swallowing, chewing, and digesting, then we would agree on the meaning of Francis Bacon's statement, "Some books are to be tasted, others to be swallowed, and some few to be chewed and digested." Similar results would follow from comparing the literal with the possible metaphorical meanings of each of the following: "The empty vessel makes the greatest sound" (Shakespeare), "Born with a silver spoon in his mouth" (proverb), "To hitch his wagon to a star" (Emerson), "Don't fire 'til you see the eyes of the whites" (Sorel, caricaturist). These statements exemplify the fact that every sentence can be understood in other senses than those provided by the observational facets of the words contained within it. Because the simplest observational report is, at the very least, a two-termed relation (e.g., "This chair is brown") and thus subject to error, some kind of judgment is always required. No event is merely observed but depends upon a context of previously experienced judgments, a durable stock of discriminating categories against which it is perceived and appraised.

The same problem applies to the observational bases of social action, a central construct in the repertory of sociological analysis.

Obviously, every action must be broken down into parts or units if the observer is to arrest his attention long enough to record what is before him. Without considering the serious difficulties which ensue from attempts to dissect cultural changes or mass behavior into action units, let us look at the far simpler activity of walking. People do more than walk at the same pace and in the same manner. Some shuffle, some bounce on their toes, some rock or toddle, glide or meander. Others may trudge, stalk, tramp, trip, and stagger. And then there are those who step briskly, march, or promenade. Although words like these are among the sociologist's clearest terms of reference, they cannot be easily distinguished; their meanings so frequently coalesce that for most purposes it is wiser to use the more abstract term "walking." Compared, however, with other terms used to describe situations in which people act, the word "walking" is highly empirical. It is much more difficult to describe *who* does *what* with *whom, when* and *where.* Assuming that social action refers to the process of moving from someplace through something to someone, once its several aspects are distinguished, the problem of recomposing them in the media of stable linguistic structures remains. Included as candidates for such structures are various combinations of conditions, means, ends, and norms; attitudes, role expectations and goal achievements; scenes, agents, agencies, purposes, performances, settings, and audiences; egos, alters, selves, and social objects; exchanges, interactions, transactions, motoric and consummatory responses. These terminologies characterize processes which transcend any observable part or unit; by amalgamating the elements and relations of social action they create the semblance of wholeness.

Perhaps, then, we have our own "indeterminancy principle" spawned by the attempt to observe, simultaneously, both the elements and the course of social action, including its conditions and consequences. Were it possible we would grasp the sense of an entire system by direct observation; since this is impossible we use words to describe it as if we had actually observed it. However, no system is scientifically useful by virtue of the allegation that it was

[80]

directly observed. Observations of social action are inescapably joined to past and future expectations, no portion of which is reliable without the others. To observe a situation is tantamount to scrutinizing the available fund of human experience for purposes of eliciting its hypothetical possibilities. It is understandable, then, why we dwell on the portents rather than on the social acts, per se, of such events as the Vietnam war, urban disorders, student activism, and political assassinations. Our greatest concerns are vested in their possible social causes, their possible effects on various people, their possible public outcomes, and their possible international ramifications. We are captured less by the naked factuality of these events than by the anticipation that they may presage surprise, alarm, distress, or destructions; that they may portray joy or sorrow, heroism or cowardice, praise or condemnation; that they may provoke vengeance, greed, or villainy; that they may signal the possibility of something indescribably cruel and ugly.

Our lives are most fully consigned to those occurrences which betoken hidden potentialities by trumpeting the limits of credibility. Without the enchantment of illusion and fantasy everyday happenings would be empty of flavor and gusto. "Where did we go wrong" and "What are we coming to" are asked more often than the unimaginative query, "Can you describe what you observed and nothing else?"

The problem may be pursued in another direction by asking how we know that anyone has a certain characteristic, that a particular person is, for instance, "alienated"? In most cases, we have his responses to "tests" purporting to measure alienation, or we can describe his actions in familiar situations. Now every person has countless contacts with a great variety of people and things, many of which are entirely beyond our range of observation. These contacts are the outgrowth of associations extending from childhood with people who, like himself, have had thousands of unseen contacts with others. This means that the "alienated" person (if identifiable) is observed but a small fraction of time and on these occasions the skeins of relationships interlining his life cannot be

[81]

clearly detailed. And if the observation of a single person poses insurmountable difficulties, note how these difficulties are multiplied when groups, social classes, and communities are "observed."

The consequences of this condition can hardly be overestimated. If the sociological observer can see only part of what two or three individuals in a delinquent gang are doing at any one time and then must turn quickly to observing another part of their activity and cannot be very sure of all he is seeing (beyond the attribution of commonsense labels), how useful are his situationally slanted reports as definitive criteria of scientific significance? Can any sociologist observe the continuous, multidirectional activity of several individuals in the span of even a few minutes without imputing "observations" drawn from his life experiences? Imagine the sheer quantity of imputed observations that must be introduced by the empirical researcher when he reports on the activities of bureaucracies, the characteristics of American society, including its "integrative" aspects, and the signs of modernization and ethnic conflict around the world! Surely no reasonable person can hold that field observations will sustain more than a small fraction of research certified as sociological.

These limitations are magnified in the uncritical attitude taken toward those undergoing observation and those engaged in observing. Neither group is ever subjected to the kinds of analyses scientsists have made of human behavior in other contexts, analyses which should be instituted *prior* to their entrance in the field, if the perspectives of scientific and ordinary experience are to have relevance. In their research, sociologists act as though the concepts they apply to others have no consequence for their own endeavors. The researchers' reference groups, dramatistic interests, class attitudes, professional values, and styles of socialization are, for the little we hear of them, quite insignificant determinants of the results he obtains. Deutscher, not to mention others, has summarized much research which points to the conclusion that there is little or no correspondence between what people say and what they do. Have these results no bearing on the correspondence between sociological reports and sociological observations (the operational side of empirical research)?

Why have we failed to assess the import of thousands of studies committed to explaining the reactions of observers? What are the effects of such complex concepts as sensation, learning, motivation, and judgment upon our "observation" of constancy, surface and shape, direction and distance, and how do these condition our description of people and events including, to begin with, body images, facial contours, vocal intonations, and other physiognomic cues? The problem of depth perception alone has given rise to horrendous problems of optical, neural, and brain functioning in which the choice of descriptive vocabulary plays a large part. Does a language of transitions, transformations, intensities, and "energy difference" adequately represent the observable layout? What is the bearing of information from contradictory sense and conceptual modalities, of different thresholds of awareness and subliminal discrimination, of verbal and figural aftereffects, of sensory unfamiliarity interference, delay, isolation, distortion, and deprivation upon the reliability of reported scholarly observations? (Consider, for instance, lower-class informants.) Indeed, how salient are these words for identifying "empirical phenomena," given the alterations of meaning which eventuate with their adaptation to various theoretical contexts. When attention is directed to the position of "observation" in learning theory, psychoanalysis, self-theory, Gestalt theory, linguistics, and ethnology, one begins to appreciate the magnitude of what is excluded when sociologists confine themselves to current methods of empirical investigation.

If between momentary instances of direct observation the researcher is occupied with a mosaic of images supplied from past experience, where does he obtain his "knowledge" of social phenomena? The reply, I presume, is to be found in the reservoir of his experience, a largely unknown composite of bio-environmental interrelations. Insofar as the experience of each day, month, or year adds some increment to one's total experience, just so much is added by the period devoted to field research. In exceptional cases, field experience may be so startling or traumatic that it leads to a major reorganization of the researcher's outlook, but we do not now have any criteria for deciding when this occurs. Without such criteria we cannot know whether the reorganization would have occurred, in any case, from the individual's continual re-arrangement of his conceptual apparatus or through the sudden reappearance of previously buried experiences. In the absence of contrary evidence, we must conclude that the results of field research are most probably dependent upon what the researcher "brings with him" when he undertakes his studies. Even though his views may be changed by the things he sees and hears in the field, these changes must be accommodated to his "matrix of experience," to ingrained categories, verbal habits, learned modes of perception, and established paths of behavior.

The more interviewers take into account the typicality and uniqueness of their respective social backgrounds, the longer they are engaged in team participation, the more they articulate the cultural sources of their understanding, the more their work is replicated in different neighborhoods, communities, and societies— the more fully must they move away from the empiricism that is, by declaration, the cornerstone of sociological research. For these steps are, in essential respects, comparative and analytical; they reach outward toward the formulation of significant generalizations, the vindication of which rests on subjective judgments, corroborated by others. If everything we do is empirical in the sense of experiential then nothing is to be gained by the oft-stated charge that a particular problem must be resolved "empirically"— by referral to survey data. To be sure, we need "more" empirical research but "more" should mean access to the total fund of human experience together with improved standards for critically appraising it.

The preceding assumptions will explain a prominent feature of today's sociology. If our empirical data provided the scientific support claimed for them, there would be less controversy on what constitutes significant research. Charges of bias, with or without ideology, would not be so frequent. In all areas of sociology—ecology, social stratification, collective behavior, etc.—disparities of interpretation are widespread. This is, of course, what must be expected from observational data that is idiosyncratic, fleeting, fragmentary, and spatiocentric. The experiences sociologists share enable them to communicate; those unshared give rise to differences of viewpoint. The ratio of shared to unshared experiences (academic and everyday) determines the range of professional acceptance.

It is doubtful whether satisfactory experimental tests can be found for judging the comparative contributions of generic experience and field research to any author's study, since the choice of experimental designs will reflect the very problem the author seeks to solve. Nevertheless, the experimentally minded may find the following procedure suggestive. First, define the general boundary conditions of a particular field situation in terms of demographic categories (time, place, age, sex, ethnic membership, etc.). Second, ask a number of sociologists of diverse backgrounds to write "hypothetical" analyses of "findings," prior to any contact with one another or the field situation in question. Third, ask each of them to enter the field situation, separately observe what is happening, and provide an "empirical" analysis of the results. Finally, compare the "hypothetical" analyses with the "empirical" analyses. If the variance of the empirical analyses is significantly less than the variance of the hypothetical analyses, some claim can be made that the field situation played a constraining role in the study results. This "experiment" assumes that the specific boundary characteristics of a particular field situation cannot contribute to the development of scientific generalizations until they are compared and categorized theoretically. However, for those who assume that these characteristics are important elements of interpretation, experiments in which their admissibility is systematically varied may produce instructive results.

Suggested Alternatives

Having expressed misgivings about the current use of logic and empirical research in sociology, I should, no doubt, assume the burden of suggesting alternative routes to firmer ground. We might, I believe, begin by freely conceding that field observations, however important, represent but a small portion of the arsenal of sociologically relevant experience. Observations that are responsive to no more than a narrow sector of space and time should not be taken as decisive for evaluating knowledge cumulated from history, culture, and daily experience, especially when the latter are judged by standards drawn from the sweep of philosophy, logic and mathematics, literature, art, and rhetoric. Such standards are more nearly rational, ethical, or esthetic than they are "empirical" in their derivation and instrumentation. Commanded by an infinity of vicarious experiences, including countless indirect observations, they are too well entrenched in our intellectual storehouse to be jettisoned by the changing way stations of local empiricisms.

In earlier paragraphs, I indicated that our language sustains the search for clarity and precision, explanation and prediction, observation and confirmation. Sociology, likewise, is sustained primarily by a body of word-word relations rather than of word-thing relations, because the former allows for the construction of many more "things," in a different sense of the word "thing," than the latter. Since we are constantly confronted with misleading nuances of meaning, expressible in symbols generally beguiling, our language should, I believe, be probed repeatedly for those avowals of human experience that petition the widest allegiances. For me, this is less a question of discovering expressions that are "correct" or "true" to experience (myths, rituals, and rules are correct or true for those pledged to them) than of ministering to the singularity, typicality, and near universality of all varieties of experience. Information is needed on the efficiency with which common expressions summon and engrave old experiences, activate and epitomize present experiences, announce and disclose future experiences. Language is most dexterous when it inscribes modes of interpretation that are attentive to the range and depth of distinctive human experience, when it evokes ways of acting that enable us to extract particularized meanings in the situations through which our several encounters are carried forward. Its potentiality is revealed in its power to restructure, by transactional process, the destinies of programs and plans; in its facility to adumbrate colloquial utterances by casting them into a wider ambit.

Insofar as universals and categories, quasi-universals and subcategories are mutually binding, they may serve as interchangeable guides for terminological analyses. On this assumption, it is possible that the nomenclature of archetypes, prototypes, exemplars, templates, models, paradigms, homologies, images, word coalitions, experiential constants, or root metaphors will, each in their way, prove illuminating. By using them as screens to inventory sociohistorical experience one may be more fully prepared to examine the productivity of social science vocabularies, especially the broadly gauged constructs of social action and behavior, social evolution, social systems, functionalism, symbolic interactionism, stratification, information theory, latent factor, componential, cross-sectional, and other forms of content analysis.

Perhaps the basic question is this: How or in what ways are things to be identified and related, assuming that what can be said about any one depends upon what can be said about an unspecific (but not necessarily unspecifiable) number of others? If a sign is "something which stands to somebody for something in some respect or capacity" (Peirce), the problem of naming the social conditions among which things can be taken as signs for other things becomes of paramount importance. Around what conditions should a vocabulary of connections, associations, affiliations, collaterals, equivalences, inferences, applications, referrals, coalescences, convertibilities, reciprocities, synonymities, resemblances, repetitions, continuities, translations, disparities, paraphrasings, semblances, concordances, coterminations, reproductions, or congruences be favored? The decisions made on the choice of these categories have much to do with the form, slope, and prolixity of primary, secondary, and peripheral vocabularies.

Categories can serve not only as captions for grouping and mediating the passage of words but as beacons for mobilizing and implementing social policies. By not referring to things as static elements but to the primary of certain senses and sentences, they may do for experience what is wanted from experience. Together with dominant and latent subcategories, they may provide the foci from which and through which the shape and drift of experience can be understood. Those that are prescriptive or privileged in the history of thought, society, and nature will extend beyond contemporary communities, local events and private experiences.

The clustering, differentiation, and recentering of experiences in ascending categories may enable the sociologist to locate the imperatives, infirmities, and contingencies through which his discipline has developed and is likely to develop. By cataloguing word gradients and language strata in various populations, it may be possible to link memory and imagination, tradition and transformation, prologue and prophecy. Everyone's experience is lucid and opaque, gathered and dispersed in varying degrees. It is a mixture of mutable and immutable, compatible and incompatible, coherent and incoherent aspects or phases of itself. It is used to act upon itself, to talk about and to extend itself. The denial that oneself or others have or have not had certain experiences clearly rests on the articulation of experience. Likewise, the claim that experience realizes inherited endowment but does not produce it is a distinction drawn from educated experience. All this everyone "knows" from experience, except those whose experience is such as to hold them unfamiliar with these words or to lead them, for anomalous reasons, to contest their usage. Moreover, everyone who contests word usage must use words anchored in his own and other's experiences. Nothing new or paradoxical can be expressed without instantaneously expanding experience and including the product within the compass of experience. The correspondence of a narrow verbal image with an observational slice of experience must be reactive to the mosaic of verbal images applicable to multiple slices of experience. And when correspondences are thus augmented, coherence with or of experience becomes the programmatic source of all standards.

Conclusion

I end this essay keenly aware that I have, in many instances, failed to strike the right note. But, then, who can speak of ideas without tilting them in manageable directions? Far from attempting to rectify a chasm of omissions, let me name if not explain what I might have said in a longer essay. I would surely say something about the considerable influence of Kant, Russell, Dewey, Hempel, and the university community on my thinking. I would explore the influence of memorable and miserable people, self-autonomy, nature, physical labor, tragedy, and death of my conceptions of the future. I would emphasize the personal conviction that we are abysmally ignorant about the most important things in life, all too ignorant to clinch the probabilities we claim for our research. We know too little about what people should want to become and not enough about the subtle ways they enhance or harm others; in part this is the question of trust and treachery—ideas but dimly understood. In this era of overspeak, we put a great deal more into words than we can understand and we understand many things we cannot put into words. Accepting this, we need ways of communicating with reason, anguish, absurdity, negation, and nothingness; of scanning and monitoring the fragments of experience which we may, in our frailty, grasp as irrefragable rays of light.

Lest the above remarks appear improvident, I hasten to list a few things of which I am fairly sure: (1) In this age, there is no visible resolution to the spiral of increasing aspirations and rewards, translated either as the limits of noblesse oblige, Christian charity, and the golden rule; *or* rich and poor in their own manner are

[89]

goaded by relative deprivation; *or* "you owe me what I expect to get from you"; *or* something else. (2) The manifest forms of human life and culture are bleakly unbalanced by the asymmetry of creation and destruction. The time and effort required to achieve human maturity or to build a great edifice exceeds, by far, the time and effort required to destroy the world. Joined to this is the kernel of truth in the maxim, "Thousands are hated while none are loved without a real cause"" (3) Everything must be seen through a double image, if not through a prism of shifting perspectives. Nothing stands alone; meaningful things are jostled and transformed by the interfaces and interstices of other things, by the porous substances that unite and divide them. This is the meeting place of ignorance and sociological inquiry. What we do here bears witness to the responsibilities of scholarship.

6

THE SOCIOLOGIST
AS NATURALIST

LEE RAINWATER

THE PRINCIPAL ATTITUDE which directs my work is one of puzzled curiosity. I have always felt that I don't understand the people around me very well, and with that feeling has come a strong curiosity to try to figure out exactly what they are doing and why they are doing it. This attitude is perhaps not particularly distinctive to me, but the form by which I have sought to resolve that puzzled curiosity during my professional life is perhaps more distinctive. I have always been drawn to styles of sociological and psychological work that partake of the naturalist's approach—that is, an approach in which there is an effort to observe the forms and behaviors in which one is interested until one feels one understands how they hang together, and then to depict as accurately as possible what one thinks he has observed so that others may apprehend that reality, and perhaps by replicating the observations validate it. This kind of activity has seemed socially worthwhile, as well as personally gratifying, for three reasons.

The first, and I suspect the most enduring for me, is a belief in the intrinsic, almost esthetic value, of an accurate and penetrating depiction of reality. In this I think perhaps I was influenced by my father, who was an historian, and who, in his own way, impressed me with the effort to see things as they are, just because they are that way. In addition, I have always felt that if men are to achieve their goals, if they are to avoid troubles and construct a society which meets their needs as fully as it might, they need to understand their world better. The particular part of the country in which I grew up can impress an observer with the extent to which men are their own worst enemies. If one for some reason does not become fully socialized to a particular world view, one can never lose the sense of puzzlement and anger at how men in that society hurt themselves and others to no good purpose.

Finally, I have always hoped that if the social naturalist's task is done well, he provides the best kind of grist for the mill of the social theorist. As a person who has neither interest in, nor talent for, doing other than heavily grounded theoretical work, I nevertheless feel that the other fellow, the theorist, would be more successful in his work if he could draw upon good descriptive work. Unfortunately few theorists have pursued this strategy systematically, although I would still feel that the best correction for much of the nonsense that passes as sociological theory is the use of work in the ethnographic tradition as raw material for theory.

There are any number of ways one might be led by the puzzled curiosity I have described. A further distinctive characteristic of my work has been the reliance on qualitative data—from participant observation, open-ended interviewing, and projective techniques. Such methods have always seemed to me to more closely replicate human life as it is experienced than the more controlling techniques of questionnaires, laboratory experiments, and the like. Since these kinds of data have been the ones that have impressed me most—whether in the psychoanalytic case study, the ethnography of the great anthropologists, or the field studies of men like William F. Whyte, or Howard Becker—it is ironic that I happen to be a rather poor and indifferent field worker. Were it not for an accident of career development I might never have circumvented this impasse—I might have had perforce to become a survey researcher! The accident was that during graduate studies in the Committee on Human Development at the University of Chicago, I became intrigued with the work being done at Social Research, Inc., in Chicago, a private research firm, then involving such people as Burleigh B. Gardner, W. Lloyd Warner, and William E. Henry. This organization was devoted to applying the combined techniques of an anthropologically informed sociology in the style of Warner and a psychodynamically oriented social psychology to studies of "ordinary social life" for such diverse clients as manufacturers, advertising agencies, the movie industry, and government agencies. (This kind of research some five years later came to be called "motivation research," but at the time we saw it as simply an extension of more academically oriented community studies.) Because Social Research, Inc., carried out numerous small projects in short periods from beginning to completion (ranging from two months to six months) the organization had adapted survey research techniques to the qualitative approach. I was able, therefore, to make use of a staff of interviewers trained to do focused and nondirective interviewing and to administer specially designed projective techniques, and consequently to work with the kind of data that was meaningful to me without having to collect it myself.

As I have worked as a "secondhand" observer, my respect for the field worker's ability has increased year by year. Apparently my ability to analyze this kind of data has also increased, so that I am often flattered by readers of my work who take it for granted that I myself collected the data about which I write and are surprised and a little unbelieving when I say that I have not. (My most recent experience as a field worker, a study of the Moynihan Report controversy, again impressed me with how much better other people are at collecting the kind of data I like to work with; fortunately I had a collaborator who is an excellent field worker.) My training in the analysis of projective techniques, particularly the TAT and sentence completions, went a long way toward developing the particular kind of sensitivity to interpreting the lines in between the lines of written material which is the sine qua non of working with qualitative data.

Curiosity and Psychiatry

How did I end up in a place like that? The intellectual and organizational coordinates of my career are hardly typical for a sociologist, except perhaps in that I, no more than other sociologists, aspired to that profession as a child—almost none of us knew it existed! From about twelve years of age I had expected to become first an electrical engineer and then a physicist. But by my first semester in college I had changed my mind. I think I now see that such a choice was a constricting defense against the anxiety that accompanied the puzzled curiosity which I felt about the world. It was a defense that didn't work for me, although, of course, it does work for many others, including quite a few men who have shifted from the physical sciences to productive careers in sociology and psychology. So from physics I shifted to psychiatry; that was about the only model of how one might go about making a career of understanding the what and why of people that penetrated to me in Mississippi. I knew, of course, from having grown up with discussions about history and political science that those, too, were fields that dealt with man, but in the South even an adolescent could get the feeling that such studies were directed more toward justifying the region and its peculiar institutions than to getting at the guts of human behavior. Psychiatry, of course, meant undergraduate work in psychology, but I found that incredibly dull. My interest was sustained only by out-of-class reading of Freud and his followers. Finally, a co-worker at the State Department, where I worked the midnight shift in the code room while studying at George Washington University during the day, told me that given my political and racial views (which put me in a highly argumentative minority against my conservative co-workers who were mostly trainees for the Foreign Service) I should study sociology. George Washington's one sociologist was in the army at the time, so I began reading through the entries that struck my fancy under sociology in the card catalog at the Library of Congress and the Public Library. This sent me eventually to the University of Southern California (Emory S. Bogardus had more entries in the card catalog than anyone else) and finally to the University of Chicago, where I see-sawed back and forth between sociology and psychology, finally settling down for doctoral work

[94]

in the Committee for Human Development which regarded both interests as legitimate.

If I had been a somewhat less superficial reader while still in Mississippi, I might not have had to take such a circuitous route to sociology. In my senior year I had read the new book, *An American Dilemma,* and had been fascinated to learn that there seemed to be a great many people who didn't share most white Mississippians' views about white supremacy, segregation, and all that. (It must have taken a courageous librarian to buy that book for the Jackson Public Library—fortunately I don't think many people besides myself read it that year.) I knew, of course, from sketchy readings of history, the *Reader's Digest,* and *Time* magazine that I was not alone in believing that there was something tragically destructive about how Negroes had been and were being treated in the South, but I had not realized that there was a scientific way of trying to understand all that and perhaps of doing something about it. Myrdal told me that there was, but somehow I did not realize that the pivotal science involved was sociology, and therefore, had to rediscover it some years later. The book that finally persuaded me to a sociological career was *Deep South,* which led me to *Yankee City,* and eventually to the University of Chicago to study with W. Lloyd Warner, Allison Davis, and Burleigh Gardner. Like many Southerners who become sociologists, the irrationalities of race have been a continuing sociological concern for me. I am pleased, however, that the contingencies of my career took me away from the study of race relations into a broad range of studies of specific aspects of the life styles of Americans of different social classes. These studies ranged from subjects of substantial social importance such as attitudes toward political candidates to trivia such as attitudes toward breakfast cereal. This research experience provided a kind of perspective which I have found extremely valuable during the past five years, when I have been able to return again to the problem of race that initially sparked my interest in sociology.

As for "influences," they are as varied as the career sketched above might suggest. At the University of Chicago I remember particularly Albert J. Reiss, then a beginning teacher whose courses in urban sociology and "social pathology" were so well organized and presented that one came to feel at home with and impressed by the broad range of traditional Chicago school sociology. I learned more than I knew from Everett C. Hughes, whose work I have come to appreciate increasingly as the years have gone by. The principal influences on me were Allison Davis, William E. Henry, Burleigh B. Gardner, and W. Lloyd Warner; the first as a teacher and model, the last three as both teachers and co-workers over a thirteen-year period. As I look back on it, I regret the influence of the unfortunate Chicago tradition of faculty rivalry and schism. The result was, from the student's point of view, not a dialectic among contending points of view, but rather a series of chasms. As a result, it was not until some time later that I began to appreciate fully the work of men like Louis Wirth, Herbert Blumer, and E. A. Shils.

For the first fifteen years of my intellectual life by far the strongest influence on my thinking was that of Freud and other psychoanalytic writers. That influence is still strong, but increasingly blended with more traditional sociological perspectives. (This psychoanalytic exposure continues to provide me with delight at the unconscious, or perhaps conscious, cribbing of psychodynamic ideas by the most unlikely sociologists.) Almost as important as the psychoanalytical influence was that of the anthropological writers of the thirties, particularly Ralph Linton and the culture and personality school represented by Ruth Benedict, Kardiner, Kluckhohn, etc. Later the work of Eric Erikson impressed me as a more truly social integration of psychodynamic and anthropological insights. In the past few years I think I have begun to pay increasing attention to people whose work I overlooked because of the feeling that there was some kind of necessary conflict between psychodynamic formulations and the symbolic interactionist social psychology, and therefore, I have been increasingly influenced by the works of men such as Anselm Strauss, Erving Goffman, Howard Becker, and Edwin Lemert.

Sociology and Social Problems

I like best my first book and my last one, but each for quite different reasons. The first book, *Workingman's Wife,* represented a combination of researches conducted over a number of years with my colleagues at Social Research, Inc. I enjoyed working with my collaborators, Richard P. Coleman and Gerald Handel, and the book pleases me as an example of what can be produced from comfortable continuing collaboration. I think I like the book most, not for what is unique to it, but for what it shares with the work of a number of other sociologists who were studying the working class at about the same time and without knowing what each other was doing. I continue to be impressed by the similarities, the replication if you will, among the working-class studies of such diverse sociologists as Bennett Berger, Herbert Gans, Mirra Komarovsky, S. M. Miller, and Frank Reissman.

The second book, *And The Poor Get Children,* I simply thoroughly enjoyed doing. It represented the application to a particular problem, family planning, of findings developed in previous working-class research and somehow all the pieces fell together right. I think I like the book also because of its shock value, its demonstration that such presumably "sensitive" topics as sexual behavior and contraceptive practice are quite available to qualitative survey methods. Finally, I enjoyed it because I made such a colossal error of prediction—cautioning that large numbers of lower-class women could not be expected to adopt the oral contraceptive because of the demands of the daily pill-taking regimen. That mistake has been a very instructive one for me, and has strongly influenced the way I derive practical implications from social-psychological findings in the research in which I am now engaged.

Finally, I enjoyed the *Moynihan Report and the Politics of*

[97]

Controversy because it gave my coauthor and myself an opportunity to experiment with sociological journalism and because it represented one of the few occasions on which I have strayed outside the area of the sociology of "private" behavior. It has always seemed to me that one of the most profound divisions within sociology is between those who study private behavior (the family, informal social relations, deviant behavior, and the like) and those who find such concerns trivial and instead concentrate on the larger questions of formal institutional behavior, political behavior, community power structures, etc. Although I have long had an interest in the operation of government bureaucracies and private cause groups, I had never had an opportunity to shift my focus from the private behavior of individuals and families to this level of social organization. The Moynihan controversy study provided an opportunity to test a number of hypotheses which I had been developing over the previous few years about the operation of the government and civil rights groups in connection with an event which had made the people involved highly self-conscious about what they were doing.

The question of impact is a difficult one for the person concerned to assess, particularly in the case of one who is not concerned with the development of theory. I believe that my efforts have had an impact in three areas. In family sociology my studies of lower-, working-, and middle-class family life have helped to break down the stereotype of one dominant American family life pattern. The particular focus of several of my books on contraception and family planning has, I believe, helped considerably to establish this area as a crucial part of any meaningful effort to understand family behavior.

I believe my work has had some constructive effect as an example of the value of qualitative methodologies. Particularly through the early 1960s, qualitative methodology enjoyed very poor standing in sociology. My work has fit in with that of a number of other sociologists who persisted in the use of these methods and who now seem to have captured the attention of an important segment of the younger men in the field. One hears much less often today than ten years ago the notion that qualitative studies are suitable only for the pilot phase of larger investigations.

Finally, I feel that my recent work has begun to have an impact on policy diagnoses concerning the race and poverty problems. In all of these areas it would be presumptuous to consider that my sociological efforts have had an impact in "reshaping" the field, but such information as I can gather concerning how my work is being used does encourage me to believe that it is playing its part in fostering standards of greater naturalistic accuracy and detail in sociological presentations, and more careful and systematic attention to policy implications.

The relationship of sociology to social problems was at the heart of my initial interest; for many years I functioned as an applier of social science knowledge and research techniques to the concerns of highly varied clients, and more recently I have been concerned to develop knowledge into sociologically informed programs for undoing the damage of racial oppression and economic exploitation of the poor. Even so, I value the wide range of styles of work in the field—from the men who do not want to move out of the ivory tower to those who are willing to work actively for change by getting their hands dirty in political movements and bureaucratic organizations. A sociology which strives so hard for relevance and application that there is no play for pure curiosity must inevitably use up its intellectual capital; a sociology in which application is either rejected or considered "dirty work" better delegated to other professions like social work or planning runs the very real risk of losing touch with the reality its theories are supposed to encompass.

I value the increasing sophistication about application and policy relevance that I think the field has begun to show in the past half-dozen years, with the increasing understanding that policy relevance also involves moral commitment on the part of the sociologist which he needs to acknowledge and address consciously.

But I think the central issue has been and will be the one that Horowitz points to in his emphasis on the autonomy of social science. And it is the autonomy of the practicing sociologist, and not just of the field in the abstract, that is important. Sociology is extremely fashionable these days—with undergraduates, with the mass media, and with government. But, its popularity comes not so much from an understanding of what sociological knowledge has to offer, as from the belief that other branches of knowledge have failed to "solve" our problems and because sociology talks about some of the most obvious ones (race, poverty, alienation, bureaucracy, etc.) it has the solution. The autonomy of the sociologist to pursue knowledge and develop theory will be seriously threatened by this popularity—not only by the threat of co-optation by the powers that be, but also by the threat of ideological co-optation in the service of the powers against the powers that be. Sociological knowledge is potentially extremely embarrassing to all of these forces since it seldom neatly confirms the preferred world view of any of the contenders in the political process. Sociology is in a position today to make crucial contributions to changing society, but it is in that position only by virtue of several decades of empirical and theoretical work which was relatively insulated from *direct* political interference by the society at large or on the campus. Now the pressures to interfere are strong. And the more accurate sociological depiction becomes, the stronger these forces will be. Sociologists will need a strong sense of solidarity no matter how varied their own individual pursuits of sociological knowledge. If they are to weather these pressures, they will need a deep and sensitive commitment to each other's freedom of responsible inquiry, and an insistent resistance to distortion of their findings by those who perceive themselves to be adversely affected by "sociological truth."

7

PERSONAL REMARKS ON
SOCIOLOGICAL
RESEARCH
IN THE THIRD WORLD

CHARLES C. MOSKOS, JR.

AN UNSUNG BURDEN of the "underdeveloped" countries of the third world (roughly defined as Latin America, Asia, and Africa) is that they have become research locales for legions of American social scientists. Graduate students writing doctoral theses, as well as established scholars, pursue their peripatetic studies in growing numbers. It is to be hoped that as the number of social scientists going abroad increases there will be an effort to report the implementation and theoretical assumptions as well as the results of their studies. In this way the interaction between theory, methods, and findings can be understood more fully. And hopefully, some of the unstated premises of much of social science can be subjected to closer scrutiny. The following account, then, deals not so much with the empirical findings of my study (1967) of West Indian nationalism, but rather with some specifics on the manner in which the research was conducted and my views on how this research is related to the ongoing sociological enterprise.

My study sought to uncover the forces affecting attitudes and actions toward political independence among the top leaders of the emerging nations of the British Caribbean: Jamaica, Trinidad, Guyana, Barbados, and the smaller islands comprising the Leeward and Windward island chains. The study revealed a diversity of beliefs; a dynamic and changing system, and a problematic future within which the hopes people have and the actions that they take can affect their future in significant ways.[1] How is it that certain members of colonial society begin to question the old order and take steps towards its termination? Why is it that the other persons in the same society look on with alarm at this course of events? And why do still others acquiesce to the shift to nationhood without being personally committed to it? It was to questions of this sort that I sought answers.

Being myself a "bird of passage," as the West Indians say, candor compels me to say that I originally came to the British Caribbean because it seemed like a pleasant and interesting place to do field work. Though the anticipated pleasures of my travels were more than realized, I also became morally committed to the efforts of the West Indian peoples to try to shape their own destiny. At the same time, I was forced to confront and reappraise many of the methodological tenets and theoretical assumptions so widespread in social science as it is practised and taught in the United States. For in addition to the inevitable personal culture shock one experiences in a foreign society, there was another culture shock concerning my sociology, my *American* sociology.

Much time, too much, was spent before leaving in formulating a research design which attempted to be "theoretically significant" as that term is currently misused. Attempts to operationalize the various grand theoretical schemes so popular back home either resulted in ending up with a trivial problem, or something so abstract that there was little connection with social change in the West Indies. These formalistic approaches—so consciously trying to avoid cultural bias—paradoxically underemphasize the most important causal factors of change in the third world: modernizing ideologies; the forms of power, control, and violence; and international economic relationships. In my case, I found it necessary to abandon orthodox conceptualizations once I began to face the realities of the West Indian scene. For it is incumbent upon the inquiring mind itself to make an order out of facts, and not to force data into a priori irrelevant pigeonholes.

A related problem is that much of the training in methodology (a result of its being oriented around team research?) excessively stresses the principle of reliability (i.e., standardizing data collection by reducing inconsistencies in measurement) to the detriment of validity (i.e., getting the truth by measuring what one is looking for) in sociological research. Methodological rituals cannot substitute for the inventiveness which the field researcher must come up with when he is out on his own. Conventions and never-to-be-deviated-from research designs can perform an important function for the growth of science, but they cannot result in the creative act on which science also depends.

The Politics of Developing Interviews

IDENTIFYING TOP LEADERS

An important methodological feature of the study was the procedure used to identify the top West Indian leaders—those to be eventually interviewed. In each of the societies in which research was conducted the same procedure was used. Initially, interviews were held with five persons, each located in a different institutional sector, who on the basis of their *position* ought to have been society-wide influentials. These initial interviews were with persons in: (1) the incumbent political group, (2) the political opposition, (3) major economic enterprises, (4) the civil service, and (5) the mass media. Each of these initial interviewees were asked who they thought wielded widespread influence in their society. The reason for using persons located in different institutional sectors during the early interviewing period was to reduce the likelihood of bias in the identification procedure toward particular institutional sectors. There was, however, little "halo" effect. On the whole, perhaps because of the small scale of West Indian society, there was general agreement on who were local leaders even if located in institutional sectors other than those of the respondent. Those influentials most frequently mentioned in the initial interviews were in turn interviewed, and asked to identify other society-wide influentials. Thus, the identification procedure developed into a *reputational* method.[2]

Departing from customary practise, I have reported in the published findings the actual names and rankings of the West Indian leaders so identified (though, of course, responses to questions in the interview are not identified with individual names). Such a public listing of societal leaders allows for an informed evaluation of the identification procedure by residents and observers of the West Indies.

ARRANGING INTERVIEWS

The period in which the field work took place (1961-62) was a particularly favorable one for interviewing. None of the leaders identified in the manner described above refused to be interviewed. There was an atmosphere of political excitement which even the casual visitor could not escape noticing. It was a time when the issue of independence was on everyone's mind; as I was to learn, it was a time when West Indians of all levels were willing to talk about where they thought their society was heading. By the time the field work was completed, I had interviewed prime ministers, cabinet members, leaders of opposition parties, heads of labor unions, wealthy merchants, large plantation owners, newspaper editors and columnists, leading members of the clergy, ethnic spokesmen, heads of voluntary organizations, prominent professionals, high-ranking civil servants, and leading intellectual and artistic figures.

An indispensable help in arranging interviews was the genuine interest of most West Indians with whom I became acquainted during my stay in the area. In every island I visited, prior introductions removed many of the obstacles I had feared. These introductions were of particular value in the smaller islands where strangers are quickly heard of and almost as quickly labeled to be helped or avoided. Many times an interview difficult to obtain was made possible by running into someone at a social gathering who was able to intervene for me. I discovered that one should not be bashful about explaining what one is trying to do. Most people are interested and if they can help they generally will. Somewhat surprisingly, I believe my relatively short stay in each island helped rather than hindered my research. Since I was leaving soon, people had to act quickly. Moreover, for those who befriended me there was no possibility that I could turn into a long-term burden.

There are occasions, however, when all available personal contacts have been used, and the interviewer himself must seek out his quarry. After some trial and error, I realized that the best procedure is simply to go to the respondent's office or home and ask to see him. If you have referred leads or letters of introduction, well and good; if not, go anyway. Rather than try to make appointments by telephone or mail beforehand, it is best to present yourself personally. The interviews themselves averaged over an hour in length and many were much longer.

Most of the interviews took place in the respondent's office, but in many cases arrangements were made to meet in other locations. Some of the more memorable interview situations were: talking to the editor of one of the West Indies' leading newspapers while a demonstration against him, bordering on a riot, was taking place outside his office; quizzing a prime minister alternately waist and shoulder deep in the Caribbean surf; passing the better part of an hour with a Roman Catholic bishop while he was waiting to officiate at a funeral; meeting a leader of a black racist cult at a political rally and then moving into the back room of a poor man's bar where the interview went on into the early hours of the morning.

THE INTERVIEW SITUATION

At the outset of the interview, before beginning any questioning, I tried, when possible, to set a leisurely mood. Our meeting was presented as an opportunity for the respondent to take a little time off from his busy and hectic schedule to philosophize, meditate, and think aloud. I was talking to him, it was understood, because he was obviously an influential person whose views mattered. In fact, few of my interviewees displayed any false modesty concerning their importance in their society.

No attempt was made to stress anonymity, such as telling the respondent that his answers would be reduced to statistical tables. It was also made very clear, however, that any desire to keep certain remarks confidential would be honored. Indeed, excessive emphasis on anonymity may create doubts in the mind of the respondent as to the candor he should exhibit. After all, no matter what the interviewer says about impartial anonymity, the respondent correctly realizes that the interviewer can subsequently report whatever he wants. For this reason, the interview must be pitched on a level of mutual trust. One should try to establish a man-to-man relationship stressing the uniqueness and importance of what the respondent is saying. And this requires that intelligent comments be made during the interview by the interviewer himself. My natural "one-down" position was somewhat overcome by the fact that during my research I had picked up a great deal of information which was of interest to my interviewees. Because I learned that I too would be questioned, and because my own information was cumulative, I reserved my most important interviews for the terminal period during my stay in a particular island.

Because the interview itself is a rapport builder, the sequence of questions is of great importance. Particularly when one is working in a foreign society, the researcher's common sense is not always a good criterion for determining how questions vary in the anxiety they may cause among his respondents. This knowledge can be effectively gained only through pilot interviews. Once one has an idea of the anxiety various questions produce, it is possible to maximize valid responses by attempting to control anxiety levels during the interview.

I found the following sequence to be best suited for eliciting information when talking to West Indian leaders. At the start of the interview, moderately high-anxiety questions were asked. This was done to gain the respondent's attention and to remove temptations to slip into clichés. But the anxiety produced at the start of the interview must not be so high as to cause the respondent to become unduly apprehensive. After the initial set of questions, the anxiety level is reduced and rapport established as firmly as possible. In the third phase of the interview, the highest-anxiety-producing questions are asked. By this time, the respondent is usually involved in his answers and has committed himself to the interview situation. At the close of the interview, the questions are of a very low-anxiety potential. The interview should end on a pleasant note and a mood of mutual good feeling. And, as any interviewer knows, some of the most significant responses come after the notebook is closed.

CONFIDANTS

Regardless of how well the interviews appear to be going, one's interpretation of them needs to be supplemented with outside opinions. It is essential to know one or more local persons with whom one can discuss the study in depth. These confidants will tend to be personal friends. Usually, but not always, they are individuals whose ideological viewpoints are close to those of the researcher. The background information these confidants can give makes it easier to piece together isolated data into a coherent picture. Frequently, such confidants are able to prevent the researcher from completely misinterpreting some finding, although one must also beware of too readily accepting interpretations which are often versions of locally accepted social myths.

Contact with confidants should be maintained even after one has left the area. In particular, published accounts of the study should be sent to persons who assisted in the gathering and interpretation of the field materials. Not only does common courtesy require that one keep in some touch with those who befriended you, but the kind of impression one leaves behind can either clear or muddy the waters for subsequent researchers. Too often I heard, "There was another chap who come down from America to do some sort of a study, but we never heard from him again."

The Passing of Traditional Research Methods

A major impression I had after completing my field work in the West Indies was that many of the principles taught to apprentice sociologists in the United States are open to question. This is not to say that our graduate programs are to be categorically damned, but it does mean that many of the standard tenets set forth in professional training are inappropriate when one does field work outside the United States, or more generally, when one's research differs from the usual social science endeavors.

A study dealing with leaders, elites, and influentials involves "upward interviewing" from the viewpoint of the researcher's status. Yet, most methodological maxims seem to be premised on "downward interviewing." (Perhaps, because so many of our subjects are housewives and college students or members of some dependent population such as prisoners, slum dwellers, old people, etc.) Attitudes of individuals are gauged by circuitous and veiled questionnaire items. My West Indian experience, however, indicated that the best questions were the most direct. Likewise, scaled or forced-choice questions proved to be uneconomical in terms of time consumption, not to mention their well-known validity problems. Yet, questions must be specific enough to allow for the comparable collection of information between persons. One must not become reconciled to "stream of consciousness" interviews just because it takes some effort to keep the questioning structured.

My study involved, along with a standard statistical treatment of the data, the utilization of a sociological method which has been variously termed "the quest for universals," "the genetic perspective," or, most commonly, "analytic induction." Unlike the conventional handling of data, the analytic induction method tries to go beyond finding statistical correlations by providing explanatory theories of causal relationships. There is an assumption that the most desirable form of knowledge rests on formulating generalizations that apply to all cases of the phenomenon under consideration. Hypotheses are constructed, tested, rejected, reconstructed, and retested until a set of preconditions is found that apply universally to the phenomenon being described during the collection phase of research. Thus, this method entails an ongoing clarification of the explicit character of the data. Moreover, there is an incorporation of the negative cases, or "exceptions," by either changing the explanatory hypothesis, refining the phenomenon to be explained, or both.

Although the analytic induction method has been customarily used (see Lindesmith, 1947; Cressey, 1953; Becker, 1963) to explain types of social deviancy (e.g., drug addiction, marijuana smoking, embezzlement), this procedure may be especially suitable for certain kinds of behavior studies in the third world. Our understanding of these areas is handicapped because of the inappropriateness of the constructs developed within American social science. Analytic induction, however, is a parsimonious method which identifies behavioral variables as they reveal themselves within a particular cultural and social context. Because analytic induction possesses a kind of dialectic dynamic and is inherently fluid, much more flexibility in the field is required than is the case with conventional survey designs discussed in most methodology primers. Later, of course, these variables can be formulated into testable propositions amenable to further examination based on large-scale sampling procedures.

American Values Abroad

As severe as the problems posed in adopting a meaningful methodology are, third world studies are faced with even more

[109]

profound questions of theoretical appropriateness. The epithet of ethnocentrism is one of the oldest in social science and, as is to be expected, it is a source of special controversy in the theoretical literature on underdeveloped areas. Writers on emerging nations are frequently criticized for forcing non-Western phenomena into Western-derived categories. It is proposed, however, that much of the controversy concerning ethnocentrism has been misdirected. The question is not so much the utility of general Western concepts to studies of the third world, but the more subtle one of the relevance of social science assumptions that are uniquely American.

In contrasting European with American sociology, the German sociologist Ralf Dahrendorf (1961) has listed six "missing traits". in American social analyses: violence, revolution, class, history, elites, and intellectuals. Many of these traits are also absent in the literature on the third world, even though they are especially germane in examining the social changes occurring there (and increasingly so, in the United States as well). Thus, despite the revolutionary situation in many of the emerging nations, a large number of American social scientists have focused their studies on requisites for stability; despite the far-reaching transformations in the social bases of power, we hear of psychological determinants and problems of personal identity; and despite the global historical processes that have divided the world into rich and poor nations, the consequences of international inequalities are discussed *sotto voce*. Even the terms "elites" and "intellectuals," which are widely used in the literature on emerging nations, are so watered down from their European usages as to lose much of their explanatory power. Where European theorists dealt with intraelite conflict and the forms of dominance, American social scientists speak of the elite-mass gap. Where intellectuals in the European tradition were seen as carriers of ideologies, studies on emerging nations focus on personal frustrations of Westernized individuals.

Along this same line, C. Wright Mills (1942), over a quarter-century ago, discussed the prevailing assumptions in American studies dealing with social disorganization on the domestic scene.

These same tendencies have been transplanted into the literature on underdeveloped countries. One of the assumptions that Mills noted was conceiving society largely as a cultural system. In the writings on the third world, there has also been a strong emphasis on continuities in value orientations. Social determinants are placed in the realm of amorphous psychocultural entities which preclude the volitional control of social change. A second assumption pointed out by Mills was that undesirable consequences, especially the deterioration of *gemeinschaft* norms, accompany urbanization. Likewise, a persistent theme pervading much of the literature on underdeveloped areas is the supposed deleterious effects on social integration and personality arising from the rapid social change. One wonders whether American social scientists are more worried over the psychological costs of change than are the peoples they are describing. A third assumption of American sociology that Mills indicated was an emphasis upon the solution of problems through individual effort and adjustment, and a disregard for the efficacy of political action to implement structural changes. In the writings on the emerging nations as well, the role of the social scientist is rarely seen to include bringing his knowledge to bear on how problems of individuals are related to public issues which can be collectively resolved by structural alterations.

Such a comprehension of developments in the third world complements another of the persistent features in the analyses of most American social scientists—the failure to explore, if not acknowledge, the contingencies on development resulting from the gap between the rich and the poor nations of the world. Indeed, evidence points to an increasing rather than a diminishing gulf between the economically developed and underdeveloped countries, and this gap cuts across both communist and noncommunist countries. Not only are the political systems of emerging nations discussed in a vacuum with regard to global realities, but there is little consideration of the alternative courses of development which would open up in the poor countries if the structure of the international stratification was changed.[3]

Even the self-consciously "comparative" studies that have been made almost always have been *horizontal*—comparing nations at the same "stage" of development. *Vertical* comparisons—explaining how events in industrialized countries and in the third world are intermeshed—would seem mandatory, but when such studies do appear they are typically written by foreign social scientists, or by journalists, ideologues, and others on the periphery of social science in the United States.

Another feature in much of the literature on new nations is a misrepresentation of the motives behind the nationalist or revolutionary movements in the third world. To the disadvantaged of the emerging nations, invidious comparisons are drawn between their current strivings and the earlier ideologies of the West. There is a strong similarity, in the explanations of the motivating forces underlying the movements in the third world by many contemporary social scientists, with the neo-Machiavellian sociology that arose in the wake of the nineteenth-century European socialist movements. In both cases, the egalitarian, altruistic, and national components of the change-provoking movements are belittled, while the elitist, self-seeking, and irrational aspects are stressed.

Such cynical interpretations of the ideological underpinnings of the political independence movements in the emerging nations are directly contradicted by the findings of my study. The data revealed that, at least in the case of the West Indies, the movement toward independence was based on an ideology anchored in the values of the Western Enlightenment, and is to be understood as a scale-increasing movement linked with humanitarian ideals. This, of course, does not mean the future development of West Indian nationalism will remain within the humanistic mold. For in an earlier era, a turning away from the values of the Enlightenment transformed the initial humanitarian nationalism into subsequent exclusivist movements. Unfortunately, imitation may still be the sincerest form of flattery. Already there are dismaying signs that the current nationalisms of the colonial peoples may in some instances follow the road of their European and American pre-decessors.

The Civil Social Scientist

At this stage of history, though, the meaning of the West Indian political independence movements goes beyond the spread of equality of opportunity and political rights within the emergent Caribbean nations. Rather, it is to be viewed as the working out in one particular region of the broader worldwide effort of colonial peoples to obtain dignity and improvement in their lives. Moreover, the modern-day strivings of the colonial peoples serve as a mirror by which the wealthier nations themselves can reassess the worth, consequences, and timeliness of the humanistic values which they profess to cherish—values that are now being put to new tests as they become really human in scale. No longer can the social science of the wealthier nations enjoy its accustomed splendid isolation. In the United States, both the race crisis at home and the Vietnam war—each with its colonial overtones—are indicative of the need for American social science to adopt a responsibly critical stance toward the direction of our society.

To bring my remarks to a close, then, it is perhaps appropriate that I try to indicate a few of the students of society who have strongly influenced my own thinking. Among the classic writers, the insights of Karl Marx and Max Weber have had a deep impact. The utility of Marxian analyses—its emphasis on underlying economic determinants, its focus on contradictions and social conflict, its view of ideology as both unself-conscious reflection of social conditions as well as narrow, self-interested rationalization—remains powerful even (especially?) in understanding pre- and post- as well as industrialized society. Although Weber's intellectual life can be properly considered a running battle with Marxian analyses, Weber was amazingly astute in highlighting the pervasive trends in modern history: in religion, a rationally argued ethic; in economics, rational calculation of interests; in politics, the rule of law and administration by an impersonal bureaucracy; and that only certain ideas out of a broader set may be selected in a society undergoing change because they fit the interests of certain "status groups" and such groups can shape the moral ideas of large numbers of others.

Among contemporary sociologists, the influences are more diffuse. A few have already been acknowledged, but four individuals need to be mentioned directly: Eshref Shevky, who as my teacher at UCLA, awakened me to the ramifications of the changing scale of contemporary society and the meaning of a humane social science; Wendell Bell, who as a teacher and collaborator set personal standards of scholarship and moral responsibility which continue to be a model for my own efforts; C. Wright Mills, whose practised use of the "sociological imagination" (i.e., relating facts of cultural and social structure to personal behavior within an historical framework) continues to inform and inspire; and Irving Louis Horowitz, who despite a sometimes hurried style has the rare ability to come unerringly to grips with the really significant issues of our time, of getting down—in today's vernacular—to the "nitty-gritty."

As typified by the above men—and there are many others—it is my belief that scholarly output and the social use of critical intelligence cannot be separated. When studying such issues as nationalism, the distribution of power, the drive toward equality, or the conditions of democracy, the effective researcher cannot be detached from the consequences of his work. Objective and intellectually honest, yes—but detached, no.

Indeed, an uncommitted posture will actually hamper the social scientist who is doing research in the third world. A person who is not self-conscious about the implications of his work will be looked upon with suspicion and distrust. As a step toward reducing this likelihood it may be well for us to consider some sort of "participatory sociology" in third world studies. That is, a plan of research in which the subjects themselves help define what are proper and needed avenues of investigation. (Although I have intentionally ignored here the role of the social scientist at home, the implications for domestic social science should be obvious.) The natural and correct question of people in the third world is, "What are you doing here?" Certainly the social scientist must always ask himself just what it is that he is doing. And if he cannot satisfactorily answer that question for the people with whom he is dealing, as well as for himself, his research is betraying both his humanity and his science.

NOTES

1. This approach is amplified in Wendell Bell and Ivar Oxaal (1964), and Bell (1967). For a study of our own society using a related perspective, see Raymond Mack (1967).
2. This method of elite identification was pioneered by Floyd Hunter (1953 and 1959).
3. A notable exception is Irving L. Horowitz (1966).

REFERENCES

BECKER, H. (1963) Outsiders. New York: Free Press.
BELL, W. [ed.] (1967) The Democratic Revolution in the West Indies. Cambridge, Mass.: Schenkman.
BELL, W. and I. OXAAL (1964) Decisions of Nationhood. Denver: Social Science Foundation, University of Denver.
CRESSEY, D. (1953) Other People's Money. Glencoe, Ill.: Free Press.
DAHRENDORF, R. (1961) "European sociology and the American self-image." Archives Européenes de Sociologie 2: 324-66.
HOROWITZ, I. L. (1966) Three Worlds of Development. New York: Oxford University Press.
HUNTER F. (1959) Top Leadership, U.S.A. Chapel Hill: University of North Carolina Press.
––– (1953) Community Power Structure. Chapel Hill: University of North Carolina Press.

LINDESMITH, A. R. (1947) Opiate Addiction. Bloomington, Ind.: Principia Press.

MACK, R. W. (1967) Transforming America. New York: Random House.

MILLS, C. W. (1942) "The professional ideology of social pathologists." American Journal of Sociology 49 (September): 165-80.

MOSKOS, C. C., JR. (1967) The Sociology of Political Independence. Cambridge, Mass.: Schenkman.

A NATURAL HISTORY
OF ONE
SOCIOLOGICAL CAREER

JAMES F. SHORT, JR.

IT IS NOT IRRELEVANT to point out that I was born in an Illinois prairie farmhouse on land homesteaded by my great grandfather and in the same house in which my mother was brought into this world some twenty-four years earlier. That proud heritage—its strengths and its weaknesses and my attempts to sort these out and to cope with them—inevitably is reflected in my personal and professional socialization, in the work that I do and my assessment of it, in my "style" and in my vision of sociology.

My background is about as WASPish as one can get, and small town in addition. My father was the high school principal in that small town throughout my twelve years of public school. He was called "the professor" by some, and he ran a tight ship at school. As the principal's son, I learned very early at least some of both the advantages and the disadvantages of being identified with "the establishment." I hope I profited from both types of experience. We were a minority, too, in an important sense—non-Lutheran protestants in a town whose largest and most influential ethnic groups were Irish-Catholic and German-Lutheran. Probably this was one of the factors which made possible my father's long tenure with the local school system.

It was common knowledge in this little town—and publically boasted by some—that a black man had never spent the night within its boundaries. I don't know whether this was true, but I remember vividly the first and only night in my memory when it was not true. A touring quartet from Piney Wood College, a small southern Negro Institution, arrived to perform at the Baptist church. After the service my father and some of the other men made certain that they could stay the night in their trailer on the church ground. History—at least for some of us—had been made.

Like Huck Finn, I suppose, I never knew my own prejudices and was very little worried about such matters. But I did admire what seemed to me to be the courage of those men because I knew the public boast. My humanitarian conscience developed very gradually under the strong impact of a conservative (but not fundamentalist) religious tradition, and a strongly moralistic but pragmatic approach to many problems. My parents were tithers, even during the depression, and enjoyment of life's plenty—on a meager but steady school teacher's salary and a small farm income —always was tempered by concern for those "less fortunate," both here and elsewhere in the world.

The religion of my childhood was tempered, also, by a firm belief on the part of my parents concerning the right of individual conscience, and a fundamental faith that science and religion were compatible. The faith that "the truth shall make you free" led to a continuous search for knowledge, and education was placed alongside religion and the family as a proper cornerstone of life. Education was a practical, as opposed to a scholarly, matter, however, and the high school course in sociology which first piqued my curiosity was a blend of social problems, social welfare, and education.

Until the time that I entered graduate school, my own conception of sociology was heavily freighted by these same concerns. Sociology, as such, did not exist at the first college I attended, Shurtleff, in Alton, Illinois, a small Baptist school which has since closed for lack of adequate support. The marines sent me to Denison University as part of a V-12 unit, and I returned there after the war to finish my degree. At Denison I met Frederick G. Detweiler, an "old Chicago" sociologist who still preached often on Sundays, but who did expose me to the "Old Green Bible" of Park and Burgess, thus beginning my education in sociology as a discipline.

The greatest influence from the Denison years, however, was W. Alvin Pitcher, who, in 1946-47 recognized and took under his wing a very confused young man just returned from the service. Pitcher, now on the faculty of the Divinity School of the University of Chicago, helped me to cope with a variety of problems which at the time were bothering me a great deal—religious and philosophical questions, emotional, moral and ethical problems. More than anyone else during this period, he made possible for me a type of personal and spiritual liberation by opening for me a world of scholarship and intellectual inquiry I had never imagined. He also introduced me to my wife-to-be, for which my gratitude knows no bounds.

The University of Chicago

Pitcher also steered me to the University of Chicago, and to sociology rather than social work, where Professor Detweiler would have had me go. I knew so little sociology at the time that it is a wonder I survived the first quarter. That I did so is a tribute to several people, among them Samuel C. Kincheloe who taught a course on Sociology of Religion which I took for a variety of fairly obvious reasons. Kincheloe was a marvelous teacher, whose enthusiasm for field research was infectious. He taught me many things, but none more important than a fundamental skepticism. During a seminar to which I was presenting preliminary results from my master's thesis, I once made the mistake of referring to some feature of the phenomenon I was describing as "natural." Dr. K's question was instantaneous: "What do you mean natural? Anything's natural if you sleep with it long enough!"

I met Andrew F. Henry during that first quarter, and his was perhaps the greatest influence of all throughout the graduate school years and for some time after. Andy and I came from somewhat similar backgrounds in important respects and we were both struggling with some of the same types of problems. My "emancipation," intellectually and emotionally, was probably due as much to the association with Henry as to any other single factor.

A third person who helped me a great deal during that first year was Ethel Shanas, then working with Ernest Burgess on the study of aging (which Burgess preferred "for personal reasons" to call "later maturity"). As part of the first course in field methods of research, I was assigned to interview for this study. I worked hard, succeeding in gaining interviews with a number of "hard to reach" respondents, and Ethel and I became friends for life. During that same course I pounded the streets and doors of Hyde Park, for some purpose I cannot recall, with Harold Wilensky and I found him a most pleasant and stimulating colleague.

The department at Chicago was the most famous research department and the best published in the world at the time I entered as a graduate student in 1947. I was at once fascinated and awed by this fact and terrified by the thought that something of this sort might someday be expected of me. At the end of my first year in graduate schoool, despite the sustaining warmth and interest of "Dr. K" and a few others, and the spark of intellectual commitment fanned principally by Andy Henry, I wanted nothing so much as to finish a master's degree and to devote my life to teaching, preferably in a small college where research was not a part of the normal expectations for tenure. Clearly it was a style of life that appealed to me rather than the intellectual attractiveness of teaching, per se. I wanted, in effect, to escape. My wife held firm, however—there would be no leaving Chicago and no babies until I finished the Ph.D.

During my second year at Chicago, fortunately for me, I became "hooked." The discipline of sociology ceased to be onerous and became an exciting enterprise, particularly through research. My master's thesis was only moderately successful sociologically, but it helped me to bridge the gap between my earlier life and what I hoped to become.

[120]

The master's investigation was, upon the insistence of Dr. K, a field project. I chose as a subject a church with which I had a close personal relationship, focusing on its adjustment to a changing community. The project taught me a good deal about a variety of research techniques and it provided a new role for me (in terms of my earlier involvement with it) in an institutional context toward which I was becoming increasingly ambivalent as a result of my developing sociological perspective. Everett Hughes returned from Frankfurt that spring after the field data were all collected and a draft completed. Hughes attempted valiantly to get ~~ !~ assess the sociological significance of the data, rather than focusing primarily on their implications for the particular institution in question. He was not especially successful in the effort, I fear, but I made a stab at it and I am eternally grateful to him as mentor and as friend. Something rubbed off, and in later years I have been most concerned with the body of knowledge of behavioral science and with the development of general knowledge rather than simply with the accumulation of data concerning whatever phenomena are under study.

William F. Ogburn and Ernest W. Burgess probably had the greatest influence on me in this regard. I may have been the last Chicago Ph.D. whose thesis committee consisted of these two. What a man Ogburn was! Not the most inspiring teacher in the classroom, his bearing and manner were enormously impressive, and his hard-headed empirical approach, a model. The scope of his interests was astounding, ranging from psychoanalysis to the broad sweep of social change, and concern with a variety of "big questions" which he regarded as in some sense more fundamental than those to which we often devote more attention. My course outline agrees with the listing provided by Dudley Duncan (1964):

(1) What to do about big business.

(2) What should the functions of government be?

(3) How to raise the standard of living?

[121]

(4) How can nations get along with each other?

(5) The education of children and the character of a people.

(6) The elusiveness of happiness.

(7) Our shifting beliefs and ideals.

(8) Morals in a changing world.

(9) Machines: masters or slaves?

(10) The caveman in the modern city.

I had come to regard Ogburn as a friend in the course of the dissertation, despite—perhaps because of—one devastating session in which he referred to my first draft of three chapters as the worst writing he had ever seen. (Andy Henry confided later he had been told the same thing, and I have heard that others received much the same encouragement.) At the retirement dinner held for Ogburn and Burgess in 1951 Ogburn helped me to resolve what had remained a fundamental problem in my life, viz., social science versus social action. Prior to this time I had been unaware of Ogburn's history in this regard, and of his earlier commitment to social reform. I found most persuasive his conclusion that scientific study of social ills was far more effective as input to their solution than were individual efforts at reform, no matter how well motivated. It is a fundamental principal I have sought to follow to this day. I have argued for some time that sociologists can neither be "silent partners" to "action programs" related to social issues nor can we stand in splendid isolation from these programs or issues. I believe, however, that we must "stick to our sociological knitting" by providing systematic and objective sociological data and analysis—knowledge, if you will—if our role is to be effective in such efforts. (See my discussion of these issues, 1967).

Burgess was chairman of the department during this period and I got to know him better after completing the Ph.D. than before, I wrote one chapter of my dissertation at his request, and it later became my first publication in a sociological journal (1952). When I first brought the chapter to him for review, Burgess took the copy, thanked me, and to this day that copy has never been found! I admired Burgess greatly, personally for his gentle tenacity and courage, and intellectually for his flexibility in approaching a variety of problems with different methodologies. (See the essays published in memoriam by Everett C. Hughes, Robert E. L. Faris, Leonard S. Cottrell, Jr., and Philip M. Hauser, 1967.) In this respect, I suppose I was influenced by Burgess more than by anyone else.

I met Clifford Shaw during the first of several evening courses which I took from him at the downtown center of the university. I was immediately attracted to him and we were friends until his death. I was tremendously flattered when Shaw gave me an opportunity to work for the Chicago Area Project and the Illinois Institute for Juvenile Research, but decided that I preferred an academic career and so did not accept.

Earlier, as I was completing my master's degree, Shaw provided the opportunity and the crucial recommendation which led to my appointment as secretary of a newly formed advisory group to the Chicago Planning Commission—the City Planning Advisory Board, a group of 200 citizens throughout the city appointed by Mayor Kennelly. The first thing I did on this job was analyze the occupational and ecological distribution of these 200 citizens, which demonstrated the gross underrepresentation of nonbusiness and nonprofessional occupations, representatives of labor, the poor, and nonwhites. A few appointments in these categories later were made but the overall distribution remained decidedly skewed. I enjoyed the contact with city planning people—especially Harold Mayer, Jack Melzer, Morris Hirsch, Charles Blessing, and several of the artists who became bosom friends—and I briefly considered a career in the field. One of my best friends in graduate school, Jack C. Smith, did just that. A successful dropout from the University of Chicago, he became head of city planning for New York City and now operates his own consulting firm in this area.

Shaw was by temperament more humanitarian than scholar, a man of action more than researcher. When he engaged in research it was in the service of these ends, and his advocacy of case study methods, "the boy's own story" was consistent with this perspective. The statistical studies which began his research career set the background for this type of work. Shaw became the charismatic leader of the Chicago Area Project, and so the intellectual godfather (though often unrecognized as such) of the philosophy and at least some of the underlying assumptions of current programs stressing "maximum feasible participation of the poor" in the solution of their own problems, involvement of delinquents in rehabilitation and prevention efforts, etc. (See my discussion of "The Chicago Area Projects as a Social Movement," 1969.)

Through Shaw, I met a number of other people who have influenced me greatly, especially Henry D. McKay and Solomon Kobrin. McKay's persistent questioning of evidence and ideology and his insistence on bringing to bear systematic data and analysis contrasted sharply with Shaw's humanitarian zeal and skillful operations within "establishment" systems, and the two complemented each other beautifully. Kobrin brought to this enterprise analytical skills and perspectives which have become increasingly important in later years to understand delinquent behavior and social response. Kobrin represents the continuity of the Shaw and McKay tradition linked with current theory and research in this area, to which he has made signal contributions.

Of the younger faculty at Chicago during my graduate years I found Albert J. Reiss most stimulating, and he has continued to be a valued adviser on many projects, articles, and other enterprises over the years.

It will be clear from these remarks that I regard the University of Chicago as a great university and I am proud to have been associated with it. The sociology faculty during my more recent tenure with the institution, as a visiting faculty member, probably has influenced my own work as much as the earlier associations of which I have spoken, but this is difficult to judge.

On Research and Publications

I find research and teaching hard work, but exciting, so long as they are directed to problems which I believe are important. I like to write, but find I write slowly and with great effort, first drafts always in longhand. The "publish or perish" problem as it often is argued seems to me to miss the point. If one has something to say, the printed word is an important medium of communication, and communication within the discipline and outside it is an important obligation for sociology as for any discipline. I believe that the quality of our communications, including its content—whether by formal lecture, seminars, in learned journals, or in other types of relationships—is the fundamental basis by which we must judge and be judged as sociologists.

As for my own communications in article and book form, I have been inordinately fortunate in the sometimes haphazard process of collaboration. Andy Henry and I were close friends and chose to write dissertations with Ogburn who was kind enough to permit us to do so. We did not realize until after my dissertation was completed—a year later than Henry's—that his interest in suicide and mine in homicide represented in some sense opposing extremes on a continuum of agression. The idea for a book came first from Henry who was then at Harvard, where he was greatly stimulated, especially by Stouffer, Parsons, Inkeles, and Whiting, and by two graduate students in the Department of Social Relations, C. M. Heinicke and Stanley H. King.

We brought together two sets of findings from our dissertations which suggested that suicide and homicide behaved very differently in response to cycles of economic conditions and were distributed differently among significant social and structural categories of people. The theoretical synthesis developed largely out of Henry's dissertation and his subsequent work while at Harvard. We both did a great deal of theoretical and empirical work in addition to our dissertations. When we had finished *Suicide and Homicide,* we felt we had come close to a fundamental understanding of the nature of aggression. I still feel the book was a very creative theoretical work and I am proud to have worked on it.

Andy continued to work on leads from *Suicide and Homicide* until his untimely death in 1957. In the meantime, I had joined the department at Washington State University and, with the encouragement of a three-year Faculty Research Fellowship from the Social Science Research Council, had begun what turned out to be virtually a career in studying juvenile delinquency. Shaw had urged upon his students that we needed a "Kinsey report" study on crime and delinquency and I proposed to follow up earlier efforts in this area by Porterfield, Wallerstein, Wyle, Murphy, Shirley, and Witmer. My interests were twofold. Methodologically, I felt efforts in this direction might help to solve some of the measurement problems associated with the use of official statistics. Toward this end, questionnaires and interview schedules were developed, and college, high school, and training school populations sampled. When Ivan Nye undertook to study family relationships and delinquency we joined forces and worked together on some of these problems. I never cease to be amazed when some investigators apply "the Nye-Short scale" to their own data, apparently assuming that we had established some sort of universal scale of delinquent acts, unbound by time, place, or population. Nothing could have been further from our minds. Ours was a first effort to employ a particular measurement technique to this type of data. Certainly it was our hope that others would study a broader range of behaviors and populations and relate them to other measures of delinquent behavior in order to develop a more versatile array of behavioral measures in the constant search for more adequate representations of reality. I believe some progress has been made in this regard and I am happy that a number of investigators have pursued this matter.

While measurement problems have long fascinated me, I have

[126]

been guided in my work primarily by the hope that I might contribute to the testing and refinement of statements of theoretical significance. This was my purpose in focusing on differential association some years ago. I must admit that I have never been especially happy with that research. Our "testing" of the theory was very crude, and I believe those who have sought to develop the theory by relating it to other theoretical statements more in the mainstream of behavioral science are perhaps on a more fruitful track. We were more successful, I believe, when Albert Cohen and I began looking at varieties of delinquent subcultures, stimulated largely by Cohen's book, *Delinquent Boys,* and research I had done in Chicago at IJR in the summer of 1954. The association with Cohen continues to be most rewarding, despite our failure to complete "that book" and despite the fact that part of his theory has been dealt with none too kindly by some of the research with which I have been associated. Cohen was a trusted adviser to the Chicago gang project which has been so important a part of my life since the fall of 1958. Fred Strodtbeck first approached me about the matter at the ASA meetings in Seattle for which Cohen and I had prepared a paper, "Research in Delinquent Subcultures." The proposition was a natural because Cohen and I planned further research in this area. The academic year 1958-59 was spent preparing proposals and planning an elaborate research program. We consulted with many people, but Strodtbeck and I did most of the work during this period.

The Chicago project eventually involved far too many people and other significant experiences to be catalogued—more, I am sure, than I am aware of. All of the faculty and several of the graduate students most closely associated with the project have appeared as coauthors of publications resulting from it—Fred Strodtbeck, Desmond Cartwright, Kenneth I. Howard, Robert A. Gordon, Ray Tennyson, Ramon Rivera, Harvey Marshall, and Ellen Kolgar. But there were many others. We had our "dropouts," but by my latest count, three Ph.D. dissertations have been written directly from the project, and nine master's theses.

[127]

We started out in Chicago to bring data to bear on recent theoretical formulations concerning juvenile delinquency, and particularly that which was associated with "gangs." Among the theoretical formulations which most influenced our research designs were those advanced by Albert Cohen, Walter B. Miller, and Richard Cloward and Lloyd Ohlin. All except Cloward were formally on our advisory group, as in addition was Phillip M. Hauser. *Group Process and Gang Delinquency* tells much of the story of that research, though several other publications have followed that report, and a good deal of unpublished work has been done. In addition to the opportunity to shed some empirical light on theoretical formulations which differed significantly from one another, we wanted to "keep a window open" on the gang boys through our access to the detached workers of the YMCA. The point was not so much that we aspired to a longitudinal study of those groups. The planned period of observation (three years) was too brief. It was, rather, that detailed contact over such an extended period permitted observations as to the nature of group interaction, as well as continued access for a variety of research purposes. I believe we succeeded in extending the perspective which William Foote Whyte so skillfully portrayed in *Street Corner Society* and I have always thought of our work as being in that tradition. Strodtbeck's small group research perspective led us to look for phenomena in the field which had been found in the laboratory, somewhat after the style of Muzafer and Carolyn Sherif whose manner of moving back and forth between the laboratory and the "natural" situation in the field appeals to me greatly.

I learned a great deal from the entire Chicago experience and it was rewarding in many other ways. I feel the project made several contributions, the significance and impact of which probably are better judged by others. A partial list would include the social scientists spoken of in the previous two paragraphs.

I think we now know a little more about the nature of the groups in which delinquency occurs. The continuing debate on this matter among investigators and others who seek to understand these phenomena promises to be lively and fruitful for years to come.

I would like to think we made some contribution to exchange theory, particulary in terms of the cultural-institutional context of social behavior. I believe we demonstrated that the values of gang boys, and the relation of these values to their behavior, is a much more complex matter than previous theoretical statements led us to believe. We demonstrated, not too surprisingly, that existing theoretical statements are much too simplistic to comprehend the complexity of the phenomena under study, and our data and analyses suggest some of the ways in which they need to be revised. The group process perspective, and the mechanisms we found operative, require much greater specification and "further research" before they can be properly assessed. Here we are consistent with, however, and for the most part more specific than, other recent work which suggests that we must direct more attention to the "situational elements" involved in social action. I believe group processes and a variety of situational elements are appropriate additional considerations, along with personality, to the sociological S-R proposition, in which S is the state of society and R the resultant rate of any social phenomenon (as discussed in Inkeles, 1959 and 1963).

University Administration, National Commissions, etc.

Some comment seems necessary concerning my brief (four years) venture into university administration. I will not claim that I entered this arena in order to "study from within," and I'm certain that occupying the graduate deanship did not enhance my sociological productivity, at least in an immediate sense. In some ways, I think the experience has made me a better sociologist. Clearly, however, this was not the reason I accepted the job. It was, to begin with, a flattering and challenging request from a man I admired and respected a great deal. The man was C. Clement French, President of Washington State University. We had worked together—all too frequently, for both of us—when I was chairman, for three years, of the Student-Faculty Discipline Committee at WSU.

I enjoyed some aspects of the deanship, but others nearly drove me to distraction. For a variety of reasons, I decided to return to full-time teaching and research and, at this writing, I am happy with this decision. I do not rule out returning to administration at some time in the future, however. It is rewarding and frustrating, but most of all, terribly important. I note, finally, in this context, that I have been extraordinarily fortunate in being associated over these years with Washington State University, where I have been given every opportunity to work at what I have felt important amidst congenial and stimulating colleagues. Life has been pleasant, indeed, and I have been much honored by these associations.

Most recently I have been involved in an intensive course in "practical political sociology" and sociological retreading, as Co-director (with Marvin Wolfgang) of Research for the National Commission on the Causes and Prevention of Violence. I am learning a great deal, and I hope to keep doing so for the remainder of my life. If I have a credo, I guess this is it.

Service with the commission is relevant to a number of the questions posed by the editor of this volume—to the manner in which we "do sociology," the relation of sociological theory and social application, and sociologists who influence one's work. Jack Gibbs and I worked together on some research for the President's Commission on Law Enforcement and Administration of Justice, but this was a very indirect type of involvement in the work of the commission. The Violence Commission experience has been of particular importance to me in several respects. I will limit my commentary to but one of several issues which might be addressed.

I am acutely conscious of the belief by some of our younger colleagues that sociology has become too identified with and servile to "the establishment." I believe we must search our sociological consciences in this regard and find ways of carrying out research on problems and issues which may be threatening to or not of interest to "establishment" funding sources. My experience with several "establishments" suggests that objective research and sound theory many times are welcomed as bases for changes in policies and practices which are found not to be responsive to needs of constituencies. One cannot proceed naively on such an assumption, but I remain convinced that sound research and theory are the most effective tools of the sociologist in the field of social application. I believe, too, that we have a responsibility to participate in important policy-making processes such as are involved in the work of national commissions, recognizing that the work of such bodies is fraught with great uncertainty and it is surely not the way to live if one prefers a life of serenity and equanimity.

Conclusion

I hope in the course of this narrative I have replied in some measure to all of the editor's queries. I confess to a good deal of ambivalence concerning this exercise in baring one's sociological (and inevitably personal) soul. It is almost too painful, the recollections and emotions of early years and the sometimes agonizing decisions which are so easily summarized—and just as easily distorted.

Certainly one's background and development are relevant to understanding the nature of one's work, but I am struck by the subtlety and complexity of the personal and professional influences on my life. Surely one's influence on students, colleagues, clients, and others is no less subtle and complex, and properly included in the sociology of sociology, as are other aspects of our discipline.

REFERENCES

DUNCAN, O. D. [ed.] (1964) William F. Ogburn on Culture and Social Change. Chicago: University of Chicago Press.

INKELES, A. (1963) "Sociology and Psychology." Pp. 317-87 in vol. 6 of S. Koch (ed.) Psychology: A Study of a Science. New York: McGraw-Hill.

——— (1959) "Personality and Social Structure." Chap. 11 in R. K. Merton et al. (eds.) Sociology Today. New York: Basic Books.

SHORT, J. F., JR. (1969) "The Chicago Area Project as a social movement." In C. R. Shaw and H. D. McKay (eds.) Juvenile Delinquency and Urban Areas (2d. ed.). Chicago: University of Chicago Press.

——— (1967) "Action-research collaboration and sociological evaluation." Pacific Sociological Review (Fall): 47-53.

——— (1952) "A note on relief programs and crimes during the depression of the 1930's." American Sociological Review (April): 226-29

HUGHES, E. C. et al. (1967) Ernest Watson Burgess: In Memoriam. Chicago: University of Chicago Press.

9

SOCIAL ANALYSIS
AND SOCIAL ACTION

AMITAI ETZIONI

MY INTEREST OVER the last ten years has moved from the study of smaller social units to that of larger ones, from greater concern with conceptualization to an emphasis on the social relevance of social *science*, and from a fair segregation of the role of the sociologist and the active citizen to a greater effort to articulate the two. In so doing, I believe my work reflects trends which affect social sciences in general, sociology in particular. I shall focus first on these trends, then briefly discuss a contribution I might have made to their extension.

Many a sociological article opens with a definition of a new concept (or relationship) and a discussion of methods to be employed to measure it. This is then frequently followed by presentation of some data relevant to the new concept and relating to it familiar sociological variables (e.g., "the distribution of elephantiasis by age and sex in cities with a population of over one hundred thousand"). Most sociologists, the author included, feel that such combination of theory and methods is the very foundation on which sociology as a science ought to be built and is in fact being constructed. But many of us also feel that something is lacking.

What is lacking most is *social analysis,* the systematic exploration of social issues; that is, concern with the methodological questions of sociological analysis of the great issues of our age, which tend to involve the study of macroscopic units. The subject of social analysis, though, is the issues, not the sociological building stones; the focus is on the instruments to be utilized to elevate the analysis of societal issues, to improve on amateur, intuitive, or journalistic sociology. Traditional training in sociology is no more a preparation for social analysis than training in biophysics or biochemistry is for medical practice. Social analysis requires special training as well as distinct methods, knowledge, and a professional tradition. It requires more than a simple application of an existing body of knowledge to the study of a set of problems; it is also a question of studying the problems that application of sociology engenders. When sick, one would hardly exchange treatment by one M.D. for that of two Ph.D.'s in biology. Hence, the call for social analysis as a new element of sociological study and training is a call for the professionalization of sociology—for adding to sociology as a science (as the institutionalized desire to know) the systematic concern with application of knowledge (the institutionalized desire to help) [see Parsons, 1959].

The *subject matter* of social analysis is all of substantive sociology. However, social analysis as a discipline is not to replace the fields of political sociology, race relations, or the study of stratification, but is to deal with the *generic methodological, intellectual, and professional problems which the substantive sociologies raise.*[1] Each of the substantive fields combines—in addition to information about the subject matter—three essential elements: to study politics, draw on a general theory and methodology, *and* be prepared to handle the generic problems of substantive analysis. The same problems would reappear if one were to study other substantive fields—for example, the sociology of religion or criminology—but would not obtain if one were engaged in sociological theory per se or pure methodology.

Analysis: Substance and Problems

What is the substance of social analysis and what generic problems does its study raise? The focus and raison d'être of social analysis are the problems of the age, the application of sociology to the understanding of society, its major subcollectivities, and a society's place in more encompassing communities. Biochemistry views the blood as having varying chemical compositions; medicine sees it as infested with illnesses. One day—when our knowledge of hematology is much more advanced—the distinction might disappear; meanwhile somebody had better be concerned with how to cure illnesses, using the very partial biochemical information available. The methodological question of medicine is hence how to act under *partial* information. Sociological theory and research slice society into social systems, role sets, and reference groups; social analysis is concerned with applying such concepts to the evolution of a world community, the redistribution of social wealth, efforts to advance the growth of human rights, the development of "have-not" countries, etc. In general, we quite correctly train students to achieve higher levels of precision by drawing better samples, using more refined measures, more specified concepts, etc. As a consequence the trained sociologist often shies away from major segments of social data because for one reason or another, he cannot obtain the kind of precision we taught him to look for. The field of analysis of societal problems is thus often left wide open to social commentators who have no methodological training at all. We should develop and teach the methods to be applied when information is fragmentary and vague, as it so often is, because the trained sociologist can still do much better—especially when he is trained to face this problem—than the uninitiated social observer.

A hardly novel historical approach to sociology serves to emphasize our position. We started with grand social theories, formulated in emotion-laden terms (e.g., progress), covering no more and no less than all of history and all of mankind. We began by flying so high on the verbal trapeze that most of our propositions could not be pinned down and those that could often did not withstand empirical tests. Our grandiose designs collapsed (see Mills, 1937).

Then, we foreswore high jumps; we preferred to advance step by step, even if it should take us a hundred years to learn to walk firmly, rather than engage again in breathtaking but also neck-breaking gymnastics (see Dexter, 1958). We sharpened our tools on

[135]

the radio-listening of housewives and focused our concepts by observing small groups of college sophomores. *Such concentration was essential for a transition period;* but behavior which is quite suitable for student days becomes an adolescent fixation when it dominates the behavior of a mature man. While sociological theory ought to be further extended and methods of collecting and analyzing data improved, we should recognize that our wings have sprouted; we are now ready to fly. It would be an overreaction to our earlier misadventures to remain earthbound to a restrictive interpretation of our discipline, to delay a new test flight of social analysis.

Another reason we, as a profession, shy away from social analysis is our fear of value judgments which, we sense, are more rampant in social than in sociological analysis. In the brief period which has elapsed since the publication of my theoretical book *The Active Society,* one question has been raised much more often than any other—how can I maintain that the theory advanced is both critical (i.e., normative) *and* objective. My answer is that we are critical in that we take the human needs and values of those subjects to our study, the members of society, as our basis for evaluation. We compare various social structures in terms of the extent to which they are responsive to their members; asking what factors prevent them from being more responsive than they are, and the conditions under which their responsiveness may be increased. We thus do not evaluate a social structure in terms of *our* preferences but in terms of those of its members.

This position is hardly a novel one—Gunnar Myrdal (1944) followed a similar approach in *The American Dilemma:* He did not state that Americans were failing to live up to *his* creed, to his conception of equality, but to theirs. We shall now show in a future publication that Marx's and Mannheim's positions are not too remote from this approach.

The theory is objective in the methodological sense that all empirically minded observers will reach the same conclusions.

Whatever their varying personal values, they may observe the same discrepancy between the values the members of society hold and the way of life their society and its component institutions promote or tolerate.

In the past, mainstream sociologists argued that sociology must be neutral to be objective; the critics, on the other hand, have posited that it cannot be neutral and urged that one's normative position ought to be explicitly stated. As long as this course is followed, sociology is either normatively sterile (at least claiming to be), or subjectively based, which undermines its scientific foundation. We suggest that *using the subjects' values rather than our own allows sociology to leave behind this either/or position.*

Another problem arises though. Members of society, the subjects of our study, may be inauthentically committed and unaware of their real needs and preferences. Our proposition is that (a) one can *empirically* test when the declared preferences are the real ones and when they are inauthentic (e.g., when there is a significant gap between the declared and real needs, respondents tend to be defensive about their positions), and that (b) the attributes of the real needs can be empirically determined.[2]

The last point is essential to the whole approach and raises a surprising amount of emotional resistance among many mainstream sociologists while it is considered almost self-evident by many psychologists and psychoanalysts, as well as by anthropologists. One reason for the resistance is that many sociologists subscribe to what Dennis Wrong called the "oversocialized" conception of man, i.e., they assume that human needs are highly pliable by society and culture. Individuals, groups, and subcultures may deviate, but the society never does; it sets the norms. As we see it, the social demands (or role expectations) that one society advances may be less responsive to human nature than those another society fosters. In this sense, the first society may be said to be deviant, or more conflicting with human nature, than the other one. Of course, both society and human nature affect each other, but neither has a prior logic nor normative claim for the adjustment of the other.

Practice: Needs and Roles

Empirically, the gap between human needs and social roles may be measured by socialization costs, social control costs, and the direction of pressure to change. To assess these, take 100 freshmen and put 50 at random into highly bureaucratic roles and the other 50 into a highly particularistic, diffuse, affective "organization." If our position is valid, you will see that it will be more difficult to train the freshmen to behave in accordance with bureaucratic norms than with particularistic ones. Sustained conformity will require more agents of social control and more frequent use of sanctions, and when control slackens there will be much more pressure in the bureaucratic organization to shift toward particularistic conduct than in the particularistic organization to shift toward bureaucratic patterns. This would indicate that bureaucratic norms are less fulfilling of human needs than particularistic ones. The same method can be applied to other sociocultural differences and other populations.

There is one catch—if the subjects come from a society which is highly bureaucratic (e.g., Prussia in the late nineteenth century), they *may* initially feel more "comfortable" in highly bureaucratic roles.[3] However, if the study is continued, we expect, they will adapt to nonbureaucratic norms much more easily than subjects from a highly particularistic background will to bureaucratic ones. We frankly do not know how long it will take, but surely longer than the four times forty-five minutes many laboratory experiments last, and less than a generation, the extent of many "natural experiments" conducted by society. Finally, we expect those individuals in roles more suitable to human nature, at least after a period of accommodation to their new roles, to be happier and less anxiety ridden than those in less fulfilling roles.

Two more arguments in favor of the present transformation toward a more critical sociology need to be examined. It is said that sociologists, by learning to walk, will find out how to fly. You can learn from the fruit fly, it is correctly suggested, new laws of genetics that apply to all animals and plants. Similarly, we can derive from sophomores' chit-chat universal laws of interaction which enrich our understanding of social behavior in general. But while it is true that in this way we can learn the "universal" elements of our theory—all the universal chemical characteristics of water are represented in any drop—we cannot study the emergent properties of complex units in noncomplex ones.[4] We will not learn much about the anatomy of elephants by studying that of fruit flies. Hence, while we ought to continue to study small groups for their own sake and for the light they cast on social behavior in general, *we ought to invest more of our resources in macroscopic sociology.*

But, as a second line of defense in favor of our present low (though rising) investment in social analysis, it is said you cannot direct scientists and tell them what to study. If sociologists find race relations an unrespectable subject, unless it can be used to perfect survey methods or to redefine the concept of prejudice, what can we do? What we can do is to realize that the distribution of scientific resources is not random, does not follow a laissez faire pattern, and is "interfered with" regularly anyhow. The distribution of sociological manpower is directly affected by the advantage of required courses, which as a rule include theory and research techniques over optional courses; by Ph.D. committees that approve and encourage some subjects and discourage others; by foundations and federal agencies—which we advise—who support some subjects to the neglect of others; by space awarded in our journals; as well as attention granted at professional meetings, to some subjects over others. All these are occasions where theory and methodology are celebrated while social analysis is given, at best, second-class citizenship.[5]

Finally, sociological scientism is revealed in the aloof attitude toward social action of many members of our profession. This is a severe case of elephantiasis in which the scientist role of the sociologist has made deep inroads into his role as a member of the educated elite of the community. This is not only a question of being a bad citizen but of not living up to a special social obligation we have as persons who know society expertly. To indicate more clearly what I have in mind, let me point out another helpful (for social as well as sociological analysis) term, that of role pairs. *Role pairs* are roles which appear frequently together in a society, in the sense that they are carried out by one and the same actor. The importance of such combinations is that they provide the most effective means of communication known between two roles—personal union. They also allow economy of resources, such as that found in the housewife-mother pair, security and elevator boy combination, teacher-researcher, doctor-medical professor, etc.

The role pair of sociologist-intellectual is a particularly effective one. Not that all sociologists were ever intellectuals or vice versa, but there seems to have been a much higher degree of overlap in earlier generations. The growing tendency to dissociate the two roles is particularly regrettable because the virtue of such role combination is greater now than it used to be in the days when it was more common, for now we command a body of theory and methodology as well as a store of validated knowledge about man-in-society which can provide much-needed background for speculation about society.[6] The social analysis of Daniel Bell, Lewis Coser, Nathan Glazer, David Riesman, Dennis Wrong, and other contemporary sociologists who fill this role pair is much more hardheaded, soundly based, and politically sophisticated than that provided by earlier generations of social analysts or by their former college mates who majored in English literature and still interpret the American scene in the light of moods revealed in *Moby Dick* or "understand" the Soviet union because they suffered with Dostoevsky.

As a discipline we do not encourage, or at least do not train for, the sociologist-social-commentator pairing of roles. In earlier days the clergy and radical movements provided the sparks that fused sociological training with social concern. Today, in the age of specialization, more and more sociologists feel that what is proper

[140]

behavior in their role as scientists is the proper behavior in their community role as well; the only way they face a social problem is through the lenses of theory and methodology. Civil defense, for example, becomes a subject for study of attitudes ("People who fear war more are also more in favor of fallout shelters.") or an occasion to try out a new computer program in mass dynamics.

The sociologist's role is preempting time, energy, and resources that belong to his role as intellectual, as one who is committed to societal issues and expresses his concern about them more effectively than other observers since he knows more than they about the society he is commenting upon. Thus he not only is against nuclear war, but applies his knowledge of society to understand why nations become inflexible in the face of such a danger and freeze rather than act; sharing his analysis with those who seek to reduce the danger through political action, but lack the benefits of the sociologist's training and expertise.

NOTES

1. Compare the concept of social analysis to that of "informal sociology" advanced by Herbert J. Gans (1958).

2. This is spelled out in chapter 21 of *The Active Society* (Etzioni, 1968).

3. There is no evidence that this is the case. Actually, we may find that just as the "happy guildsman" in the preindustrial world was found to have been quite miserable, so the Prussian citizens did not enjoy their bureaucratic roles despite deep socialization to prepare them for these roles.

4. This point is elaborated in chapter 3 of *The Active Society* (Etzioni, 1968).

5. My practical suggestion is that some space in our journals be given to social analysis essays; there is really no danger that the nonprofessional publications will be deprived. Similarly, social analysis books written by sociologists (or on subjects sociologists ought to write about) should be systematically reviewed, and review essays dealing with the generic problems they raise be invited.

[141]

6. For discussion, from various perspectives, of how the role pair of sociologist and social analyst operates, or fails to operate, see Alvin Gouldner (1964). For discussion of how the two roles inform one another, see Robert Merton (1946: 185-89, and 1961).

REFERENCES

DEXTER, L. A. (1958) "A note on selective inattention in social science." Social Problems 6 (Fall): 176-82.

ETZIONI, A. (1968) The Active Society: A Theory of Societal and Political Processes. New York: Free Press.

――― (1965) "Social analysis as a sociological vocation." American Journal of Sociology 70 (March): 613-22.

GANS, H. J. (1958) " 'Informal sociology': a proposal for a new publication." American Sociological Review 23 (August): 441-42.

GOULDNER, A. W. (1964) "Anti-Minatour: The Myth of a Value-Free Sociology." Pp. 196-217 in I. L. Horowitz (ed.) The New Sociology. New York: Oxford.

MERTON, R. K. (1961) "Social problems and sociological theory." Pp. 697-737 in R. Merton and R. Nisbet (eds.) Contemporary Social Problems. New York: Harcourt, Brace & World.

MILLS, C. W. (1937) The Sociological Imagination. New York: Grove Press.

MYRDAL, G. (1944) The American Dilemma. New York: Harper.

PARSONS, T. (1959) "Some problems confronting sociology as a profession." American Sociological Review 24 (August): 547-59.

10

FROM SOCIALISM
TO SOCIOLOGY

SEYMOUR MARTIN LIPSET

THE STORY OF THE WAY I became a sociologist is quite simple. I first entered the City College of New York in February 1939. The Great Depression was still on, and my father, who was a printer—a member of the Typographical Union, had been without regular employment for many years. The family livelihood came largely from the money which my father earned as a substitute or irregular worker in various printing plants and newspapers in New York. Since such work was irregular with peaks and severe periods of almost total unemployment, we were forced to depend for assistance on relatives, principally an uncle of mine who had a lucrative dental practice in Westchester. This uncle happened to be a bachelor, and the family decided that his practice ought to remain within the family since it was the principal economic asset we possessed. As a result, I decided to take an undergraduate science degree with the idea of going on to dental school helped by my uncle. It did not take very long to discover that science and my interests did not agree. My grades were low, and I dropped out of the science curriculum after one year. I then shifted to taking social science courses with a principal interest in history.

A more important influence on my attitudes, values, and general knowledge at the time, however, were my political concerns. As a high school student in Townsend Harris High School, the preparatory school of the City College, I had been active in the Young Peoples' Socialist League, then the Youth Section of the Socialist Party, and the American Student Union. I had dropped out of the YPSL before leaving high school as a result of disillusionment with the severe factional fights that had occurred within the organization stemming from conflicts with Trotskyists and near-Trotskyist groups. On entering college, however, I decided to become active again and join that wing of the Young Peoples' Socialist League which had been formed as the Trotskyist-controlled section. One of my closest friends in the organization was Peter Rossi, who had also been a classmate of mine in Townsend Harris. Both of us dropped out of the organization after a year or less of membership, after it had split over the issue of support or opposition to the Russian invasion of Finland in the winter of 1940. We remained, however, involved in what was a loose, unorganized grouping of anti-Communist leftists ranging from anarchists through Social Democrats, left-wing Socialists, and Trotskyists. This grouping functioned regularly in one of the alcoves in the City College lunchroom engaging in rather vehement, almost continual discussion among the members of the group who hung out in the alcove, and in sharp conflict with the Stalinist members of the Young Communist League who were in the next alcove. The principal subject of our discussions and debates was the reasons underlying the failure of the Socialist and Communist movements in the Soviet Union itself, in Spain during the Spanish Civil War, and in various countries in Europe and elsewhere. While we disagreed as to the reasons, we all agreed that the various organized movements had been total failures either creating totalitarian oppressive states such as the Soviet Union, or failing to successfully resist Fascism or influence the structures of power in other countries.

These various discussions had a comparative sociological flavor. We all read closely the texts of Marxism, including many of the works of Lenin and Trotsky. And given our awareness that the various movements had failed because of the seemingly self-aggrandizing behaviors of their leaders, we were impresssed by Robert Michels' book, *Political Parties.* Michels' work came to us as a revelation. He seemed to have the clue to explaining the common factors underlying varieties of Stalinism in Russia, the degeneracy of the Communist movement outside of Russia, and the ineptitute and failures of the Social Democratic Parties. Interest in Michels' work led a number of the people in the alcove to study sociology.

However, I cannot claim any such high intellectual reason underlying my decision to major in sociology. I can still recall the way in which the decision occurred. Peter Rossi came to me one day with the announcement that we should major in sociology. I asked him why. And his reply was that this was the one field which would guarantee us employment after graduation. For City College undergraduates of that day, sociology was conceived not as a field which might lead one to become a professor in it, but rather as the discipline which prepared you to become a social worker. And Rossi pointed out that the more unemployment the more likely we were to be guaranteed jobs if we qualified as social workers. This argument that sociology had a more guaranteed economic future than majoring in history or other social sciences appealed to me. My principal source of personal income at the time was working for the National Youth Administration, The Youth Section of the WPA, of the Works Progress Administration, or work relief. It was, I suppose, the equivalent of the Poverty Program for college students which exists today. One could earn $30 a month on this program by working sixty hours, which I did. Issues of employment and unemployment were real and personal for me and other students of that day. Consequently, I do not find it surprising, in recollection, that I decided to study sociology because it seemingly would guarantee a social work position.

The next decision pertaining to my sociological career occurred as a result of World War II. I was scheduled to graduate in 1943. I had about a year and a half to go when Pearl Harbor occurred. Under the rule set up by the college for those going into the services, I could graduate if I completed a year's courses, since the college gave students close to graduation a semester of credit for entering the armed services. My draft board was surprisingly generous and gave me a deferment for a year, one which was then extended over another additional six months without my asking for additional time. I fully expected to go into the army at some point, and hence made no specific plans for further study or employment after graduating. When I was finally called up by Selective Service in the summer of 1942, I found out that I did not qualify on physical grounds. I am very nearsighted, and one of my eyes was classified as technically blind, although it is correctible with glasses. Upon my informing some faculty members of City College of the fact that I was going to be deferred because of my eyesight, I was offered a fellowship in the City College Sociology Department. The fellowship, which paid $400, was essentially a research assistantship in the Laboratory of Social Research at the College. This award, plus encouragement from some of my teachers, particularly Gerhart Saenger, with whom I worked, gave me the idea of applying to Columbia for graduate work. I continued working in the Laboratory of Social Relations with Saenger on some early voting studies in 1943 and 1944. I had entered Columbia as a graduate student in the fall of 1943.

By that time, I had a pretty fair acquaintance with what sociology was all about, and some sense of politically relevant problems that I would like to study. I recall that my first contact with anyone at Columbia was with Bob Merton, whom I saw in September to consult about my program. Although it was my first contact as a student, I told Merton that I had two topics in mind for my Ph.D. thesis. He seemed surprised to find an entering graduate student with definite topics but asked me what these were. My answer was that I could not yet decide whether or not to study the factors behind the rise of the CCF, the Cooperative Commonwealth Federation, the Socialist Party of Canada, or the reasons underlying the perpetuation of the democratic two-party system in the International Typographical Union, the union to which my father belonged. The first topic was motivated by my interest in the general problem of why there was no socialism in the United States. As an active socialist, I had been interested for a long time in this issue, and was therefore fascinated with the fact that the Canadian Socialist Party had suddenly taken on a spurt of growth in 1943. It rose up in that year to become the official opposition in the Ontario legislature, with thirty seats. In addition to its victory in Ontario it gained considerably in various other provinces and even temporarily became the second largest party in Canada according to the Gallup Poll. The American socialist papers were of course very interested in this and reported on it. I was subscribing to Canadian socialist papers and had some fair acquaintance with what was going on there. The general notion I had in mind was to see what it was that made a socialist party successful in Canada when all the efforts in the United States had been miserable failures.

The second topic, as I explained it, was derivative from my interest in Michels' work and in the general sources of oligarchy and authoritarian behavior in trade unions and left-wing political parties. Following Michels' and my own general interest in the labor movement, I had of course become aware of the fact that oligarchy characterized much of the labor movement. I knew something of the operation of the Typographical Union from my father and his friends and from having attended meetings with him in New York. Consequently it struck me that a study of the Typographical Union might shed light on the ways in which one could inhibit or prevent authoritarian practices in the labor movement.

As a graduate student, my political interests continued to determine the work I did as a student. In my first year at Columbia, I wrote a paper for a course of Merton's which dealt with the Typographical Union. This paper particularly impressed him at the time and was instrumental in the strong support which I received from Merton and others to gain a fellowship in my second year at Columbia. My income now rose to the magnificent sum of $1,000, which permitted me to live separately from my family. During my second year at Columbia I worked closely with Robert Lynd, largely because he was extremely sympathetic to my political concerns, but also because he was especially supportive, psychologically, of my work. Like most graduate students, I was extremely insecure, anxious as to whether I had the ability to do anything as a sociologist. Lynd was especially reassuring on this score, constantly setting my aspirations at a much higher level than I had originally set them.

It is difficult to tell students of later generations what the Columbia Sociology Department of the later part of the war looked like. There were not many more students in residence than faculty members. Although many of the faculty were extremely busy, involved in research projects which stemmed from the war effort, and were housed at the Bureau of Applied Social Research, then located at some distance from Columbia, on 59th Street, it still was relatively easy to see anyone one wanted. Most classes and seminars were extremely small. And although I probably spent more time with Lynd than with anyone else at Columbia, I was able to get a great deal from the other people on the faculty, such as Paul Lazarsfeld, Bob Merton, William Robinson, and Ted Abel. In fact, if students of my generation had any complaint it was that one was too visible as a student, that the faculty knew exactly what you were doing or not doing. One had a sense that if one decided not to take a seminar or not to work with someone that this was an act which the individual concerned would know about right away. I think many of us at that time would have said that we would prefer to be in a larger department in terms of number of students, with less visible contact with faculty.

Although my sociological interests remained tied very closely to my political values while I was a graduate student, there's little doubt that my years at Columbia led me to define research in a very different way from what I thought when I first entered graduate school. The commitment to an effort at objective scholarship, to learning the techniques to test hypotheses, to relating one's work to broader bodies of theory, all became meaningful, real objectives in this period. Although I never then or since have accepted the idea that value-free, research or academic, concerns are possible, I did then learn largely through our discussions of

Max Weber and his ideas that a scholar, if he was to be creative, had to try as consciously as he could to negate his political and other biases and prejudices insofar as they affected his work. I remember being especially struck at the time with a discussion by Weber in which he argued that it was the obligation of the teacher not to present "party truth," that is the beliefs about society which stem from his political orientations. Rather, Weber argued, an honest teacher and scholar should be more receptive to presenting in public findings about society which contradicted his political hopes and values. One should be suspicious, he argued, of findings which coincided with what one wanted to find in terms of one's opinions. If one found what one hoped to find, one should double-check it, and then still be suspicious. On the other hand, he enunciated the dictum that results which contradicted one's anticipations were more likely to be valid since presumably one's unconscious as well as conscious biases would be pressing the researcher to locate data which fit his predilections. If in spite of this he still produced results which contradicted them then he could feel fairly certain that these were valid. In addition, Weber believed and argued that a professor, because he was in a superior status and authority relationship to his students, should not try to influence the students politically. Professors should particularly seek to separate their role as political activists and citizens, from those of scholars or teachers because they were dealing with young people who had a right to make up their own minds without being influenced by the personality or authority of their teachers.

These judgments struck me, a student who was interested and involved in radical politics (I was once again a member of the Young Peoples' Socialist League), as extremely sensible. Teachers should stay out of student politics, but, even more important, a scholar should try to do objective research in spite of his political commitments. Such a conclusion, of course, did not mean that one could not choose one's research topics in accordance with one's values and interests. If anything, the opposite was true. One chose one's study because of beliefs about what was most important to find out, so that research could lead to action. On the other hand, the commitment to action-relevant topics did not contradict agreeing with Weber that one should try to avoid letting one's values affect one's conclusions.

In accordance with such concerns, I continued to be interested in the two topics that I had first mentioned to Merton in September of '43. That is, I was still interested in doing a doctoral thesis either on the CCF or on the Typographical Union. I thought, at the time, that it was more likely I would study the union since I could do this while remaining in New York and continuing to work part time at the Bureau, or in some other capacity. To study the CCF would mean going to Canada and I did not see any way to do that. Robert Lynd, however, thought that the CCF was a much more important topic than democracy in the Typographical Union. While I was at Columbia, in June, 1944, the CCF won power in one province, Saskatchewan. My original notion had been to study the Ontario CCF, which had become the second largest party in the province, comparing groups in Ontario with comparable ones in the United States, e.g., auto workers in Windsor who were socialists with their compères in Detroit who were not, or steel workers in Ontario and Pennsylvania. Lynd, however, thought that studying a socialist movement which had actually come to power, even if just in one rural province, would make a more interesting project. He encouraged me to apply to the Social Science Research Council for a predoctoral field fellowship. I did so and was awarded the fellowship.

Shortly before I got the fellowship I married Elsie Braun who was then completing her undergraduate work at Hunter College. She was majoring in history, but had also been active in the Young Peoples' Socialist League, and had political interests similar to my own. Both of us welcomed the idea of being able to go to a section of the world ruled by a socialist party and see what it felt like to live in an area where the socialists were the major party rather than a small insignificant sect as in the United States. On being awarded the SSRC Fellowship, we left for Saskatchewan in

[150]

June, 1945 and stayed there until August 1946. The fifteen months I spent in Saskatchewan were among the most exciting and informing of my life. Saskatchewan in 1945-46 was an exciting place for a young sociologist and socialist. The party had recently come to power, and had attracted to Regina, the provincial capital, many young socialists not only from Canada, but some even from the United States and Great Britain to work in the government. Here was the first attempt at a socialist experiment on the North American continent and those who were privileged to take part in it felt that they were making history, that they had an opportunity to influence the future politics of not only Canada but North America as a whole and consequently the world. As a fellow socialist, I was welcomed by the members of the government in both elective office and in various appointed positions. There was little that went on that I was not privy to. I often sat in meetings of the party or the government. For fifteen months, I became simply another one of the young intellectuals who had come to Saskatchewan to help take part in the Socialist experiment.

Although I was involved to some extent in the situation as an active participant, my wife and I still kept in mind the fact that I was also gathering material for a Ph.D. thesis at Columbia. As I saw my task, it involved two separate efforts, first an attempt to explain what it was about the social situation of Saskatchewan which made it possible for a socialist party to win majority power in 1944. The second job was to analyze the actions of the government, sensitized by my awareness that the record of most socialist parties elected to office was one of relative moderation or conservatism, that is of backing down from their commitment to radical social change. The second topic, in a sense, was a follow-up on the concerns of Michels. The first task, the analysis of the social movement, involved working over the historical record, tracing through the emergence of the party from its precursors, the way it changed as it moved to power, the kinds of groups that supported it at different stages in its history, the sources of its leadership, the nature of its ideology, etc. My wife, who was trained in history, spent a great deal of time in the library helping me gather the material for the historical record. We also did a rather painstaking job of gathering voting statistics for the thirties and forties which could be correlated with other statistical data. This job was not easy since it involved getting precinct-type data and adding it up to form the equivalent of the units for which we would find census materials. As part of the historical analysis, I had many long and fascinating interviews with founding members of the CCF. Many of these older people had been pioneer settlers of the province. The province itself had been settled largely at the beginning of the twentieth century, so many of the first-generation settlers were still alive. A number of them had been active in socialist, radical, and labor movements in other countries before coming to Saskatchewan.

The effort to analyze the work of the party in power involved spending a great deal of time with party and government officials. While much of this work consisted of formal interviews with different people, a great deal of the most useful insights were gathered through taking part in all sorts of informal discussions and social gatherings. The most memorable of the latter occurred at the home of a high government official one Saturday night at a party at which I became stone drunk. Those who know me well will testify that drinking is not one of my usual assets or liabilities. I have no memory of why I happened to get drunk at this particular party. However, I do recall that during the evening I decided to compare the romantic attractions of various of the women at the party by going around and kissing each of them. Apparently at some point or another I passed out. I awoke the next morning on a cot in a room in which the other occupant was the baby of the household, then less than one year old. He was busy cooing and gurgling happily. When I recalled where I was and why I was there and what I had done the night before, I was convinced that my research and my career were finished. In spite of having elected a socialist government, Saskatchewan was an extremely moral place in which, for example, men and women were not supposed to drink together in public facilities. There was a strong strand of puritan moralism and prohibition sentiment within the CCF. Much to my surprise, however, this episode did not upset my rapport with those I knew. If anything, I think it helped since it gave me an undeserved reputation for a quality of behavior which was not typical for me.

In the fifteen months I spent in Saskatchewan, I did almost no writing or even detailed outlining of what the study was actually about. In a sense, I had a number of general questions grouped into the two main sections of the study and simply tried to gather as much data as I could into these categories. Some of this collection was of course formal and rigorous. In addition to collecting voting statistics, I gave out questionnaires to the delegates at both party and co-op conventions. I also tried to interview many of the leaders of the party and gather systematically comparable materials on them.

I left Saskatchewan at the end of the summer of 1946 to take a position as a lecturer in sociology at the University of Toronto. This job stemmed directly from my Saskatchewan work, since I first visited Toronto while on a trip back to New York in the middle of the year. I went there to look over the materials collected by the Canadian Gallup Poll. I wanted to see whether I could possibly use these materials by grouping Saskatchewan data so as to build up a big enough sample of Saskatchewan respondents to analyze party support and attitudes. While in Toronto, I decided to visit the university to find out whether anyone there was doing research on related topics. I introduced myself to the sociologists, and as a result some months later they decided to offer me a job. Being in Toronto was extremely useful since I continued to have access to Canadian materials. I could get a detailed look at another part of the CCF, the then rather strong Toronto organization, and I had an extremely light teaching load while working on my thesis. The thesis was written up during the next two years. I finished it about January or February, 1948, and successfully defended it at Columbia in the spring of that year. I was then offered a position at the University of California at Berkeley which paid considerably more than the $2200 a year I was earning at Toronto. Upon moving to Berkeley I was also offered a joint position with the Institute of Industrial Relations there, then under the direction of Clark Kerr. This joint research position was attractive to me not only because it freed me from some teaching and gave me access to some research funds and assistance, but also because I thought I would now work on the other topic which I had designated for a prospective Ph.D., namely, the political system of the Typographical Union. I did, in fact, begin such work, limiting myself initially to a detailed analysis of the history of the union, seeking to find out how the two-party system of the union began and to try to look for mechanisms which enabled it to maintain itself for well over half a century.

This work at Berkeley resulted in a rather lengthy article which I hoped to expand into a book. It also brought me in contact, for the first time on an overt level, with some of the competitive problems and behavior of academe. I submitted the article which I wrote on the ITU to a major political science journal. The editor wrote back that he and his fellow editors liked the article very much and intended to publish it, but that before doing so they decided they ought to submit it for a check on its accuracy to an authority in the field since none of them knew anything about unions or their politics. Some months later I got a letter back from this editor in which he reported that their referee had written a rather detailed and negative criticism of the article and recommended that it not be published. He said that while he still thought it was a good article, in the view of this criticism they could not publish it. He submitted a copy of the criticism; they were rather vitriolic in tone and contained what I thought was an extremely petty set of detailed corrections of supposed errors of fact which I had made. In a few cases the critic had detected some real errors, but most of those which he claimed were errors were in fact, accurate. I redid the article and sent it out again, this time to a journal which specialized in labor topics. Sometime later the article was returned again with a negative judgment and again with a copy of rather harsh criticisms written by the critic to whom they had sent the article. Clearly, whoever had criticized the article knew the ITU and its history and was a specialist in the subject. I of course could not prove who it was. I had some suspicions, since my article criticized other materials which had been written on the ITU as naive, and I assumed that there was a good chance that the article had been reviewed by someone whom I had criticized. I escaped my critic by sending the article to the *British Journal of Sociology* where it was published. The editors of the British journal presumably never referred it to an American authority on printing union history.

For the record, I should note that some years later a sociologist colleague then teaching at another university told me that a particular individual at his university had a strong dislike for me. He reported to me that the individual in question, who was in fact an authority on labor history, had told him that I had written an article which had criticized him, and that he had attempted to stop its publication. Beyond this, he told my friend that he had written to the chairman of the Sociology Department at Berkeley at the time, and to Clark Kerr, telling them that I should be fired since I was not a proper scholar as evidenced by my criticism of his work. Those in authority at Berkeley naturally ignored this letter and also never told me about it. The story, however, is of more than personal autobiographical interest, since I would guess that similar reactions occur from time to time within the academic profession. Academic men have nothing but their scholarly reputations and when these are challenged by the young men of another generation who bring to their work new ideas, techniques, or other orientations, and in effect place the work of older people in the wastebasket as outmoded, they create a tension which can result in the kind of extreme behavior that took place in my case. I should indicate, however, that as far as I know this incident had no negative repercussions on my work or career. If I had known about it when it happended I probably would have been upset and it might have affected me. By the time I found out what was behind the whole affair and how far my critic had gone I had already written the book about the Typographical Union; its reception left me with no concerns about this particular negative reaction.

The work which I did on the Typographical Union's political system was not the only or even the principal research that I undertook at that period at Berkeley. The Institute of Industrial Relations had committed itself to doing a study of labor and social mobility in conjunction with some work being sponsored by the California Department of Labor. I was asked to serve on an interdisciplinary committee guiding this research. For reasons which are not relevant at the moment, the other members of the committee were unable to spend much time on the project and the study ended up in my lap. Since I had long been interested in the general topic of stratification and social change, and wanted to get involved in an actual research survey, I was willing to take part in the study. Much of my time at Berkeley, particularly in 1949 and 1950, was spent collecting data for this particular investigation. The study eventually resulted in the book, *Social Mobility in Industrial Society*, by Reinhard Bendix and myself. Much of the book was written, however, on my second stay at Berkeley, which began in 1956. The year 1949-50 was more notable at Berkeley for being the year of the loyalty oath fight. At the time, I was somewhat involved in the fight against the oath, which was supported by most of the members of the Sociology Department and of the Institute of Industrial Relations. Also during this year, I was invited to come back to Columbia for a year as a visiting assistant professor. I agreed to do so and after spending a period of time at Columbia I decided to stay there on regular appointment. One reason for my decision to stay at Columbia was that I had become involved in a rather elaborate study of the Typographical Union which was supported by a grant from the Rockefeller Foundation.

CLASS AND CONSERVATISM

I've described much of the intellectual history and events involved in the study of the Typographical Union which led to the book, *Union Democracy*, in an article published in *Sociologists at Work*, edited by Paul Hammond. I will not repeat what is already in print there. I should only note that this study represented continuity and culmination since it involved following up on the knowledge which I had gathered as the son of a printer, and on the topic which I had been interested in as a Young Socialist and which I had wanted to do as a doctoral thesis. The comprehensive character which this investigation took, however, was made possible by the fact that I could collaborate with Martin Trow and James S. Coleman, both then graduate students at Columbia, who wrote their dissertations as part of the project of the study of the ITU.

Politically, my years at Columbia overlapped with the Korean War (1950-1954) which was also the era that has come to be known as dominated by McCarthyism, the crusade which Senator Joseph McCarthy waged to eliminate what he called the Communist conspiracy in government. The McCarthy era had a major impact on American intellectual and academic life. Many became interested not only in fighting it, but trying to understand how McCarthy and the support which he received were possible. The Fund for the Republic, a subsidiary of the Ford Foundation, became interested in the possibility of supporting a comprehensive study of the phenomenon of McCarthyism and asked the Columbia Bureau of Applied Social Research to undertake a preliminary investigation to see to what extent such an undertaking was feasible and to detail what substudies ought to be done. I took part in a Bureau committee which supervised this preliminary study. As part of the work I undertook some investigation of the social background of McCarthyism, both historically and contemporaneously. This work resulted in a long memorandum, revised version of which was eventually published as an article, "The Sources of the Radical Right," in the *British Journal of Sociology*. It also appeared shortly thereafter in slightly revised form in a book edited by Daniel Bell on the *New American Right*. This paper was, I believe, the first time that the term "radical right" was applied to extremist movements in the United States. In terms of my own intellectual development, it also has some importance in that in the course of examining the data concerning the bases of support for various extremist movements which advocated bigotry and intolerance, both in the past and present, I came to realize that many of them derived their support largely from the underprivileged and less educated elements in society. Much of the evidence for this statement was summed up in a very long footnote in that original article. These data sensitized me for the first time to the possibility that the less privileged groups in the society were not only potential bases of support for leftist movements advocating what I thought to be progressive social change, but that they also constituted a potential mass base for reactionary authoritarian movements. Subsequent work on the subject resulted in an article which has gained a great deal of attention both positively and negatively, depending in some part on the political orientations of the critics, "Working Class Authoritarianism," which has also appeared as a chapter in my book, *Political Man*. The study of McCarthyism never came to fruition since the Fund for the Republic decided not to support it.

My next major piece of research, an effort at systematizing the bases of political cleavage on a comparative perspective, stemmed from a project which was also located at the Bureau. The Behavioral Sciences Division of the Ford Foundation, then under the direction of Dr. Bernard Berelson, decided to support a number of inventories of knowledge in different areas of social science. Berelson gave the Bureau a grant for an inventory in the general field of political behavior. Paul Lazarsfeld was largely instrumental in getting the grant for Columbia, but assigned its implementation to a committee composed of Richard Hofstadter, Herbert Hyman, David Truman and myself. I decided to use this opportunity to look into the literature bearing on the factors determining the political orientations of occupational classes in Europe and America. Juan Linz, then a graduate student at Columbia, worked closely with me during the years 1955-57 on this inventory. In 1955-56, Linz and I went out to Palo Alto to the Center for Advanced Study in the Behavioral Sciences, where we spent the year writing up and trying to systematize the materials bearing on the factors which differentiated support for different political tendencies among various strata, that is within the working class, farmers, professional groups, business classes, and the like.

In a real sense, this effort was a follow-up of an interest I had had ever since I was a Young Socialist in high school. During my years in the Young Socialist movement, I had been interested in the general topic of why the "revolution" failed everywhere. This ultimately meant that I had worked up a series of lectures which dealt with Germany, Italy, Spain, and many other countries. When I started to teach courses in political sociology, I found that much of what I lectured on was an academic translation of this topic. The topic translated, however, not as a study of revolutionary movements, but rather as a study of the behavior of social strata. In a sense, I was now trying to find out why large sections of the workers in different countries supported conservative parties, which was another way of asking why the socialists did not come to power. Or conversely, what made other strata diversify their political allegiances. By looking at the issues comparatively, one could relate such differences to variations in national traditions, levels of industrial development, patterns of political party organization, and the like. Since many of the questions that Linz and I were trying to answer were not covered by existing research, we sought to locate sample surveys of voting behavior and political opinions in different countries. We were then able to do a great deal of secondary analyses of these data, to look at issues such as the differences between income groups, people of different educational levels, and the like, within the same strata in different countries. Our major concern at the time was basically in the

[159]

factors which affected allegiances to different political orientations or parties. It was a study of the sources of cleavage, of conflict. This work, largely done at the Center in 1955-56, resulted in a two-volume mimeographed manuscript which we regarded as a research first draft. It was a manuscript which contained a great deal of data brought together within a rather general conceptual framework, which we hoped to elaborate on in much more detail subsequently.

In 1956, following my year at Palo Alto, I returned to Berkeley rather than to Columbia. Once back at Berkeley, the pressures to finish up the book that I had originally committed to the Institute of Industrial Relations there on social and labor mobility were strong. Reinhard Bendix joined me in working up these materials, which we ultimately published in book form. Some of the work in this book reflects my interest in comparative politics. It includes a fair amount of material dealing with the effect of social mobility on political behavior. Although I think that this book is a good book for the state of the art at the time it was done, it is not one which stemmed from any fundamental drive or intellectual interest of mine which had to be fulfilled. Rather I would describe it as a chore arising from having once gotten involved in the project and feeling committed to finishing it off. During the period that I was working on *Social Mobility in Industrial Society,* I continued trying to rework some of the data which Linz and I had collected during the year at the Center. Linz, who joined me at Berkeley for another year, spent most of the time working on his doctoral thesis, which was an outgrowth of the larger project. His thesis dealt with the social basis of party cleavage in Germany. In my effort to find a way of systematically reworking the comparative political data, I began to write a number of papers on different subjects drawing on the original materials. Sometime during this period, that is, around 1958, Nathan Glazer, then an editor of Anchor Books, approached me with a proposal that I put together various of my papers on politics for a book of essays. I agreed to do so and turned to either rewriting some of the existing essays or writing new ones which might logically fit into such a book. When I submitted the book of essays to Anchor, my editor there, Anne Freedgood, suggested that I really ought to spend more time reworking them, trying to make a more compact and unified book rather than just a collection of essays. I did this and the ultimate result is the book, *Political Man.*

Political Man presents a somewhat different orientation from the way in which Linz and I first conceived of the comparative cleavage project. As I was working through the cleavage materials, it struck me that looking at these materials solely from the point of view of cleavage was a mistake, and in some ways was even unsociological. That is, in studying such data one is looking essentially at the operation of a social system, namely, the system of political conflict in democratic societies. Such a social system operated through different tendencies gaining the allegiance of various groupings within the society; it also required that there not be a high correlation between social position and political allegiance. In a sense, the Tory workers, the workers who voted for the more conservative parties, were not simply deviants who had not yet come to some sort of true political class consciousness as viewed by the Marxist model, but rather their existence was a requisite for a stable democratic order. As I argue in *Political Man,* democracy requires that the major political parties seek to be responsive to all major groupings within the society. Otherwise one has a state of civil war rather than democratic tension. Observations of this type led me into looking at the conditions for the stability of democratic political systems as well as the conditions supporting cleavage. That is, it involved the study of consensus and cleavage, a concern which interested Tocqueville. The introductory chapter to *Political Man* outlined some of the intellectual concerns which are represented in the book. *Political Man,* thus, represents an attempt at analyses of the operation of a total system. The various chapters in it follow up on a variety of topics with which I had dealt in some of my earlier writings. Thus it contained some detailed analyses, of right-wing movements, which continued and elaborated on my original concerns with the radical right. It also contains a chapter trying to deal systematically and generally with the problem of the political process in trade unions and private governments, an attempt which follows up on *Union Democracy*. And most of the book deals with the competitive struggle of parties in democratic societies both specifically in the United States and around the world. This latter section took off from the discussions in the draft manuscript written by Linz and myself.

Political Man also contains a long section dealing with the social requisites of democracy, which focuses primarily on the differences between underdeveloped and developed countries. In it I tried to compare the characteristics of systems which were democratic with those which were undemocratic or unstable. This work, which pointed out the fact that democracy was largely an attribute of highly developed societies with a high income and level of education, while authoritarianism was a characteristic of poorer systems, led very directly to an interest in the politics of developing countries. Rather than turn directly to a study of some underdeveloped countries, I thought that an analysis of the political development process in the history of some developed countries might contribute to an understanding of the interrelationships between development and political systems. In a discussion at a program committee meeting planning the agenda for the Fifth World Congress of Sociology, which was supposed to deal with the sociology of development of new nations, I suggested that one ought to include a discussion of the United States since from the point of view of the concept of a new nation, it was the first new nation. Some of my colleagues on the program committee of the International Sociological Association, who were from Europe, questioned the utility of this idea of the United States as the first new nation. I promised, therefore, that if they would include a place for the topic on the agenda that I would write a paper on the subject. This commitment led me to begin working on American history and development and ultimately resulted in the work which has been published in my book, *The First New Nation*. *The First New*

Nation represented an effort to see the United States in historical and comparative perspective. That is, it is an effort to try to understand some of the elements of American values and politics which are seemingly different from other countries by pointing out what is unique about American history, and what is special about American social structure. The first part of the book is, therefore, historical, dealing largely with events and structures that are an outgrowth of the first couple of decades of American independence. The last part of the book, however, represented an effort to systematically deal with specifying the value system in the United States as contrasted with that in other countries and to point up the way in which a value system which is historically derivative determines and affects the institutional structure of a country. In looking for ways to compare countries systematically, I came to the conclusion that the Parsonian pattern-variables formed the most useful set of classifications for such comparative analysis. I also argued that to fruitfully use them in the context of comparing highly different countries, e.g., India and the United States, was not really terribly useful. Rather, a comparison of countries which are highly similar, such as the English-speaking democracies, might offer a better indication of the utility of emphasizing superordinate values of a country as an explanatory framework. The last section of *The First New Nation* involves an attempt to do just this, using data which are essentially illustrative rather than hard evidence.

After finishing *The First New Nation* I decided that I wanted to follow up on the work that I had done in the last section of the book by gathering systematic primary materials in order to test out the hypotheses concerning value differences among various countries. My original plan was to secure funds to do a large comparative survey of attitudes and behavior in a number of countries. I thought that focusing on the Latin American countries might make sense in this connection since the fact of a common language and cultural tradition, at least among the Spanish-speaking countries, would enable one to eliminate some of the methodological problems that would occur if one tried to compare countries with different languages and different cultural traditions. The cost of such a study on a comparative basis, involving looking at many countries, was very high, and it proved to be difficult to raise the money for the study. Looking for ways of achieving the same results more cheaply, it struck me that analyses of the attitudes and values of university students in various countries might be the cheapest way to obtain systematic comparative data. University students seemed to be a good group to look at comparatively since they are in a similar position in their countries, thus reducing the variability that might be involved in dealing with a variety of occupations, and they also constituted the future elite of their countries. One should be able, therefore, to say something about how countries will differ in the future as well as in the present by such comparisons of university students.

About this time, the University Committee for the Study of Labor and Economic Development, which involved four labor economists, John Dunlop, Clark Kerr, Fred Harbison, and Charles Myers, became interested in the study of student behavior. They offered me funds to begin an investigation of the attitudes of university students towards politics and careers in underdeveloped countries as reflected in various attitude surveys which had been conducted in these countries. Their interests and mine seemed to jibe, so I began looking into the general problem of student activities and behavior. This concern with the attitudes and behavior of students, particularly in underdeveloped countries, began in 1963. As I did preliminary work on the topic I became aware of the enormous importance of students as a political force in emerging nations both contemporaneously and historically. I must confess now that I assumed that their political role in developed countries was largely a matter of historical interests. I was on leave from Berkeley in 1964-65, but I remained at the university to work on this project. This was, of course, the year in which the Berkeley student revolt took place. The Berkeley revolt had enormous impact on the situation in the University of California and in many other places around the world. It also, of course, could not help affecting my interests and knowledge and concerns with student activity. To some degree it shifted my attention for a considerable period of time away from the underdeveloped countries as such. I became more interested in the general phenomenon of student politics both in American and in various other countries. This led to my dropping the specific interest in Latin America with which I had begun my investigations and turning over the work in this area to various graduate students and colleagues who have continued working on the subject. Trying to deal directly with ongoing and changing student politics made it much more difficult to set up one formal project of studies of student behavior. In effect too, it killed off my early notion of using studies of students as a way of testing out hypotheses about the effect of national value differences on other types of behavior within countries. Most recently, I have been working on a book with some colleagues dealing with the general problems of students on a comparative scale. This is a work which is currently in process.

Although I have dropped the idea of a systematic comparative survey study designed to test some of the basic hypotheses concerning the effect of superordinate national values on variations in institutions and practices of different countries, I have continued to follow up a number of the themes presented in *The First New Nation* and also in *Political Man.* Such work, which essentially represents some of my major effort since coming to Harvard in 1965, has been published in my most recent book, *Revolution and Counter-Revolution.* The first section of the book contains two chapters dealing with value differentiation among Latin American countries, and in Quebec. These are contrasted to aspects in the United States. The second chapter goes into detail analyzing a number of variations between English Canada and the United States which is designed to explore in much greater depth some of the themes taken up in *The First New Nation.* The title of the book, *Revolution and Counter-Revolution,* refers to the revolution in the United States and the counter-revolution in Canada. That is,

I try to explore the consequences of the fact that the two great Northern American nations came out of the same event, the American Revolution, but that one represents the victory of it, while the other the defeat. This essay is basically an effort to detail the meaning of Max Weber's insightful analogy of a loaded dice game in which he suggests that major historical events structure future developments by being institutionalized. Other essays in this book point out the extent to which I have tried to push ahead in new essays on topics which have been explored in earlier books. In my judgment, the most important essay in the book is probably the one dealing with the social stratification, which was originally written for the *International Encyclopaedia of the Social Sciences.* In it, I've summed up many of my ideas about major differences in stratification theory which I've developed over the years in teaching a course of stratification. The essay is concerned with the way in which the different theorists have related their analysis to the concept of alienation. Alienation is a uniquely important sociological concept. Basically, I would contend almost all sociological theorists suggest that alienation occurs when the system breaks down, even though they vary in their analysis of what causes system breakdown. The analysis of the sources of political diversity first explored in *Political Man* are also elaborated in this book in sections dealing with political cleavage in underdeveloped countries as well as in the developed countries and the United States. The chapters in *Revolution and Counter-Revolution,* while all representing a continuity with previous work, can be explained as a response on my part to invitations over the past five or six years to take part in conferences or symposia on topics on which I had previously written. That is, they do not represent a conscious decision to work on a variety of issues which I had covered earlier, but rather in a sense are the response to outside invitations to do a paper which elaborated on something I had dealt with earlier.

At the moment, the work which is closest to completion is a

book which I am writing with a colleague, Earl Raab, dealing with the role of right-wing movements in American society from 1790 down to the present. This work is an outgrowth of the original paper which I wrote in the mid-fifties on McCarthyism. My return to the topic was largely inspired by a proposal made to me by representatives of the Anti-Defamation League around 1960. The Research Director of the ADL, Oscar Cohen, was interested in having a major university take over responsibility for a series of students analyzing the phenomena of anti-Semitism in the United States. I was not interested in working on anti-Semitism, but others at Berkeley involved in the Survey Research Center were, and we came to an agreement that the Survey Research Center would take over responsibility for a set of major studies. At the time I agreed to do a study of right-wing extremism which, though clearly related to the topic of anti-Semitism, would not necessarily be directly involved in it. This request coincided with a decision by Daniel Bell, the original editor of the book, *The New American Right,* which had contained various essays written on McCarthyism in the mid-fifties, to put out a new and updated version of the book. Bell asked all the authors of the original essays to write new ones analyzing the phenomenon of right-wing extremism in the post-McCarthy period. I spent a good part of the year of 1961-62 working on an essay dealing with the social bases of support of the Coughlinite movement of the 1930s, McCarthyism in the 1950s, and the John Birch Society in the late fifties and early sixties. This study essentially involved reanalyzing public opinion data which presented evidence concerning individuals who supported each of these phenomena. At the time, I assumed that the book which Earl Raab of the San Francisco Jewish Relations Community Council and I had agreed to do would largely deal with relatively contemporary, post-World War II radical movements. Because of other research commitments, Raab and I did not do much on this work until after I went to Harvard.

THE RIGHT WING AND THE ILLUMINATI

In 1966 I began working on what I thought would be a long historical chapter dealing with precursors of right-wing extremism in American history. As I began to go through the literature, and particularly in reading through many unpublished theses and dissertations that had been done on various types of right-wing organizations in universities around the country, I realized that there was a fascinating and coherent story of the role of right-wing extremism in America which essentially began with the beginning of the republic in the 1790s and has continued down to the present with the American Independent Movement of George Wallace. The historical analysis pointed to linkages in theory, ideologies, particularly conspiratorial notions, among the various tendencies which I would classify in the category of right-wing extremism from the beginning of the republic.

The most facinating of all turned out to be the longevity of the conspiratorial theory involving the Illuminati. The Illuminati were an organization formed in Bavaria in the 1780s which historical records suggest was dissolved after a few years by the government. It was essentially an organization of Enlightenment intellectuals designed to further social reform and intellectual change, and was affiliated with the Masons. For reasons which it was difficult to understand, a literature emerged first in the 1790s which credited the Illuminati with being behind the French Revolution and all other revolutionary plots in various countries in Europe. This literature reached the United States and was seized upon by leaders of the then declining Federalist party and Congregationalist Church in New England. They charged that the Illuminati were present in the United States and were behind the growth in influence of Jeffersonian infidel revolutionary notions and the decline in traditional religious beliefs. The belief in the Illuminati conspiracy reappeared in the anti-Masonic movement of the late 1820s and early thirties. The anti-Masonic movement also arose during a

[168]

period of rapid social change, which witnessed the growth of a liberal political movement, this time the Jacksonian Democrats. These changes were identified with a plot of Masons and to some extent the Illuminati.

For the most part, belief in the Illuminati conspiracy is reduced to a minor theme for the rest of the nineteenth century. It was replaced among right-wing groups by the belief in Catholic conspiracies. However, it should be noted that anti-Masonic and anti-Illuminati writings and organizations continue through the nineteenth century. Anti-secret-society organizations emerged after the Civil War and reprinted much of the earlier literature. The theory that the conspiracy of the Illuminati is behind all revolutionary change emerged again after the Russian Revolution, and was picked up in the United States. The staid *Christian Science Monitor* actually published a long editorial in 1920 discussing the possibility that the Illuminati were behind the revolutionary movements and social changes of the day. Henry Ford, then in the throes of his rather virulent anti-Semitism in his weekly newspaper, *The Dearborn Independent,* also was cognizant of these old conspiratorial theories. He, however, argued that the agitation in the 1790s and the 1820s against the Illuminati and Masons only served to conceal the fact that the real enemy was the Jews, that the belief in the Illuminati-Masonic plots was really a misunderstanding by those concerned with moral decay in America.

Concern with the Illuminati took on a major flavor in the United States in the 1930s. Gerald Winrod, a pro-Nazi fundamentalist minister of the Midwest, published a number of books and articles dealing with the Illuminati conspiracy, which revived many of the old charges from the 1790s on. Father Charles Coughlin, who was much more important than Winrod, also believed in the Illuminati conspiracy and would mention the founder of the Illuminati, Adam Weishaupt, as the inspirer of the work of Karl Marx and other revolutionaries. Following World War II, a considerable body of Illuminati literature has appeared among various right-wing movements. Some of it charges that Senator Joseph

McCarthy was killed by the Illuminati because he began to be aware that they, rather than the Communists, were the real enemy, that the Communists were the dupes of the Illuminati. Most recently, the John Birch Society has taken over this ancient conspiracy as a major dogma. Robert Welch, the head of the Birch Society, has published one long pamphlet and a number of articles dealing with the Illuminati. *The American Opinion Library,* put out by the Birch Society, has actually reprinted a book first published in 1797, *Proofs of the Conspiracy,* by John Robison, which was the first major exposé of the Illuminati, and had a great deal of influence in the United States in the 1790s. Robert Shelton's *Ku Klux Klan,* the largest of the current Klans, has also printed a number of articles about the Illuminati and their role during 1968. As one reads through the right-wing literature, it becomes apparent that there has been a continuity of literature and ideas of which the Illuminati conspiracy is only the most exotic one.

A detailed historical analysis of right-wing extremism as a response by various groups in America to changes which they perceive as undermining their status, values, or economic position is justified not only by the continuity of ideas. Rather, it appeared to me as I delved more deeply into the historical record that these movements had a similarity in function and in bases of support. They also had comparable effects on the American political system. To a considerable extent in periods in which extremist groups reached heights of mass support, alliances developed between the extreme right and moderate conservatives. The latter would use the bigotry and conspiratorial notions of the extremists as a means of winning the support of the less educated and less privileged elements in the population from their political rivals, the Democrats. Thus, although I had planned to spend a few months working on the historical background of the radical right, it turned out that I spent close to two years delving into this record and analyzing it. The work as a consequence has taken much more time than I anticipated, and I had hoped to finish the book by the fall of 1968. Concluding it was held up to await the outcome of the Wallace campaign in the 1968 elections. There are, as readers of our work will discover, many parallels in the activities of Wallace and the earlier right-wing groups.

A major byproduct of the research on right-wing movements was a long article dealing with the role of religion in American politics. In my writings on American politics in *Political Man,* I have stressed basically the role of class and economic factors as differentiating the major parties over the years. As I read through the historical record pertaining to the role of right-wing movements, it also became clear to me that religious differences had formed at least as important a source of differentiation between the two major parties from the start of the republic down to the present. The Democratic party had always been more successful in appealing to the "out" groups in religious and cultural terms. This meant that the Democrats had appealed more successfully than their rivals to the immigrants and their descendants, to Catholics, and to other groups defined as minorities. Their opponents, on the other hand, have had excess support from the more evangelical, more puritanical Protestant denominations in the country. Thus, the Federalists, the Whigs, and the Republicans each in turn defended the interests and values of Evangelical Protestants in conflicts with Catholics and other religious groups, including atheists and theists. The more conservative parties also from time to time allied themselves often quite openly with nativist anti-Catholic groups and parties as a way of winning elections. The analysis of the special role of religion as a source of differentiation in America is presented in a long chapter in *Revolution and Counter-Revolution.* The work on this section was a byproduct, as indicated above.

THE RANGE OF DEMOCRACY

In looking over what I've written about my work, I note that I've tried to describe the reasons why I undertook various bodies of writing or research. I doubt that an author or scholar is the best person to properly evaluate or explain the logic contained in the work which he has done. I personally see a strong strain of consistency and effort at cumulation of comparable problems. *Agrarian Socialism* was concerned with specifying the conditions which facilitated the emergence of a left-wing, that is, innovative, movement in North American society. It began with a historical analysis first of agrarian radical movements in the United States, and then of such movements on the Canadian prairie. In it, I try to specify the kinds of structural conditions which would facilitate large-scale participation by the ordinary citizen in innovative politics designed to gain control over institutions, both political and economic. The study of the right-wing movement deals with the opposite pole, that is right-wing, or preservatist movements. These are movements of ordinary people who see themselves losing control or losing status as a result of changes in the political system. They respond by efforts to turn the clock back institutionally and in value terms. The study of student politics, like that of agrarian socialism, is also primarily concerned with innovative left-wing politics, essentially those concerned with social reform. Extreme or radical politics, however, are not the whole story of democratic political systems. If they were, such systems would be essentially unstable and unworkable. Consequently, any effort to understand political behavior in general requires a detailed analysis of the factors underlying political conflict among the moderates, that is, those who basically accept the existing rules of the political game and the larger system but who seek to gain or preserve something they value within the system. I would argue, therefore, that the bulk of my work in political sociology has been devoted to an analysis of the factors underlying the behavior of different actors in democratic society. These actors run from the extreme left to the extreme right.

Since, as I indicated at the beginning of this essay, my initial interests in the field were devoted to understanding the factors which would make innovative or left-wing politics possible, and secondly with trying to understand the factors which made democratic participatory politics difficult if not impossible. My original work was heavily influenced by the intellectual concerns and writings of social theorists like Karl Marx, Max Weber, and Robert Michels. These men and their writings have remained important as sources of ideas and concerns in my work down to the present. However, as I also came to be concerned with understanding the way in which the democratic process operated, and what made it possible to maintain a system in which the actors agree to the rules of the game even though these might temporarily adversely affect their chances of winning, the work of social theorists more concerned with problems of stability as well as of change became important. This meant that theorists such as Emile Durkheim, Alexis de Tocqueville, and Talcott Parsons took on much more importance in my work than they had originally. Tocqueville first appears in some of the analysis in *Union Democracy* since it became clear that many of the conditions which seemed to help maintain a stable democratic system in the ITU were highly comparable to those which Tocqueville presented as sources of American democracy in his classic, *Democracy In America*. Durkheim, though not a political or stratification theorist, is of crucial significance in any effort to understand the bases of conservatism in society. Parsons also has been important for attempts to understand the stabilizing mechanisms of the social order, but in terms of my own work he has been even more influential as a source of concepts and ideas about ways of categorizing social systems comparatively in order to understand the differences in institutional structures among them. The social theorist whose work has probably come closest to bridging all the various interests which I've had, as well as the different concerns of the various theorists whom I see as important in my own work, has been Robert Merton. Merton, though properly seen as primarily a structural functionalist in his theoretical orientation and, hence, closer to Durkheim and Parsons than to anyone else, has also been concerned in much of his writings with problems of social instability and of innovation. His writings, as I try to suggest in my essay on social class, bridge the concerns of the Marxian tradition with those of the Durkheimian one.

In discussing the sources of my scholarly work, I have stressed the extent to which they have been responses to political events and to political concerns. In the quarter of a century since I first began graduate work in sociology, the political scene has obviously changed greatly. In the late thirties and early forties students and intellectuals who saw themselves as men of the left and who took as their dominant political objective the attainment of a more democratic and more egalitarian social order faced the twin menaces of Stalinism and Fascism as represented by the regimes in the Soviet Union and Germany. These totalitarian movements existed in most countries as domestic political forces. With the defeat of Fascism in World War II, Stalinism remained a major threat to the existing democratic societies. It appeared to be expansionist and totalitarian. Hence, many concerned with social change felt it necessary to combat first Fascism and then Stalinism in order to defend the existing democratic systems of the West. In spite of their manifold deficiencies from a moral point of view, these societies clearly permitted a more democratic and egalitarian existence for both mass and intellectual elite than did the totalitarian regimes. The breakdown in the cold war which followed the divisions within the communist world upon the death of Stalin is the beginning of de-Stalinization. Liberal movements within Eastern Europe, and the split between Russia and China, not only changed the character of communism but also affected domestic and foreign politics among Western states. The moratorium on sharp radical criticism which in effect existed from the late thirties until the late fifties has been broken. The break came first among students and intellectuals, and is in fact still limited largely to them. An understanding of the character of radical movements both on the left and right has become a more important issue both for social analysis and social action than was true in the period dominated by the totalitarian threats. To some considerable degree, I would think, my own recent work represents a response to such changes in the political climate.

11

ELEMENTS OF A SOCIOLOGICAL SELF-IMAGE

JOSEPH BERGER

WHEN THE EDITOR of this volume suggested doing a paper on my sociological self-image, he activated in this respondent two strongly conflicting reactions. Surely I am too young to be writing about my self-image as a sociologist. Properly, this is a task of the elder statesman looking back on his career, searching and finding coherence in his particular sociological odyssey, and, of course, setting forth to the younger generation "what is still to be done." On the other hand, am I really that young? I certainly have already formed basic orientations which guide my work as a sociologist and are part of my self-image. And since at least some of these orientations are still matters of debate in our field, shouldn't they be given expression? The resolution of this conflict is, in the first instance, reflected in the title of this paper, particularly in the phrase, "Elements of." It is also reflected in its organization. Most space, in one section or another, is devoted to simply presenting some positions that are constitutive of my general research orientation. A smaller proportion is spent on my own work, and in particular on that special subclass which I "like best," and still a smaller proportion is devoted to the question of "impact on reshaping the field." All in all, this particular allocation strikes me as quite reasonable, given the task of picturing the self-image of a sociologist in progress.

On Defining Characteristics

Insofar as there is something special in "my way of doing sociology," it arises in part from the fact that I have come to hold certain general research orientations and interests that are still to some extent matters of controversy in our field. Among these is my interpretation of and commitment to the "generalizing orientation" in sociological research, and my interest in formalization as a theory-building strategy.

THE GENERALIZING ORIENTATION IN RESEARCH

As a research sociologist, I have been guided by what I am here referring to as a generalizing research orientation. I have been concerned with formulating and developing general and abstract theories about various types of social processes—occupational mobility, evaluation-expectation processes, and status processes. I have also been concerned with constructing formal models (where possible) for such theories and with devising experimental situations (where appropriate) in which such theories and models can be tested.

Such activities have always seemed to me to be both reasonable and natural. In part, this follows from my belief that whatever sociology is (and it is certainly other things), it is also a generalizing science. As such, its practitioners must be concerned with the state of theoretical knowledge in the field, and in particular with the cumulative development of that knowledge. Still, it is clear that there is much sociological research that is not explicitly addressed, per se, to developing abstract theories of social processes. There is also much sociological research, important and legitimate to the sociological enterprise on other grounds, that has surprisingly little payoff with respect to the task of developing cumulative theoretical knowledge in our discipline. How are we to understand this situation? I want to argue that there is a fundamental distinction between a generalizing and historical orientation in research; that the historical orientation may be much more common in sociological research than the generalizing orientation; and that this fact may, in part at least, explain the slow development of cumulative theoretical knowledge in our field.

The distinction between the historical and generalizing orientations in research does not involve a difference in the *structure* of explanation or prediction. I believe, with others, that whether the research focus is generalizing or historical, the same type of formal components is involved. As long as we are concerned with explanation, prediction, or postdiction, we make use of: (1) general propositions or "law-like" statements; (2) statements describing initial or antecedent conditions; and (3) statements describing events to be explained. Independent of the nature of the research focus, the inferential character of our activity (whether its form be logical deduction, probabilistic inference, or mathematical derivation) involves using assertions like type 2 in conjunction with those like type 1 to infer those like type 3.

The research significance of a distinction between a generalizing and historical focus hinges on which of these formal components is of primary concern to the researcher in his task. For the investigator with an historical focus, statements of type 3 are typically his primary concern. These may concern a particular event or set of events, and these events may be simple or complex. From his standpoint, this event (or set of events) is the "given" in his problem. It is often the case that the event is in some sense important or socially significant. Be that as it may, the event is of *intrinsic* interest to him, and he is concerned with explaining it. For the most part, the task of explaining such events involves establishing statements of type 2. That is, it involves constructing hypotheses describing the occurrence of certain initial or antecedent conditions, and then determining whether these hypotheses hold. Just as the event to be explained in this type of orientation is of intrinsic interest, so too are the "explaining" antecedent conditions of intrinsic interest. However, in terms of this research focus, statements of type 1 are of secondary importance. If they *are* made explicit (and often they are not), they can usually be shown to consist of general propositions from various social science sources, or fairly broad commonsense assertions about social behavior. My intent is not to criticize the use of such assertions. I believe that the use of such a mixture of general propositions and commonsense assertions (from whatever source) is a both necessary and standard feature in this type of enterprise. However, calling attention to their character does highlight the claim that type 1 statements are of secondary importance in this research situation. In a strict sense, such generalizations and broad assertions are not being tested in this type of research, although they can be used in conjunction with type 2 statements—statements about antecedent conditions—to explain the events of concern. It should not be surprising, therefore, that this type of research focus, as important as it may be in its own right, has been the basis of so little general theoretical knowledge in our field.

As I have already said, I suspect that this historical orientation in research is far more common in our field than the one which I think of as the generalizing orientation. For the investigator working within a generalizing focus, it *is* the case that statements of type 1, either singly or in the form of an organized set constituting a theory, are of primary concern. From the standpoint of this particular interest, there are the "givens" in his problem, and it is the statements of this type that are of *intrinsic* interest to him. In his concern with formulating and establishing such statements, he must also be concerned with statements of type 2 or 3. However, his interest in such statements is primarily of an *instrumental* nature. He is concerned with statments of type 2 and 3 in order to obtain empirical tests that are relevant to his general propositions or theory. Such empirical tests, of course, are necessary to evaluating his theory; and even more significantly, are necessary to providing the information required in refining and reformulating specific assertions.

Nevertheless, it is typically the case that theories can be tested under different conditions, and that there are different types of tests which can be applied to a theory. As a consequence, the investigator working within a generalizing orientation may have considerable latitude in the choice of the particular type 2 and type 3 statements which will be of concern to him. His selection of a set of initial conditions for study (which, therefore, determines the type 3 statements that constitute a particular test of his theory) will probably rest on his answer to such questions as: (a) How sensitive a test does a particular set of initial conditions provide for this theory? (b) Can he experimentally control the behavior called for by a given set of initial conditions? (c) What kind of data can he obtain which is relevant to the type 3 statements entailed by his particular selection of initial conditions? Insofar as the researcher with a generalizing focus is not concerned with *applying* his theory (an important but separate consideration), he has latitude in terms of the type 2 and type 3 statements with which he is concerned. He may indeed select initial conditions which are "manipulated" (controlled by the experimenter) and "artificial" (do not typically occur in normal interaction), and he may indeed be concerned with predicting what appear to be "very special events" (events that are possibly not defined as socially significant at a given time). But it should be noted that from the standpoint of his orientation, the investigator's concern with events that are "manipulated," "artificial," and "very special" is an instrumental one. His interest in these events is in the information they can provide in terms of which he can test, refine, and reformulate his general propositions and theories.

With many others, I share the conviction that the better the theories available to us, the more fruitful will be our historically focused research activities and the more effective our attempts at social engineering. Given the nature of our discipline, I think that there is little reason to fear that sociologists will divorce themselves from historically focused research or from applied problems; and this is certainly as it should be. But there is reason to be concerned with the present state of theoretical knowledge in our field.

There are, I am sure, many very different reasons that can be adduced to explain the slow development of cumulative theoretical knowledge in our field. But one of these, and perhaps not the least important, may be the fact that the generalizing orientation in our research activities is not as fully institutionalized as it is reasonable to expect it to be in a generalizing science.

FORMALIZATION

From a rational standpoint, my interest in formal theory follows quite naturally from my interest in developing theories of basic social processes. But from the standpoint of personal history, it has taken me considerable time to really understand the relation between these two interests. Although model-building was "in the air" at the time of my graduate training at Harvard in the early fifties, actual work along these lines was largely confined to the then pioneering efforts of Bush and Mosteller in the area of learning theory. Little that occurred in my graduate training served to promote my interest in or understanding of formalization. Then, as even today (although probably to a lesser extent), one could define oneself as a theorist while at the same time dissociating oneself from model-building. Then, as even today, model-building (in some quarters at least) was more likely to be classified as a variant of research in methodology than as a type of theory-building activity.

It was not until the late fifties that I became keenly aware of the range of possibilities that formalization provides for the development of sociological theories. By that time I had already worked with Snell and Kemeny on the problem of applying stochastic theory to the study of occupational mobility (Berger and Snell, 1957; Kemeny and Snell, 1960), so I had some appreciation of the many problems (technical and substantive) which arise in this type of research. But what about the possibilities afforded by this type of activity? Basically, this was the question we sought to answer in the research which led to *Types of Formalization* (Berger et al.,

[182]

1962). Basing ourselves on an intensive analysis of *what had actually been accomplished* in a specific area, we were able to arrive at some unexpected conclusions. Among these were that formalization had been (and could be) employed in different types of theoretical activities, that the application of formal theory need not be restricted only to the case in which a fully elaborated and extensively established substantive theory already existed, but that formalization can be used at different stages in the development of theoretical knowledge. Formalization can be effectively employed in the situation where a theorist is primarily concerned with *explicating* what appears to be a theoretically significant concept (an extremely common activity among sociologists). It can also be effectively employed in the case where the theorist is primarily interested in *describing* in a *precise* and *simple* manner some well-studied process or structure for which he may not yet have a well-established explanatory theory (e.g., the description of occupational mobility processes, or the analysis of kinship structures).

There are problems and limitations connected with formalizaton as a theory-building strategy. Some of these were discussed in *Types,* and I am sure I could add many more if I were to rewrite that book today. I do not think of model-building as a panacea for the many problems that confront us in the area of sociological theory. A theory which in terms of conceptual and empirical considerations is inadequate will normally *not* be transformed into a useful or empirically significant formulation by interpreting it within a formal structure. Although I should add that the *attempt* to formalize such a theory may well highlight its inadequacies and motivate efforts to reformulate it. Further, I do not believe (nor in my own research have I followed) the dictum that says that *any* substantively promising theory *can* be formalized. In fact, there may not exist an appropriate mathematical theory *with* a well-developed theorem structure which can be profitably used for the particular problem. Or, if an appropriate mathematical theory exists, it may entail measurement conditions which the sociologist, given the present state of his art, is unable to meet. In either case, no matter how skillful or sophisticated the mathematical exercise involved, the resulting formalization is not likely to yield a significant development in our theoretical knowledge. However, I do believe that if we have a formulation that is at least conceptually adequate (if not refined and elaborated) and is empirically acceptable (if not well established), then we have a *candidate* for formalization. If it should also be the case that there exists an appropriate mathematical theory (entailing measurement requirements which can be met), then the formalization of this formulation is likely to yield a more *powerful* theoretical structure. At the very least, formalization in this case enables us to make more precise the deductive implications of our original formulation. Insofar as this increases our capacities to test our original formulation, it enhances our ability to refine and develop our theoretical knowledge. In the final analysis, this, as I see it, is the fundamental rationale for formalization as a theory-building activity.

On Work

EXPECTATIONS RESEARCH

Of the various types of research activities in which I have been involved, that "which I like best" (if I may use the editor's phrase) is my work on expectation processes. In one form or another, I have been absorbed in this work for over a decade, and I find myself today as deeply involved with the problems posed by this research as when I first started.

My original interest in expectation processes grew out of a desire to try to explain the emergence of power and prestige orders in task-oriented groups. In particular, the research of Bales and his associates had intrigued me. He, as well as others, had shown that marked inequalities in various types of behaviors and evaluations occurred in relatively short periods of time in groups whose members were initially status equals. Early in my thinking, I became

[184]

convinced that such an order of inequalities could be explained by positing that an *underlying* structure of performance expectations developed out of the interaction in these groups, and that once formed, this structure then determined the interaction which took place.

Theoretical and experimental work on this problem has taken many different directions over the years and has given rise to many different types of products. It led directly to the development of a standardized experimental situation that has come to be used by colleagues and co-workers in their studies of a wide range of problems concerned with expectation processes (see Zelditch, 1968; Moore, 1968). In addition, it has led to developing a number of theoretical formulations and mathematical models concerned with different aspects of this problem. Probably a good deal concerning the nature and character of this research is conveyed by this list of most recent efforts: a theory concerned with the relation of performance expectations to small group behavior (Berger and Conner, 1969), a mathematical model concerned with the relation of performance expectations to evaluation processes (Berger, Conner, and McKeown, 1968), and a mathematical model concerned with the relation of performance expectations to decision-making and social influence (Camilleri and Berger, 1967).

In the course of this research I also became convinced that a theory concerned with the formation and maintenance of expectation states could be applied to a wide range of "classical" sociological problems. About five or six years ago, I started to work seriously on one of these classical problems. Sociologists have long been concerned with the effect of socially defined status characteristics such as age, sex, and race, on the behavior of individuals in face-to-face interaction situations. Further, an extensive body of small groups literature exists on this problem which demonstrates that such status characteristics as age, sex, race, and occupational class, have marked effects in determining the behavior of individuals in a wide variety of small group situations. This research (in collaboration with M. Zelditch, Jr., and B. P. Cohen) led to the development of a theoretical formulation that enables us to account for a substantial proportion of the empirical findings on this problem to be found in this small groups literature (see Berger et al., 1966). Subsequently, independent experimental tests of this theory have been carried out. The results of these tests lead us to believe that we can, with this formulation, describe a process by which status characteristics organize the behavior of individuals in *particular* interaction situations.

Now it is "clear" to us that a theory concerned with the formation and maintenance of expectation states can, if properly generalized, be applied to still other classical sociological problems. The one which has most recently interested us is the problem of explaining the structure, conditions for, and consequences of, status consistencies and inconsistencies in face-to-face interaction. And this is the way this research has evolved—no sooner have we gotten a grasp on one problem, that is, an understanding of the way in which expectations are formed and maintained for a specific set of social conditions, than we start pushing out toward still another problem. In this process it typically has not been the case that we could simply generalize a previous formulation so that it is applicable to a new set of social situations. More commonly our tactic has been to develop parallel formulations (formulations sharing many of the same concepts and assertions) for different specific problems. The hope is, of course, that eventually these formulations can be rigorously related to each other. But we have tended to be cautious in this matter. There is much to be done in developing and experimentally testing particular formulations, and the construction of a single comprehensive theory is a task still very much for the future.

What started as a concern for some "simple" problems has also over the years grown into what can properly be called a research tradition. Like other such entities, this tradition is a mixture of elements. It consists of some reasonably well-developed theoretical assertions concerning the operation of expectation processes; a fairly large set of problems, only some of which have been "solved," that are regarded as relevant to research on these processes; and a standardized experimental situation. Among other things, the latter has permitted us to carry on a wide variety of empirical investigations under basically similar information-gathering conditions. Finally, one can speak of there being a distinctive theoretical perspective in our research. This consists, among other things, of solutions which have grown out of our work on previous problems, and general ideas, concepts, and broad assertions, in short, the materials out of which new problems are formulated and, hopefully, new solutions generated.

Over the years I have been able to interest many extremely able students in the ideas and research problems in this area. I have also been fortunate enough to have had colleagues, such as M. Zelditch, Jr., B. P. Cohen, S. F. Camilleri, and Bo Anderson, who have become deeply involved with the theoretical and empirical problems of expectations research. And this fact, as much as any other, is involved in characterizing the work on expectation processes as a research tradition—namely, that there is enough commonality in problem definitions, theoretical perspective, and research procedures to allow the efforts of different individuals to easily contribute to our knowledge of what we like to think of as a "basic social process."

REDUCTIONISM

Does this type of approach to "classical" sociological problems make me an adherent of reductionism? Not necessarily, and certainly not in the sense of the traditional definition of such a position in our field. I do not believe that positions for reductionism or for nonreductionism can be established in terms of arguments concerned with such questions as "What is really the basic stuff of social reality?" In my own thinking, reductionism in sociology is a research strategy. In the final analysis, evaluation of the claims of this strategy, its importance in our field, whether it gains or loses adherents, will depend upon the degree to which its

[187]

adherents are able for any given problem to realize its objectives. Therefore, it is important to understand these claims and objectives before we entrench ourselves in noncommunicating camps arguing on "higher grounds" that it can or cannot be done.

To see what is involved, consider the following simple example. Assume that, as a sociologist interested in small groups research, I claim that sociologists have established the existence of a simple relationship between the size of a small task-oriented group and the variation in participation of the members of such a group. This relationship (call it R) is in the form of an abstract empirical generalization which presumably would hold under specified conditions. Imagine now that some sociologist comes along and argues that he can reduce this generalization to the "level of individual behavior." How are we to understand this claim? At the very least, this is a claim that he can *explain* R. But more is involved. The shock aspect of this claim (from the standpoint of the sociologist) is that he can explain R by using *terms* predicated of individuals rather than social units. What would be required for him to achieve this end? From what we know of these matters (Brodbeck, 1958; Nagel, 1961), in all likelihood the following: First, we require a set of laws or theoretical assertions involving terms predicated only of individuals. For example, these might be assertions describing how any individual in a given group situation develops a particular type of performance expectation for himself and others. Second, we require assertions describing how processes assumed to occur for one individual are related to similar processes occurring for other individuals in the given situation.[1] These might be assertions, for example, that describe the conditions and processes by which a number of individuals in the given situation develop similar or dissimilar expectations in relation to each other. And finally, we require substantive assertions which in effect relate the terms of these laws to terms which appear in R—assertions, for example, relating expectation structures as held simultaneously by a number of individuals in a group to the distribution of their participation. Given these elements, it is at least in principle possible for the theorist to explain R, and in this sense reduce it to laws and assertions involving terms and relations predicated of individuals.[2]

Now, first and most obvious, it should be noted that a reduction of this type does *not necessarily* mean that a sociological generalization or law is being reduced to a psychological generalization or law. One could make such a claim only if one chooses to regard *all* assertions involving terms predicated of individuals (as compared to social units) as psychological laws. At best, such an identification can be said to be arbitrary; at worst, it is a confusing shibboleth. Second, for any given problem, the reductionist's claim can be evaluated, and one can determine whether or not the reduction has been achieved. And finally, the fact that a reduction has been achieved in one problem area does not constitute proof that it can be achieved in all areas. Achieving a reduction in the strict sense is, in most cases, a formidable task which is not realized by simply saying it should be so. It therefore makes little sense to argue that we should eschew in our empirical and theoretical work a nonreductionist approach on the grounds that a reduction will surely be achieved sometime in the future.

For myself, I have tended to pursue a reductionist strategy in my work. This strategy has developed naturally in the course of my research on different problems, and as far as I can tell, it does not follow from general philosophical convictions concerning "the nature of reality." It is in this sense that I regard it as a pragmatic reductionism. For the problems with which I have been concerned, the strategy appears to be reasonable. If we are able to explain some of the things that we know about power and prestige order in task-oriented groups by using concepts and assertions predicated of individuals and relations between individuals, it is an obvious tactic to try to explain what is known about social interaction in still other types of social situations with the use of similar concepts and assertions. Such efforts may result in a number of *different* expectation theories. The hope, of course, is that we can eventually relate these different expectation theories to each other. This is certainly one of the motivations in following this strategy—

namely, that through these reductions we may be able to construct a comprehensive theory applicable to a wide range of social situations. And this is also a criterion in terms of which we can evaluate the strategy in any specific case.

However, it surely does not follow from these arguments that this is the *only way* to develop general and comprehensive theories for the wide range of distinctive substantive problems of interest to sociologists. It makes little sense to argue from "on high" that such comprehensive theories cannot be constructed unless the sociologist follows a reductionist strategy. I know no way of either establishing or refuting such a position. We can probably easily recognize that such a view, taken seriously, can be intellectually debilitating. But there are positions, companions, in fact, to this one, which are equally debilitating. Among these, for example, is the one which claims that to follow a reductionist strategy is to violate a basic tenet of sociology; or a related position which chooses to define some substantive area in which a reductionist approach appears to have some possibility of success as being outside the concern or interest of sociologists. Given the present state of knowledge in our field, it is surely unwise at this stage (if not always) to legislate against theoretical strategies.

On Impact

I am certain that it is not possible for me to assess what impact, if any, I have had up to now in "reshaping our field." However, *if* I do come to exert some such impact, it may well come about as a result of my activities in the Stanford sociology program. For the last ten years I have had a major share of the responsibility for shaping the goals and the content of the graduate theory program in this department. From its very inception, this program has placed heavy emphasis on providing the student with training in theory construction. It has also sought to develop in the student an attitude of "theoretical boldness"—to be able to evaluate in a sophisticated manner the various types of theoretical activities sociologists are engaged in, to be aware of the possibilities and potentialities that do exist for developing rigorous theory, and to be able to use some of the analytical and technical skills that are necessary for their own work in theory.

For almost a decade now, all of our students have gone through some or all parts of this program. What impact do I see such a program as having? Have we produced a generation of creative theorists? This is hardly to be expected, and certainly is not the case. We do expect and hope that some of these students (probably a greater proportion than is typically the case) will become active and creative theoreticians. Some, we expect and hope, will become seriously involved in doing research in the area of theory construction *itself.* Although the sociologist has much to learn from the growing literature in the philosophy of science, there is much more that he needs to know about the process of constructing theories that he will *not* find in this literature. Research on problems of theory construction is very much needed in our field, and sociologists, through their own efforts, will have to develop a usable body of knowledge in this important area. Such expectations we hold for at least some of our students; but for most, if not all, who have been exposed to this program, we hold more general and basic expectations: that they will become sophisticated users and critics of theoretical work; that they will have a *realistic* appreciation of the present state of our field in these matters; and that through their own work, as well as their teaching, the next generation will become aware of both the needs and potentialities of theory-building in our field. It is just possible that this type of orientation, if it takes hold, will have an impact on the future shape of sociology.

NOTES

1. See in this connection Brodbeck's (1958) discussion of "composition laws."

2. For an attempt to explain an empirical generalization such as the one considered here in terms of concepts and assertions involving expectations processes, see Fisek (1969).

REFERENCES

BERGER, J., B. P. COHEN, J. L. SNELL, and M. ZELDITCH, JR. (1962) Types of Formalization in Small Groups Research. Boston: Houghton Mifflin.

BERGER, J., B. P. COHEN, and M. ZELDITCH, JR. (1966) "Status characteristics and expectation states." In vol. 1 of J. Berger, M. Zelditch, Jr., and B. Anderson (eds.) Sociological Theories in Progress. Boston: Houghton Mifflin.

BERGER, J. and T. L. CONNER (1969) "Performance expectations and behavior in small groups." Appears in both Acta Sociologica 12 and R. Ofshe (ed.) Interpersonal Behavior in Small Groups. Englewood Cliffs, N.J.: Prentice-Hall.

BERGER, J., T. L. CONNER, and W. L. McKEOWN (forthcoming) "Evaluations and the formation and maintenance of performance expectations." To appear in Human Relations.

BERGER, J. and J. L. SNELL (1957) "On the concept of equal exchange." Journal of Behavioral Science 2 (April): 111-18.

BRODBECK, MAY (1958) "Methodological individualism: definitions and reduction." Philosophy of Science 25 (January).

CAMILLERI, S. F. and J. BERGER (1967) "Decision-making and social influence: a model and experimental test." Sociometry 30 (December): 365-78.

FISEK, M. HAMIT (1969) The Evolution of Status Structure and Interaction in Task Oriented Discussion Groups. Ph.D. dissertation, Stanford University.

KEMENY, J. and J. L. SNELL (1960) Finite Markov Chains. Princeton: D. Van Nostrand.

MOORE, JAMES C., JR. (1968) "Status and influence in small group interactions." Sociometry 31 (March): 47-63.

NAGEL, E. (1961) The Structure of Science. New York: Harcourt, Brace & World.

ZELDITCH, MORRIS, JR. (1968) "Can you really study an army in the laboratory?" In A. Etzioni et al. (ed.) Complex Organizations: A Sociological Reader (2d ed.). New York: Holt, Rinehart & Winston.

12

SOCIOLOGY AS
AN IDEA SYSTEM

ROBERT A. NISBET

*What do you consider the most uniquely defining
characteristics of your way of doing sociology?*

Working with ideas and idea systems. This is an enterprise that I
regard as neither more nor less empirical than working with, say,
roles and role systems or status and status systems. In terms of
human culture, we have two environments: the intellectual, composed of ideas; the institutional, composed of roles, statuses,
norms, and the like. Neither environment is intrinsically more
important than the other. Neither environment is less susceptible
than the other to objective analysis. Obviously, the two environments permeate each other; they are hardly separable. But they are
manifestly distinguishable, and should be distinguished.

Given the existence of the two environments I find it extraordinary, to say the least, that a hundred times the energy and
resources go into the study of the institutional environment that
go into study of the intellectual. John Dewey once said that every
educated mind has in it tissues of Platonism, Aristotelianism, and
Augustinianism, and that the purpose of philosophy is to make one
aware of these tissues. But the task is equally that of each of the
disciplines that today form the universe of knowledge. To become
aware of the ideas that in one degree or other mold us, shape us,
motivate us: this is surely as essential an enterprise as that of
becoming aware of behavior patterns around us. I am referring to
the intellectual environment at large and to the plurality of specialized intellectual environments that scientists and scholars work in.

Each of the latter is vital. Whatever major breakthroughs will take place, or are now taking place unbeknownst to us, that will differentiate the future of sociology from the present, will have far less to do with new institutional *data*—the sort of thing commonly called "empirics"—than they will with radical rearrangements of existing ideas. Michael Polanyi gives us this paradigm for all progress in science: *Discoveries are made by pursuing possibilities suggested by existing knowledge.* He illustrates it with Max Planck's astoundingly original quantum theory of 1900. All the material on which Planck founded his theory was open to inspection, Polanyi tells us, to other physicists. "He alone saw inscribed in it a new order transforming the outlook of man." Did Planck hate facts, data, figures, quantities? Not at all. But the new order he saw inscribed was *in existing knowledge.*

Hence the horror, the unadulterated horror, of teaching students today, undergraduate and graduate alike, that science is a matter of going, method in hand, from door to door or from census tract to census tract in search of new data, or new configurations of data to be computer fed. "Go with an open mind" is commonly the instructor's parting adjuration.

What folly! Descartes thought his triumphant *Cogito: ergo sum* was the fresh and unalloyed product of an open mind, a mind deliberately purged, he tells us, of all that he had learned. But instead of indulging in the vain pursuit of cleansing his mind, Descartes would have done better *to have become aware of what was in his mind,* and work critically from that. For his *Cogito: ergo sum,* far from being, as he thought, novel, was but another statement—an identical statement—of something St. Augustine had devoted several paragraphs to in, among other works, his *Confessions,* and with which Descartes was certainly familiar. If the history of social thought seems to run tiresomely in cycles—and God knows the history of sociology seems to—it is only because few if any of us take the trouble to become aware of what is in our minds, whether generally as human beings or more specifically as social scientists.

[194]

I am not pleading for more courses of the type known solemnly and pretentiously as The History of Sociology in one or other of its several variations. Such a course is all too often a stupefying bore, a kind of Dick and Jane reader in action: "Look, look! See, see what Ibn Khaldun said!" What killed Dick and Jane will surely, in time, kill this kind of course. The study of ideas, of what Polanyi calls "existing knowledge," is much too important an enterprise to be left to those who adjust to the onset of senility by presenting strings of names, dates, and who-said-what-when.

The past in itself is but fodder for the antiquarians. All that can possibly justify its study is the extent to which one or more of its continuities permeate the present. It is the *present* that we should be concerned with, and the only good reason I can think of—and it is a splendid reason—for the study and restudy of such minds as Durkheim, Weber, Simmel, Tocqueville, Marx, Mead, and a few others in sociology, is that they are as surely our contemporaries as though they were attending annual meetings of the ASA. The present structure of sociological knowledge is vivid testimony to what I am saying. Its central premises are their central premises; its problems are theirs.

But if we are to learn from them we must go with questions and themes in mind, questions and themes that are the product of concern with the present. Truly, as Whitehead said, the present is holy ground. In our sociological present are problems of order and change, of the macrocosmic and microcosmic, of quality and quantity. These alone should be the point of departure for study of what we call the past. Distinction of the substantive past from the chronological past is important. In Athens in the fifth century B.C., there were countless dramatists to entertain audiences night after night. Most of them are in the substantive as well as chronological past. We know neither them nor their works. But an Aeschylus, Sophocles, or Euripides lies only in the chronological, not the substantive, past.

So with knowledge; so with that small part of knowledge we call the social sciences. Either an Aristotle or an Augustine or a

[195]

Leibniz—or a Tocqueville, Marx, Weber, Durkheim—speaks to us in the meaningful terms of *present problems, present questions* about the two environments we live in—or off with his head! Let us waste no time on museum pieces.

I have been writing only of ideas and idea systems. Admittedly, gloriously indeed, the past serves one other major purpose for those interested in present problems. It is a vast exhibit of persistences and changes, of processes and structures, of stagnations and creativities, to which we can take questions grounded in present urgency. And it is astonishing how much of the past, in these terms, is usable; how much of it has left itself recorded in one way or other. For the study of social change the past is absolutely indispensable. Change I define as a succession of differences in time in a persisting identity. Each element of the definition is vital, but I emphasize here the middle element "in time." How can we possibly distinguish between mere motion or activity and *change,* how can we possibly sense the interplay of *persistence* and *change,* save through observation of some persisting identity over a significant period of time? There is more to be learned about the mechanisms of change from, say, the history of the university during the thousand years since its inception than from all the group dynamics studies put together. In fact, I should think that before any faculty committee on courses ever approved a course called Social Change, a sworn affidavit might be required testifying to the instructor's understanding of the proposition that change means *change-in-time,* and the greater the amount of time, *ceteris paribus,* the better.

In sum, the uniquely defining characteristics of my work are (1) *intellectual,* meaning ideas and idea systems and (2) *historical,* meaning, not simpleminded narration, but the uncovering of the strata of meaning, strata of different ages and sources, which compose the present.

[196]

What is your view of the current relationship of
sociological theory and social applications?

Very dim. In fact, I would like to make a plea for the frank abandonment of sociological theory considered as a separate room within our mansion. It does more harm, it seems to me, than good. Our best "theory" consists of the insights, ideas, and hypotheses that have bounced off nontheoretical studies: Durkheim on suicide, Weber on religion, Thomas on the Polish immigrant, Merton on differential rewards, and so on. It is the mark of any distinguished piece of scholarship, on whatever subject, that by very virtue of its distinguished character, some kind of transfer is effected of its own insights to other and ostensibly unrelated subjects. This, of course, is all to the good.

It is unfortunate that the word "theory" has taken on undue prestige. I am told that this is a problem in other fields, including the physical sciences. But I think it is most conspicuous in our own discipline, sociology. Self-styled ventures in sociological theory have not been very successful, it would appear. We are sometimes dazzled by their conceptual, even mathematical, clothing. But beneath the royal rainment little seems to exist. We find ourselves thinking of Roy Campbell's lines on some modern poets:

> *They use the snaffle and the curb all right*
> *But where's the bloody horse?*

Far better, I should think, to forget "sociological theory" as such—above all, get it out of the meetings of the ASA—and continue to work as we have at our best on suicide, religion, community, social class, ideas, organizations, and so on. The best studies will, as they always have, leave a residue of suggestion; the others will not, and what is the matter with that?

Having got this off my chest about so-called theory, I come to what I think is the real point of the question: the relationship between sociological *knowledge* and social application. That there

[197]

is knowledge, in every proper sense of that word, in sociology permits no doubt whatever. But I confess I find the relation between it and the major instances of social policy-making in our time rather dim also. It is easy to take refuge in some variant of the supposition of either conspiracy or obtuseness and to say that sociology suffers from discrimination in high places. Perhaps so. And I frankly do not see how prospective policy-makers—using this phrase to include a Saul Alinsky at one extreme and the Supreme Court at the other—can be educated apart from some considerable exposure to the major insights of sociology.

But the policy-makers at their greatest, whether radical or conservative, should and do draw from not merely a diversity of analytical disciplines (and sociology is by its nature one of several analytical disciplines), but from motivations and qualities of judgment—and plain old-fashioned *morality*—that are scarcely to be wrapped up in any science. And any effort to remold sociology along lines that would make it directly, unmediatedly relevant to policy-making seems to me as profound an error as to make the university an instrument of direct action in the modern state. The objective of sociology—of all science—is knowledge. No doubt a little of sociological knowledge will be, at any given moment, directly usable. But mostly the salutary policy consequences of sociology will have been effected, I think, through disciplines that are intermediate to sociology and social policy, what Znaniecki called "synthesizing" disciplines.

Even the existence of synthesizing disciplines, to convert and apply the insights of the analytical disciplines, will not effect any miracles, not at least in democracy, however enlightened it may in time become. For policy-making is a good deal more than application *of the known.* It is also response, oftentimes immediate and under conditions of emergency, *to the unknown;* or rather, to circumstances that are as preemptive as they are unique. Remember Pearl Harbor! The American government knew, having broken the Japanese code, virtually to the day when Hawaii was to be struck, and how. The knowledge was there. Judgment, policy, call it what we will, made the knowledge otiose. All was at rest on that fateful Sunday at Pearl Harbor.

And there is another, profounder, aspect to all this. The best illustration I can think of for this final point is the momentous Supreme Court desegregation decision of 1954. In that landmark of American law, there were some references to sociological and psychological "knowledge" about the deleterious effects of segregated schooling. But as Morroe Berger pointed out in a bold and brilliant article on the decision, such references were, first, dubious on strictly scientific grounds and, second, expendable. All that was really required for that great and long overdue decision was the combination of moral precept and legal precedent that the decision in its best sections exemplified. Putting the matter differently, sociology does indeed study race relations and yields us much knowledge about the subject; *but* that decision not only *was* made fundamentally on the nonsociological grounds of legal precedent and ethical consideration, but could scarcely have been improved had all the resources of an *exact science* of race relations been available.

Does this mean, then, that *no* relation exists between sociological knowledge and social planning? Of course not. It means only that we have no more right to expect sociology to be the immediate platform of social policy or social action than we have to expect physiology to be a sole and immediate platform for measures in public health. But I would be unhappy under any public health officer who had never studied physiology.

There is, finally, the relation between application and contingency. Science, as the incomparable Aristotle tells us, is concerned with the recurrent, the regular, with what is summarizable in law or principle. Policy-making is, alas, confronted by the nonregular, the nonrecurrent, by the contingent. And the contingent forms a vast area in human affairs. Barbara Tuchman has recently reminded us of a wise saying of Trotsky: Causality in history is refracted through a natural selection of accidents. Every word of that definition is vital. Miss Tuchman goes on to recall something that will

[199]

never leave the memories of those who came of age in the 1930s: the Spanish Civil War. Nothing, she says, and I can echo this in vivid memory, was more certain that that if the Loyalists were defeated by Franco and his Nazi and Fascist allies, Spain would become a base for these allies in the foreshadowed European war, Gibraltar would go, and Britain and her allies would be cut off from everything east of Gibraltar and, particularly, Suez. Well, as we know, Franco did win (a victory made possible by Hitler and Mussolini), the European war did follow, but Spain remained neutral, Gibraltar did not fall, and the Allied powers had their Mediterranean.

We said then that in addition to the moral reasons for opposing Franco there were irrefutable strategic (policy) reasons. But, as events showed, these were only the moral reasons—and they are as good and right today as they were then.

Who are the sociologists whom you are either influenced by or most respect? Further, are they the same scholars now as in your formative years?

The first scholar to influence me—and he still does—was the late Frederick J. Teggart of Berkeley. He was a great and in many ways original mind; which meant that he could be monumentally one-sided, and also driven by a sense of personal mission. Under Teggart I studied essentially—Teggart! In the process, however, I read a vast amount of the classics in just about all fields *but* sociology. At no time, as undergraduate or graduate student, did I know what it was to read a book in or take a course in any of the staple fields of sociology—rural-urban, community, race relations, etc. (Nor do I today miss them.) I never once heard him refer to Durkheim, Simmel, Weber, Tönnies, Cooley, Thomas, Mead, Tocqueville (Comte, Marx, Spencer, yes, but inevitably critically), or any of the other titans of the sociological tradition.

The consequences could have been predicted by any run-of-the-mill Freudian. I revolted, and in the process (this was after I got my degree under Teggart) fell upon Tocqueville, Durkheim, Weber, and the others as though no one before me had ever known or understood these figures—a common failing of late conversions. I acquired for them a lasting obligation that was not discharged until I wrote my *The Sociological Tradition,* discharged, that is, to the limit of personal ability. They influence me today as they did when I began the slow process of reading them. I'm sure they always will. Of them all Tocqueville is foremost in my mind. Nothing like his combination of intuitive prescience and clarity of observation exists anywhere in the nineteenth and twentieth centuries. Now, I am in a manner rediscovering Teggart, and my *Social Change and History* is, at bottom, tribute to the vital things I learned from him but put aside for twenty-five years.

There are of course living sociologists who have influenced me, and continue to, but they happen to be personal friends, and friendship is too fragile a thing in this world to be saddled with publicly acknowledged obligations.

Which of your own writings do you like best, and why?

Until my next book is published, I choose my most recent one, *The Sociological Tradition.* I like it because I sweated over it for several years; because it is, as I noted above, a modest effort to repay a debt; and because it seems to me to say what *the mainstream of contemporary sociology is about and what its sources and essential contexts are.* As I said above, my dominant interest is ideas and idea systems. Where others may see laws, methods, hypotheses, conclusions, I see ideas and idea systems— such as community, authority, status, the sacred, alienation— underlying and giving shape and meaning to the laws, methods, etc. And in order to know *what* the major ideas and idea systems are, it is necessary to know precisely what events and *perceptions of events* formed the challenges to which the ideas themselves are responses.

The book has been honored in several reviews (once in decided-ly invidious fashion) by comparison with Talcott Parsons' *The Structure of Social Action.* But in fact there is no basis whatever for the comparison. Both books, it is true, deal with, *inter alia,* Durkheim and Weber. But the rest is not comparable. Professor Parsons' objective was to take a carefully selected group of figures and, through meticulous analysis, work toward a line of highly specific analytical theory. (No one has ever misunderstood Parsons' objective more than some of his first reviewers, notably Louis Wirth!) His success in this enterprise can be measured by the immense impact the book has had in shaping books, articles, and courses in sociological theory in the thirty-one years since its publication. My objective was a very different one, one that in no sense falls in the realm of social theory, but instead in the realm of the sociological understanding of the dominant themes of sociol-ogy, considered as a major idea system in our contemporary culture. What the success of my book will be is hardly deter-minable at this early date.

The most frequent criticism of the book is the abundance of quotations from the titans. Well, having no flair for perfection, it was a choice between under- and overquoting. I chose the latter. And as the single most negative review of the book has empha-sized, the thesis of the book *is* novel. What else then but to use the *ipsissima verba* to support a novel thesis, and most especially in those sections of the book where the thesis might ordinarily seem least applicable—as with Simmel. Hence also my insistence upon using *only* those passages in the titans that had been rendered into English by other, fully acknowledged translators. *Anyone* can prove a thesis by clever paraphrase or his own translation of the original!

What impact would you say your sociological efforts have had on reshaping the field?

None. I feel no immodesty, however, in saying that some of the things I have been writing about since 1939 have arrested attention here and there, and have contributed to a perhaps more accurate understanding of what sociology *is,* considered as a historically developed system of ideas.

Thirty years ago I "discovered" the European Conservatives and, with them, the two revolutions (democratic and industrial) that they rather pathetically sought to stop through their philippics and jeremiads. Prophets of the past they were, and history is not ordinarily kind to such. In terms of what they said, irrespective of anything else, they and their feudal dreams might best be forgotten. But they did two things: in their hatred of modernism they identified it; and in their rather absurd love of traditionalism they identified it, too.

This was their bequest to posterity. In a series of articles and books, beginning in 1941, I have spent the last quarter of a century tracking down some of the influences left by this curious group—very direct and acknowledged influences—upon many, such as Comte, Tocqueville, and Proudhon, who were not in any way sympathetic to the objectives of the Conservatives. And, as I think I have amply documented, a good deal of the *thematic* character of sociology derives from currents of thought in Western Europe engendered by the reaction of the Conservatives to the two revolutions and to the Enlightenment that preceded them. It's not the whole story, of course, but it's a good part of it. And judging from a number of more recent works also interested in the genesis of idea systems in the nineteenth century, I take some satisfaction in the fact that my first explorations along this line thirty years ago have borne fruit other than my own.

These same explorations in idea systems led to *Community and Power,* which I wrote in the late 1940s. That book has been called (by the distinguished editor of this book, among others) "nostalgic." I don't think there is a nostalgic page in it, but debate would be gratuitous. Suffice it to say that what I *think* it to be is: (1) an account of the nostalgia for lost community that is so manifest in

[203]

the thought of this century; (2) a treatment of the historical rise of the idea system of political power, absolute power, in the West; (3) the threat posed by widespread craving for community in the contexts of the kind of power represented by the modern state; and (4) an unabashed plea for *division of power, decentralization, social pluralism,* and *multiplication* of more or less *autonomous groups and associations* in the social order.

That book was written twenty years ago, and it pleases me that its essential argument has far more intellectual company today than it did then. Even among liberals—not just anarchists and conservatives—the magic of the unitary state has disappeared!

13

EGO, ENERGY AND
THE EDUCATION OF
A SOCIOLOGIST

RAYMOND W. MACK

I AM A TEACHER. This probably does more to explain my style of work, research priorities, and range of interests than anything else.

Once I had abandoned the notion of spending my life as a professional musician (the earliest evidence available that I am capable of assessing data and of being objective in reaching decisions having enormous policy implications), I knew that the thing I wanted to do was to teach. Even the faculty and curriculum of the Education Department at Baldwin-Wallace College did not dissuade me. I have taught at the University of Mississippi before the 1954 Supreme Court decision and at General Electric management seminars since; I have taught general social science courses for freshmen, personnel management for business school seniors, and field research methods for doctoral candidates. My wife claims that I even try to teach sociology to my in-laws. I enjoy it. I'm hooked.

I like to teach. I consider teaching a noble calling and have no empathy for and little patience with those sociologists who treat teaching as something that interferes with their more important work.

On several occasions I have been complimented by students (bright, sensitive students, of course) on the organization of my lectures; they say that I talk extemporaneously as if the material were written. One should not argue with compliments, but they have it backwards. I don't talk from what I have written; I write from what I have said. For me teaching is a dress rehearsal for writing. I outline an idea, present it to a class, talk it over with students who find holes in it or add dimensions to it. The next time I bring it to a different class the idea may be more elaborate, or more polished, or less certain, but it gets a different feedback in its new form. I try it on my friends and my colleagues (not mutually exclusive categories). I try to phrase it for public lectures to nonsociologists. When I have been over something enough times I find writing it relatively easy. This may be why as a writer I am a spurt-worker. I wrote the first draft of *Transforming America* in less than six weeks, but in another sense it took me five years. I had been shaping and rearranging the materials in lectures for several years before I even tried to put it into manuscript form. Troy S. Duster and I worked directly from his class notes on the lectures in my "Social Inequality" course and from my syllabus to write *Patterns of Minority Relations,* and I worked from the same set of materials to select and organize the readings in *Race, Class, and Power.*

The relationship between teaching and writing is for me a total one. I cannot make good sense of viewing teaching and writing as separate activities. Sociology constitutes a way of looking at the world which provides us with new perspectives and insights. All our writing is an attempt to bring this perspective to bear on social data in such a way as to teach either others or ourselves. In the kind of writing we do in textbooks, in the *Saturday Review,* in the *New York Times Magazine,* or in *Trans-action,* we are trying to teach "laymen," be they college freshmen, corporation executives, or governmental policy-makers. We are trying to give them a look at some relevant portion of the social world through a sociologist's eyeglasses. In the kinds of writing we do in the professional journals, such as the *American Sociological Review,* we are trying to teach each other. We are writing for people who have already been fit with the sociologist's eyeglasses and are trying to improve the quality of the lens or the scope of the vision.

With increasing specialization, there is an increasing need for sociologists in one topical area to teach sociologists in another area—almost as if they were laymen. A demographer who has devoted almost twenty years to the study of fertility may be a layman in his knowledge of contemporary research in sociology of education. The need for us to teach one another also arises from the kind of research which focuses on social problems rather than being constricted by disciplinary boundaries. Such research often means that the sociologist, economist, anthropologist, and political scientist studying economic development in Latin America are familiar with each other's work, but unaware of the research of sociologists, economists, anthropologists, and political scientists on the economic development of Harlem.

Then . . .

The importance of the role of teacher was reinforced for me in graduate school by three different—very different—professors. The attribute they shared was an extremely high set of expectations. During my first year as a graduate student, E. William Noland urged me to submit for publication a paper, "The Need for Replication Research in Sociology," which I had prepared for a seminar in industrial sociology. As a result of his encouragement, my first paper was published in *The American Sociological Review* before I had earned my master's degree. Nicholas Demerath on two occasions gave me more responsibilities than I was ready for on research projects, and then encouraged me to deliver on the commitment. The first of these projects became my master's thesis and was published in *Social Forces* as "Housing as an Index of Social Class." (For those who think the discipline has not advanced much in the past twenty years, it may be worth noting that the idea of an appraisal index of housing as a stratification indicator was a brand new idea.) Professor Demerath also chaired the committee for my dissertation, which was published in *The American Sociological Review* as "The Prestige System of an Air Base." I still favor the approach to sociological research which I learned on this assignment. We got acquainted with the social system by several periods of participant observation and interviewing on several air bases, living in enlisted men's quarters on one base and officers' quarters on another and spending a good deal of the time simply

[207]

hanging around where the work was done and talking with men after hours in the barracks, the enlisted men's club, and the officers' club. We then constructed a questionnaire for quantitative analysis on the basis of what we had learned through field research. Given some of the dumb mistakes my fellow graduate students and I avoided by preceding our quantitative work with field research (not to mention the gaffes we committed anyhow), I have an abiding suspicion of the results obtained from questionnaires administered to a sample of a universe which the questionnaire designer has not observed.

Perhaps the professor who influenced me most was Rupert B. Vance, who served on both my M.A. and Ph.D. committees, and with whom I studied in seminars in social structure and in human ecology. "Ecological Patterns in an Industrial Shop," which was published in *Social Forces,* was originally a research paper for a seminar with Professor Vance. All I brought to the seminar was a set of field data gathered by participant observation in a railroad repair shop. What Professor Vance showed me was the value of theory as the explanation of data.

The social scientists whose writing influenced me most in graduate school were Weber on bureaucracy, and on class, status, and party; Simmel on conflict; and George Homans on *The Human Group.* Vance also introduced me to C. Wright Mill's work; I still find *White Collar* his most seminal contribution.

Then, too, there was a set of people whom I now count good friends, but who were distant prophets when I was a graduate student. Given the quality of such works as "Propositions on Intergroup Hostility and Conflict," "Jealousy as Sexual Property," "Some Principles of Stratification," and *Industrial Relations and the Social Order,* I assumed that Robin Williams, Kingsley Davis, and Wilbert Moore were aging giants in the field, but I learned subsequently that they were scholars who were writing good sociology in their thirties, which I was reading and learning from in my twenties. (The fashion today of lumping into a social category all those "people over thirty" lends an imprecise aura of youthfulness to those of us who are actually not only guilty of being over thirty, but even over forty.)

As an undergraduate history major, I was first turned on to behavioral science by reading Ralph Linton's *Study of Man.* Imagine my excitement, then, when I reported for my first teaching position, a second-semester appointment at the University of Mississippi, to learn that my office was next to that of the distinguished visiting professor, Ralph Linton. I cannot imagine a formal postdoctoral relationship which would have been better for me. Linton had a limitless fund of research experiences to relate, theoretical ideas to argue, and professional gossip to impart. We taught in the morning, wrote in the afternoon, and talked into the night. Linton recommended me to his erstwhile colleague from the University of Wisconsin, Kimball Young, who was chairman at Northwestern University and who became my departmental chairman, friend, coauthor, and second important postdoctoral teacher.

Linton and Young remain for me marvelous examples of what happens with the interaction of ego and energy. Given a certain intellect, productivity is a function of ego plus energy (I am speaking of ego not as boastfulness, but as internalized commitment and self-confidence). We should all want to have a well-developed enough ego to be modest; an uncertain and insecure man cannot afford to invest his limited personality capital in modesty—people might believe him when he says that he is unimportant.

. . . And Now

Since the completion of my formal education, I have had the good fortune to have Robert F. Winch as a colleague ever since I was a beginning assistant professor, and have profited greatly from his tough-minded intellectual companionship. During the eight years I was Chairman of Northwestern's Sociology Department, I tried always to hire people who were better sociologists than I, and

I feel that I was quite successful. Howard S. Becker, Scott Greer, Richard Schwartz, Arnold Feldman, John Kitsuse, Rémi Clignet, Charles Moskos, Bernard Beck, and John Walton are a stimulating set of sociologists; one would have to be seriously deficient as a scholar not to learn from such colleagues. Too, I have learned through teaching joint seminars with social scientists from other fields—men of the quality of Paul J. Bohannan, Donald T. Campbell, Richard C. Snyder, and George I. Blanksten.

More recently I have been influenced by the work of Robert Rosenthal and Amitai Etzioni. I have enormous respect for the kind of work exemplified in Ryder and Westoff's research on fertility, and in Blau and Duncan's *American Occupational Structure,* but it is not the kind of sociology I find exciting to do. At the other pole, I think Lipset's *The First New Nation,* Bendix's *Work and Authority in Industry,* and Erikson's *Wayward Puritans* splendid contributions. But for me the greatest pleasure comes in field research, in looking at human groups to ascertain what they are doing, what they believe they are doing, and what are the intended and unintended consequences of their beliefs and behaviors. Probably this is why I find the stylized rituals of racial discrimination so fascinating, based as they are on social definitions of race with all their informally learned and unspoken assumptions. (The practice of foremen wearing felt hats while laborers wear billed caps has always been a more intriguing kind of discovery to me than the data on an organizational chart.)

Assumptions

Next to saying that I consider myself a teacher, I suppose that the most revealing thing I can say about the nature of my work is that I think sociology is fun. This is one reason that I am so offended by bad writing and by dull teaching. We are so fortunate to have as our subject the inherently exciting topic of man's social life. It is terrible to corrupt into tedious discussions of methodological detail and abstract theory what is really an exciting analysis of fascinating data. I cannot share the tragic view of human society which seems fashionable among many social scientists, who see man as a subject over which the waves of history wash. According to this view, whether he floats or sinks depends on the currents and the tides, not on any decision or action of his; the social structure itself is the source of man's social behavior. Sammy runs because of the social environment in which he was reared and runs the way he does because of the social context into which his past has propelled him. In this conception of *socius,* man is controlled by social, economic, and political conditions; when he faces what he regards as a choice, his response is actually not only conditioned but also determined by what has gone before.

I find more congenial the social scientist's view of man not as tempest tossed, but as capable of swimming against the current, or at least of mounting a log swept along by the stream of history, partly controlling his destination, depending on his own determination and skill. It is an image of man as a human being being able to rearrange the parts of the universe into a new pattern, a person capable of seizing the initiative and embarking on a new course.

My basic substantive interest in sociology is in the process of stratification and the resulting rank structure. As long as I can remember having a scholarly interest in human society, my curiosity has been focused on the fair shake. What do people consider to be an equitable distribution of rewards? How are decisions reached about the allocation of resources? Who gets a fair shake and who does not? How do people arrive at their conclusions about what constitutes a fair shake, and how do their assumptions ever get changed?

I was and am interested in political and economic proposals to solve the problem of social order, from fascism to communism. I was and am interested in religious and philosophical explanations of what human society is and could be. Long before I knew of the existence of sociology, I was writing junior high school history and civics term papers focused on what I would now describe as the fair shake—or, in more scholarly language, an equitable social

[211]

order. Somewhere between junior high school and college graduation, I closed in on the idea that social science is more likely to
bring it about than any other form of "do-gooderism."

My ideal for social science approximates the research and policy
feedback of an excellent medical school: basic research findings are
applied in clinical practice, and the feedback from clinical practice
informs theory-building and research design. For this reason I am
particularly interested in deviant case analysis arising from the
exceptions to our generalizations. Most wealthy Americans vote
Republican; how, then, account for wealthy Democrats? Many
narcotics addicts are products of slum environments, discrimination, deprivation, and broken homes; what explains people from
the same environment who do not choose narcotics as a way of
life? And who are the prosperous, middle-class people who do?

One explanation lies in the existence, even within the limits of
class and cultural environments, of alternative norms of behavior.
Freedom is a product of awareness: awareness of choice, of the
possibilities, of alternatives.

This concept of human society is reflected in the titles of what
I think are the better books I have written: *Race, Class, and Power*
and *Transforming America.* I cannot conceive of my writing a
book entitled *Abandoning America,* or *Despairing of America,* or
even *Bitching About America.* I believe, as a social scientist, in the
possibility of transforming America.

And Goals

The editor of this symposium has asked each contributor to
comment on the question: "What impact would you say your
sociological efforts have had on reshaping the field?" In my case, I
hope that it is too early to tell.

One of the efforts in which I take pride is one for which a
rational man does not expect much credit; I think that the Department of Sociology is a better department now than it was when I

accepted the appointment as chairman. But we are more likely to say that a man is too good a scholar to waste his time being chairman than that he is too good a chairman to waste his time doing research. The rewards in that role, therefore, depend heavily upon knowing what you want to achieve and weighing the results for yourself.

Since, as I have said, the role of teacher is a central one for me, I am inordinately proud of the students who have worked with me and who are now applying the skills of the professional sociologist in various ways: in the Office of Economic Opportunity; in the Research Department of the Urban League; leading the independence movement for Mozambique; working in the Peace Corps; and in scholarly research and writing. I, of course, derive special pleasure in hearing about those former students who are now recognized by their students as fine teachers in institutions from Hawaii to Santa Cruz, Berkeley, UCLA, Columbia, and Oberlin.

What our editor meant, I suspect, was for us to assess the impact of our research and writing. It is, of course, rewarding to know that my research, "Do we really believe in the Bill of Rights?," has been replicated by sociologists at more than twenty colleges and universities. It does a great deal for one's morale to meet a graduate student at a professional meeting who says that he first became interested in sociology through reading the introductory text by Young and Mack. It is fun to feel part of the cumulative nature of social science when I read Joseph Gusfield's work on organizational structure and occupational role and realize that he has broadened our understanding by putting to research use the theoretical notion I published as "Occupational Determinateness: A Problem in Hypotheses in Role Theory."

Still, for me, the greatest rewards derived from the immeasurable impact of teaching. We are living, I think, in an intellectual generation when sociologists are capable of exercising an unprecedented influence on policy. I do not think that there is any conflict between our trying to be objective in the gathering and analysis of data and our having firm convictions about the kind of

[213]

social order we see as desirable.

I hope, for example, that the research and theoretical analysis some of us have done while attempting to cast race relations in a stratification framework will help us to reduce the social injustices which have become institutionalized through our social definition of race.

Those of us committed to the social application of sociological research and theory have an obligation to human society to communicate effectively what we as social scientists know. As long as physicians and clergymen, lawyers and businessmen, laborers and farmers believe things we know to be false about human nature, birth control, race differences, or the relationship between democracy and capitalism, we have not done as well as we want to as teachers. When we see the wealth of detailed misinformation with which our freshmen arrive on campus each fall, we know that our work is cut out for us.

What I aspire to for us as social scientists is neatly stated by Robin Williams in his generous foreword to *Transforming America:* "The author has not tried to write a 'value-free' book—as if he does not care whether a particular social pattern or its opposite prevails. For example, it is clear that he respects individual uniqueness, rejects racial discrimination, and approves of personal freedom. One can agree or disagree, but there generally will be no difficulty in discovering where he stands. This is as it should be. His values do not get in the way of his objectivity or his critical regard for evidence, and, of course, that too is as it should be."

Exactly.

14

TEACHERS, STUDENTS, AND IDEAS
A Personal Account

WENDELL BELL

NEAR THE END OF 1968, James A. Mau and I submitted a book for publication tentatively entitled *The Study of the Future: Explorations in the Sociology of Knowledge.* It is an edited volume, but the selection of contributions and the contents of my own chapters reveal the philosophy of sociology at which I have arrived as well as several continuities with my past work. In this book, Mau and I formulate a theory of social change which emphasizes the concept of belief, value, images of the future, decision-making, and individual as well as collective action, as these impinge on, and alter, social structures. Society is not reified. Historical social structures are viewed as a set of conditions upon which the individual, acting separately or as a member of a group, can and does—by action or default—serve as a causal agent. We call the theory "a cybernetic-decisional model of social change" and we argue that sociologists themselves are among the agents of change. We state a series of directives which, if adopted in the theoretic orientations of research, would make sociologists more conscious of their own relevance for the emerging future, more responsible for the consequences of their work. This perspective runs against the grain of the ahistorical, rigidly structuralist, and abstract

AUTHOR'S NOTE: *I wish to thank Burton R. Clark, Scott Greer, James A. Mau, Jerome K. Myers, and especially Earl Lyon and Ivar Oxaal for their comments on an earlier version of this paper.*

theories which have been taught in the United States during the last four decades or so. Moreover, the evolution of my thinking during the last few years, to the point reached in the volume in question, has been shared by my co-editor, a former student of mine. This fact illustrates another aspect of the sociological style I have endeavored to maintain: the close association in all my past work between research and graduate education. A developing philosophy of sociology, then, and an innovation in the instruction of graduate students are the two themes that inform this paper.

Now I can't help smiling at the seeming pretentiousness of such phrases as "philosophy of sociology" and "all my past work." Perhaps the skeptical outlook of the sociologist makes us wary and mistrustful of even our own deepest convictions. But the enterprise our editor has led us into, the discussion of professional self-images, can hardly be done at all without some suspension of laughter and the nagging self-doubt which tends to discharge itself in the spirit of satire. Some balance between seriousness of purpose and an amused detachment is called for, avoiding self-deprecation, however entertaining to the readers, and complacency, however gratifying to the writer. Let us agree at the outset that most of us, including this writer, when viewed through the lens of history, are at best small winners; that, however we try, we are imperfectly objective in viewing ourselves.

In the pages that follow I've tried to answer the questions that Irving Louis Horowitz suggested to the potential contributors when he was planning this special volume. He asked about the most distinctive characteristics of our way of doing sociology. My answer is divided into two parts. The first deals with some of the concepts and subjects in urban sociology and the sociology of nationalism on which my research has focused: social choice, social trends and change, anomia and social participation, urban differentiation, leadership, and the idea of social scale that, recently, has included attitudes toward equality, democracy, and nationhood. The second deals with methodological style, including comparative and cumulative studies carried out in conjunction with graduate student education.

Horowitz asked specifically about our views on the interrelationship of theory and application. My answer is that sociological theory *is* application in the degree to which it contains assumptions about the nature of social reality and the relative importance of its aspects. These nearly always have some implication for social action or, especially where the assumptions are deterministic, inaction. If this is true, then sociology is not ethically neutral and the widely held "value-free" stance can be justified only as a strategy, useful, first, to the continued conduct of research under conditions where it might be suppressed if its relevance to the conflicts of the day were understood; and second, to the enhancement of credibility among naive sources of support. Accepted as an ideology, as it has been in American sociology, the value-free stance has led to the gratuitous trivialization of much sociological work.

Horowitz asked what impact, in our opinions, our sociological efforts may have had on reshaping the field. I would have to answer "probably very little." At the age of forty-three I think of myself among the hardworking professionals who go about generating new data in a changing theoretical framework, who together make sociology as developed and sound as it is. Given our need for systematic theory of great scope, addressed to problems of moment and rendered reliable by an increasingly sophisticated methodology, I would be most happy to be one of the architects of sociology. I shall be happy if, as one of the workers, I can be moderately proud of my part of the work.

In a field, moreover, where architects are rare, imperfect, and heavily in debt to their fellows, one may hope for more. An ingeniously designed empirical study, a reformulation of theory, a methodological breakthrough, a gifted student who goes beyond one's work, each may bring the recognition that most of us value and that time may yet validate. So one may hope. In the interim, I tell myself that a certain stubborness to proceed according to my own lights should be combined with some regard for the lesser

[217]

rewards of professional and university service, the satisfactions of competence, industry, and commitment to the collective enterprise.

Finally, we have been asked which sociologists influenced us most and which of our own writings we liked best. These questions, I think, are best answered in the body of the paper, along with elaborations of the summary answers just given to the other questions. The fact that the names of many people will appear illustrates my conception of sociology as a set of complicated networks of human associations, exchange, and communication that are in motion over time and space. Sociologists become involved in each others' careers and lives in intricate ways, so that chains of relationships are established through which subtle and often unnoticed influences flow. Furthermore, brief intellectual encounters sometimes can be as important as enduring relationships or as those that are consciously recognized as significant.

Social Area Analysis

UCLA in 1949 and the early fifties was a good place to be an embryonic sociologist. In the sociology wing of the combined Department of Anthropology and Sociology, Leonard Broom had brought together a talented group of young sociologists that included Donald R. Cressey, Ralph H. Turner, William S. Robinson, Edwin M. Lemert, Philip Selznick, and John James, each of whom was to leave his mark in the years to come. The anthropologists were generally more mature and established scientists than the sociologists were at the time, and had more than the usual influence on graduate students in sociology. Especially influential were Ralph L. Beals, Walter Goldschmidt, and Joseph Birdsell. Eshref Shevky, an older man and a sociologist by adoption and recent work rather than by early training, was brought into the department on a full-time teaching basis during this time.

UCLA offered a sound and comprehensive sociological education, exciting intellectual exchange, and aspiration to be at the top of the profession. This last, I think, was due partly to the newness of the graduate program in sociology. No one had yet received a Ph.D.; Scott Greer and I were to be the first in August of 1952. Some members of the faculty may have been overly concerned about the quality of their first products. The consequences were both beneficial and deleterious. Anxiety among the graduate students, which can run high in any graduate school, was so rampant here that some graduate student performances were start-lingly impaired. Some promising students dropped out. I was moved to increase my efforts, though often joylessly, and to internalize an ideal of achievement that has been both a drive to do better work and a source of restlessness and questioning about just what really good work is.

Whatever the anxieties that stemmed from the new Ph.D. pro-gram, there were many close, personal relationships between faculty and graduate students in the department. We were fre-quently in the homes of faculty members, some of them—for example, Cressey and Turner—were almost of the same age as ourselves and some had shared our experiences of military service in World War II. I did not particularly appreciate this fact at the time, although I now know from knowledge of other universities that the degree of personal care that I received at UCLA is seldom achieved in graduate schools. Of course, my recollections of intimacy between faculty and graduate students during those early days at UCLA may be exaggerated and they may not apply to everyone who was there, but there is no doubt that the spirit behind my own efforts in this direction came from the dedication of my teachers.

Of course, the graduate students were also learning from each other, and we were fortunate in having a talented and energetic group. Graduate school was not complete without the endless sharing of interpretations about what it all meant. Scott Greer, John Kitsuse, Irving Bobb, and Burton R. Clark were among my best friends. Santo F. Camilleri and Bernard J. Fleischman, and, later, Pauline Bart, Dennis McElrath, Helen Beem (Gouldner), and

Sheldon Messinger, among others, helped set the tone and the direction of some of my future concerns through intellectual discussion and often heated controversy. Scott Greer was most influential on me at the time, and our lives and our work have intermingled throughout our careers.

Although I learned my sociology at UCLA, I had been greatly influenced by a Professor of English at Fresno State College, Earl Lyon. When I first encountered him, I intended to go to law school after graduating from college. Although I didn't change my major, which was Social Science with an English-Speech minor, I did shift my aspirations toward graduate school, first to English and then, on Lyon's advice, to sociology. Lyon was, and is, a great teacher who has affected the lives of many of his students. For myself, he remains a friend and advisor after more than twenty years. There was much that was sociological in his style, whether he was teaching courses in freshman English or advanced courses in semantics, or the Bible as literature. He was shocking. Jesus to him was a tough, witty revolutionary—an incredible heresy to our provincial ears. He needled the establishment. He tore at our most cherished and parochial conceptions, and was, of course, often misunderstood. Although he was sometimes under attack from parents for what appeared to them as vulgarity, political radicalism, or blasphemy, he was a thoroughly responsible man.

Looking back, I realize that today much of the same goes on in an introductory sociology classroom, although at the time and in that rather conservative agricultural community of Fresno, California, his message was electrifying. Also, by the highest standards of his own discipline he demanded evidence and proof for interpretations, as a sociologist would by a somewhat different set of standards. Yet, because of the particular platform from which he spoke—a classroom in English—and his particular loves—he was a Chaucerian scholar—Lyon's students received more than an appreciation of some of the perspectives of sociology or anthropology. He had a passion that we sociologists have often had cut from us during graduate school and he had an erudition and love of scholarship which provided me with an enduring critical standard in the face of the computer-blinded and intellectual tinker-toy training some sociologists receive.

When, finally, I went to him with my plan to follow in his footsteps and go to graduate school as an English major, my highest ambition being to return to Fresno State College as a faculty member, he said that his field was bankrupt and that I should instead go into sociology. Perhaps it was a polite way of telling me that I had no talent for Chaucer. In any event, he sent me to his former college roommate, Walter Goldschmidt, whom he much admired, and I was on my way to UCLA.

I'm not sure why I ended up in sociology rather than anthropology. Lyon had suggested it. He may have had a notion that anthropology had peaked by 1948 while sociology was just entering a period of rapid growth and development. Perhaps I had a nose for the modern and contemporary, and I may have thought that sociology offered a more congenial outlet than anthropology for my tendencies toward social reform. Be that as it may, after seeking the advice of Goldschmidt, I arrived, several months later, in Leonard Broom's office ready to begin graduate work in sociology.

William S. Robinson had a great impact on graduate students at UCLA. He dominated the teaching of statistics, methodology, and the logic of social inquiry there for about fifteen years. A Ph.D. from Columbia University, researcher at the Bureau of Applied Social Research, and student of Paul F. Lazarsfeld, Robinson once described himself as a Cadillac on a desert—high powered but nowhere to go. Here was one of the best-equipped methodological minds in sociology, whose infrequent articles—such as his brief paper on ecological correlations—were gems of perfection, relevance to the profession, and influence, who told his students that at the present stage of development in sociology it was of more help to the science for them to roll up their sleeves and build roads with their hands than to invest in a set of fancy wheels and high-powered engines. He taught us to suspect the statistical or methodological virtuoso as having possibly more dazzle than substance, being better for self-delusion or career advancement than for contributing to science. I'm convinced he knew what it really was to be a social scientist. He warned against the constrictions of narrow little models, the limitations of mathematical assumptions, the mental straitjackets of conventional social science methodology, the evils of mere empiricism, the faults of nominalism, the aridity of what passed as pure theory, and the inappropriate application of sociology to much of the standard philosophy of science. He inspired us to *divergent thinking* within the context of the use of formal simplicity, the hypothetico-deductive method, the critical specification of relevant data, and ingenuity. He gave us a sense of perfection toward which we should strive as sociologists—as *scientists* of society, although it was understood that few, if any, of us would ever achieve it. With such standards in mind, he taught us statistics and methodology, and could work up a towering rage at our obtuseness. I am sure that some students would have preferred less than he gave, especially by way of his ambivalence and uncertainty concerning the worth of his own skills. But most of us left UCLA with a sizable kit of tools, as Don Cressey used to say, and with the commitment to use them flexibly and innovatively. Thanks to Robinson's unusual combination of insights, a few of us left with considerably more.

At Broom's suggestion, I did *A Comparative Study in the Methodology of Urban Analysis* (1952) for my dissertation and came in close working relationship with Eshref Shevky and his social area analysis. Shevky had published *The Social Areas of Los Angeles* (Shevky and Williams, 1949), and Broom, who was impressed by it, was doing some additional work with Shevky using the method. Social area analysis is basically a framework for the analysis of urban neighborhoods. It is linked both to a theory of social change and a description of long-term social trends as broad contexts within which basic variables for the construction of a typology of modern urban neighborhoods are developed. Also, it

[222]

contains a theory of differential socialization, expectation, and opportunity as an explanation of the individual and collective attitudinal and behavioral consequences of the social areas themselves. Although to some extent emerging out of the earlier studies of the Chicago school of human ecology, social area analysis contained certain theoretically distinctive features that set off a controversy between us emerging social area analysts and sociologists associated with the Chicago tradition.[1] Various lines of research using social area analysis sprang from Shevky's original work, but they were not drawn together until 1968 when Scott Greer and others published, in a volume dedicated to Eshref Shevky, *The New Urbanization.*

The basic purpose of my dissertation was to compare the Shevky typology with the Tryon method of urban analysis. This led me to work during one summer with Robert C. Tryon, Professor of Psychology at the University of California, Berkeley, who with his students had been doing a series of studies (Tryon, 1955) of "psychosocial areas" in the San Francisco Bay region using, among other methods and data, his cluster analysis applied to census tract statistics. My dissertation included a description of the Shevky procedures to the census tract data for the San Francisco Bay region (Bell, 1953) to serve as a basis for comparing the empirical results of the Tryon and Shevky methods; factor analyses of the Shevky variables for both San Francisco and Los Angeles (Bell, 1955b); and detailed methodological, empirical, and theoretical comparisons of the Shevky and Tryon approaches. My dissertation did not deal with some of the broad issues of theory that were at the foundation of the Shevky scheme, but I could not avoid being affected by them. My concern with the idea of social scale and a theory of social choice—or as we have now called it, "a cybernetic-decisional model of social change," as well as my appreciation of cumulative and comparative studies, were to grow out of this early work.

[223]

Urban Neighborhoods and Individual Behavior

I left UCLA in August of 1952 for my new job as Assistant Professor of Sociology at Stanford University. Although I was to teach part time in the department, my chief obligation was to direct a new Survey Research Facility. Two things may be of special note during the two eventful years that I spent at Stanford. First, I became a teacher of graduate students on a rather large scale. My experience probably was atypical for a new Ph.D., but I had contact immediately with most of the sociology graduate students at Stanford, supervising a few Ph.D. dissertations and providing the required research experience for nearly all of the M.A. candidates.

Second, I was able to continue the work that I had begun on social area analysis and to extend it by the use of sample surveys. The work to date had shown that the variance between urban neighborhoods as described by census variables could be adequately summarized by three major dimensions: socioeconomic status, familism, and ethnicity. Tryon (1955) and his associates, as well as Broom and Shevky (1949), among others (i.e., Broom et al., 1955), were beginning to demonstrate the utility of the social area typology by relating a variety of other variables to it. What was needed, I thought, was a large-scale sample survey, within the social areas of San Francisco, designed to test their relationship to theoretically relevant measures of individual attitudes and behaviors. Furthermore, theoretical relevance, according to my view at the time, should be determined both by recourse to the emergent theory of social area analysis and the widely accepted theories of the Chicago school of urban sociology. This was to be my primary research preoccupation—a preoccupation that left room for little else—while at Stanford and for a few more years, as it was to be Scott Greer's major acitivity in the Laboratory in Urban Culture which he founded and directed at about the same time at Occidental College in Los Angeles.

When I arrived at Stanford, the Survey Research Facility had no name, no office, no clients, no Director (I was *Acting* Director since the Committee for Research in the Social Sciences had higher aspirations for a Director than they found in my person), and a few Ford Foundation dollars. What it didn't know it had at the time was a band of hardworking, idealistic, dedicated graduate students who were to play a major role in its activities. It is clear to me now that without them the success that we did achieve with the several surveys we conducted under contract during those two years and with the San Francisco survey of urban neighborhoods and individual behavior, which flowed from my own research interests, would never have been possible. Some of the students involved were Fred Chino, the late Harold Hoebel, Jan Howard, and Harry Kincaid—who shared the tribulations of administrative headaches; Clayton Lane, Donald L. Mills, Glenn Walker, Pierre van den Berghe, Henry Zentner—who became confidant and friend; and especially Marion D. Boat and Maryanne T. Force—who both continued working with me into the writing of the final reports.

In his famous article, "Urbanism as a Way of Life," Louis Wirth said, "Distinctive features of the urban mode of life have often been described sociologically as consisting of the substitution of secondary for primary contacts, the weakening of bonds of kinship, and the declining social significance of the family, the disappearance of the neighborhood, and the undermining of the traditional basis of social solidarity." Using sample surveys, we went into four contrasting types of San Francisco neighborhoods in 1953 aiming to test these and other assertions about urban life. Our findings, since corroborated by others including Scott Greer, brought into question the picture of city life painted by the Chicago ecologists of the 1930s.[2] The urban mode of life may be characterized by secondary contacts, but such contacts were not so much substituted for as *added to* primary contacts. We found that some urbanites were isolated from informal relationships, but the vast majority were not. The bonds of kinship may have weakened with the rise of city life, but relatives, including those not living with one another, were found to represent a significant and important source of personal relations, support, and friendship. The social significance of the family may have changed, but our findings cast doubt on the conclusion that it had declined. The neighborhood certainly has not disappeared, although some of the socioeconomic and family characteristics of neighborhoods were shown to produce different patterns of social isolation and participation. The typical urban person was not found to be lost or anomic. Finally, we concluded that in a changing society the traditional basis of social solidarity may be constantly eroded, but this does not mean that there is no basis for social solidarity or that the present is lacking or inadequate when compared to the past. In fact, despite the obvious problems engendered by urban living— some still to be faced as we approach a future of massive conurbations—the modern city brought new opportunities for economic betterment and security and it meant freedom from "small-town narrowness, smugness, and the sealed morality whose real fruit was spiritual death" (Bell, 1968).

Although the neighborhood surveys took most of my time, I revised the Shevky typology with the help of some of the graduate students, and applied it to the 1950 census tract statistics for the San Francisco Bay region. On the basis of this work, Shevky and I (1955) prepared *Social Area Analysis* for publication and the initial sampling frame for the surveys was established. Most of the work at Stanford was exhausting. Punching calculators, striving for theoretical relevance and defining concepts, writing interview schedules, block listing, selecting and training interviewers, checking on the interviewers, coding, punching IBM cards, running marginals and cross-tabulations, making tables, and punching calculators again took most of our time. Then, too, we had moved into an old building, a former residence, altered and furnished it for our use, and established services for its operation and maintenance. Even such mundane things take time. But I had one bookish and somewhat more lonely intellectual activity during the time that was pure pleasure. I had gotten involved in trying to reconstruct the mathematical basis of the Shevky segregation indexes, and with assistance from Professor Herman Chernoff of the Department of Statistics, wrote a paper showing the derivation of the Shevky indexes and proposing a revision. Although it was never much used as a segregation index, "A Probability Model for the Measurement of Ecological Segregation" (1954)[3] had a certain elegance about it that I enjoyed. It may be most useful not as an index of residential segregation, but as a measure of probable interaction, which it constitutes before normalization. As such, it could be used as a model of the probable interaction between members of the same group, between members of one group and a different group, or between members of one group and the members of that group plus members of specified other groups, and the groups could be defined by any sociological variable such as sex, age, race, occupation, education, income, etc. But this is just a passing thought for a favorite child who turned out to be an orphan.

Familism and Suburbanization

Moving to Northwestern University in August of 1954, I continued to work on social area analysis and studies of urban social life. For the most part this meant continued analysis of data collected in San Francisco and writing, including eventually an attempt to synthesize the results of all of those researchers who had used the Shevky typology to date (Bell, 1959). One new elaboration of the Shevky theory caught my attention—its application to the suburban move, and, as we shall see, a largely unplanned subject of research entirely new to me was to intrude into my concentration upon a slice of urban sociology.

I conducted two small studies—nothing like the amount of data collection in San Francisco—one in the Chicago suburbs of Des Plaines and Park Ridge and another in two Chicago neighborhoods (Jackson Boulevard and the Near North Side) and in the suburbs of Bellwood and Kenilworth to test some specific hypotheses about the decisions that people made regarding the location of their residence, especially the preference that some persons were showing for suburbia. Also, these studies were done, it should be mentioned, in a context of the widespread opinion among intellectuals, including sociologists, that the nature of suburban life was abominable. David Riesman (1958), referring to the suburban sadness, confessed that he loved both the city and the country, but not the suburbs. Deviating from the usual complaint of conformity in the suburbs, Riesman identified an aimlessness and a "pervasive low-keyed unpleasure" that were related somehow to a tacit revolt against the industrial order. Sadness was to be found in the suburbs that could not be described in terms of traditional sorrows. Work had become affectless and no longer central, consumer skills had come to dominate, domesticity and peace had become important values, the variety of work provided by the central city had come to matter less, the elite had retreated from the great problems of the metropolis, leisure had become a burden, commuting by car was vacuous and solipsistic, the housewives were captives, and both suburban men and women were more tied to residence than city dwellers.

Undoubtedly, there was much truth in what Riesman said, but the tone and judgments in work such as his led to a vilification of the suburbs, such as "split-level headaches," "cracks in picture windows," and "the eclipse of community," which made one wonder why people kept flocking to them.

The results of our studies gave an answer. They supported the hypothesis that the suburbanites of the fifties were largely persons who had chosen familism as an important element in their life styles and who were seeking, in addition, a mode to express a consumership life style and community participation on a neighborhood basis. There was very little evidence from these two studies to support the negative evaluations of suburban life which were then so widespread. Further, there was little evidence that the suburban trend represented a revolt against most aspects of the industrial order or a "back-to-ruralism" movement. On the contrary, suburbanites wanted the conveniences of an advanced technological society and the advantages of economic development and modern urban culture. Traffic, defilement of air and land by industry and auto, apartment living, noise, crowding, and lack of neighborhood groups conducive to the safety and welfare of children from toddlers to teens without constant parental surveillance were among the things that "pushed" the movers out of the city. Not that the city constitutes all of these things uniformly either in fact or in the perceptions of the movers. But in the particular types of urban neighborhoods in which most of the suburban movers had lived these features were prominent. Suburban expansion made available new neighborhoods of a certain type and thus provided solutions to many of these and other problems, and the solutions were at least moderately successful at the time for the bulk of the people who moved. Thus, the findings of our two small surveys, although revealing some complaints about suburban life and perhaps only moderate happiness among suburban dwellers, showed that in the main and judged by their own goals and standards the suburbanites could not accurately be described as sad. By their own testimony, critically assessed, most of them were much less sad in the suburbs than they had been in the city (see Bell 1956, 1958, and 1968).

At Northwestern I continued not only my work on social areas and Shevky's notions of social choice, but also my involvement with graduate students. Dorothy L. Meier, Kenneth Polk, and Ernest M. Willis were to go to UCLA, the first two to continue graduate work toward their Ph.D. degrees and the third as a faculty member. All three had done their master's theses under my direction at Northwestern, Meier (1957) on the San Francisco data focusing on anomia, Polk (1957) on "The Social Areas of San Diego," and Willis (1956) on the segregation of Negroes in American cities. Walter C. Kaufman (1961) made some excellent suggestions for further revisions of the social area typology in his doctoral dissertation and went on to work with Scott Greer, who had moved from Occidental to the Metropolitan St. Louis Survey, where he too continued extending the Shevky theory, especially

[229]

into the area of political participation. Among the other graduate students with whom I had more than passing acquaintance were Edwin Flittie, Raymond J. Murphy, who also went to UCLA as a faculty member, and Eduardo Mondlane—the son of a tribal chief —who a few years later was to become the exiled head of the Mozambique Liberation Front.

Kimball Young, then nearing retirement, was a model of hard work and productivity; Robert F. Winch encouraged proof and hard logic; and William Byron, who, though he was in his sixties, could outwalk me along the shores of Lake Michigan in the middle of a blinding snowstorm, was a zestful and dedicated teacher. Each of them taught me how to live my life better as a sociologist. The historian Ray Allen Billington and his charming wife Mabel, who "sponsored" the Bells socially, were learned, sophisticated, and warm-hearted friends. Melville J. Herskovits, from whom my wife took a course on the Negro in the New World, was more of an influence on me than he knew. But perhaps none has had as much influence as Raymond W. Mack and the political scientist Richard C. Snyder, who at a later **time** were to become advisors to the West Indies Study Program and who continue to engage in joint ventures with me. Both men are distinguished by many things, but in Raymond Mack I've always most respected his tireless devotion to the teaching of sociology, not just in the classroom but everywhere it might do some good if its uses and relevance to social action were known, and in Dick Snyder his ability to break out of present disciplinary conventions and to think with originality about the future directions of social science.

Jamaican Leaders

Before I left Northwestern, three things happened that were to change the direction of my future work. (1) I overheard a conversation at an annual meeting of the American Sociological Society. Two people, who were unknown to me, were standing by the book exhibits discussing the program on which I had a paper listed. One said, "Who is this fellow Wendell Bell?" The other replied, "He's the social area man!" I didn't linger to hear more. Scott Greer and I had thrown ouselves into our work with all of our energy and with missionary zeal. Now, he and I, our students, and the original UCLA group had contributed the largest percentage of work using the social area typology. We had felt that Shevky had not received a fair hearing when his book on Los Angeles was first published, since the field was largely dominated by persons with the Chicago persuasion. We had thought that we could single-handedly redress the presumed grievance—and we almost had! But we were scientists, not cultists; in the last analysis the social area approach must rest on its own merits as established in the eyes of others. I resolved to turn my attention elsewhere, at least for a while, and see what would happen. (This was all true, but I must also admit to a bit of restlessness to boot.)

(2) The Carnegie Corporation of New York—which had helped finance my studies of urban neighborhoods in San Francisco and was to finance my upcoming studies of elites and nationalism in the West Indies—had given a grant to the Department of Political Science at Northwestern for a self-study directed at the "problems of study and teaching in political science with a view to revision of its own curriculum and study program" (Hyneman, 1959: vii-viii). The chairman of the department, Charles S. Hyneman, invited me, and other Northwestern sociologists, to attend a series of conferences that were held in connection with the self-study in which many of the top political scientists from all over the country participated. The major topic of discussion turned out to be nothing less than the status of political science in the United States. By listening to these exchanges of views, I learned of the "various challenges confronting political scientists and opportunities available to them." Such knowledge was soon to begin shaping my work.

Finally, (3) on a cold, winter night in Evanston, my wife and I decided that we must go somewhere to warm our bones. Belatedly,

[231]

that "somewhere" turned out to be Jamaica. Broom had held a Fulbright grant to Jamaica when I was at UCLA, and I had worked on some census data from the Caribbean in his seminar. A look at the data on the distribution of flush toilets showed that it was favorable for the health of our small children, and I knew something of the area at first hand since I had been to Cuba and had flown over the Bahamas and the Caribbean as a Navy pilot in World War II. Like most compulsive professionals who seldom take a proper vacation, I set about planning a summer research trip to Jamaica that would include a further study of the social choice theory and the life styles of career, familism, and consumership that I had used in the suburbanization studies. What I didn't know then was that when the Bell family arrived at Palisadoes airport at the beginning of summer in 1956 we would find Jamaica in the throes of transition to self-government and I would have both the challenge and the opportunity to shift the focus of my research from social area analysis to Jamaican leaders and the decisions of nationhood. Nor did I know then that I was signing on for a tour of twelve years of Caribbean research.

Before leaving for my first summer in Jamaica, I received word that the Social Science Research Council had granted me a three-year half-time Faculty Research Fellowship for my proposed research, as then planned. Thus, I went to Jamaica knowing that the summer would be largely a preparation for further research. By the time the summer was over, however, I was thoroughly dissatisfied with my original plans. Back at Northwestern, I switched my topic to a study of leadership and political change, got permission from the SSRC to do so, persuaded Emily R. Smith (1957), a Northwestern graduate student, to do some preliminary work on the subject as her master's thesis, and began planning to do a quite different study from that originally anticipated.

The planning had to be sandwiched between my prior obligations to bring into print my studies of social areas and the San Francisco neighborhoods. I found that I had a great deal to learn. The political science conferences had whetted my interest, but could not have given me the background that I needed to carry out a study in political sociology. Thus, there was a period of learning, both from reading and from conversations with my friends in political science both at Northwestern and UCLA (who now included, among others, David E. Apter, George I. Blanksten, James S. Coleman, Thomas P. Jenkin, Dwaine Marvick—whose wife Elizabeth, being the daughter of Louis Wirth, seemed to close one circle—and David A. Wilson). For a variety of reasons, including some that were personal, my wife and I decided to return to UCLA in the fall of 1957, and by the middle of the next spring, in 1958, I was on my way to Jamaica for the major data collection of the study with several large boxes of questionnaires for mailing to a sample of Jamaican leaders.

I could—and perhaps did—write a book about what went wrong with that mail questionnaire survey. The troubles began when the customs inspector classified the questionnaires as stationery and demanded a large duty. ("But they're not stationery!" "You write on them don't you?" "Yes." "You put them in envelopes, don't you?" "Yes." "You send them through the mails don't you?" "Yes." Gleefully, he pounced, "It's stationery!") After some delay (the dates on my covering letter and follow-up letters were getting older), I finally was able to speak with the Collector General and he decided that the questionnaires were not stationery.

By this time, however, I had shown copies of my questionnaires to the staff members at the Institute of Social and Economic Research at the University of the West Indies and some of them let out a mild roar. A summit meeting was called, at which I was an anxious outsider, to decide whether or not the Institute should dissociate itself from my study. The question was not scientific value, but political sensitivity. Would the Institute's sponsorship of a questionnaire which touches on controversial political issues to be mailed to Jamaican leaders compromise it and the University with the government or endanger the financial support it received? The issue was resolved in favor of my study with the understanding that I should make a minor change in one of the covering letters and receive some sort of approval from government.

With my anxiety still running high, I arranged to talk with Sir Kenneth Blackburne, who was to be the last British Governor of Jamaica, and the Jamaican political leader, Norman Washington Manley, then Chief Minister. In a situation that was much too complicated to explain here, Sir Kenneth told me that the days had passed when a British Governor could give me the approval that I sought, but that he would confer with the Chief Minister. A few days later, I received a note from Sir Kenneth to the effect that he and the Chief Minister had decided that Jamaica was a free country and that I could send my questionnaires to anyone I pleased. (I later wondered if they might have "decided" differently!)

So I mailed my questionnaires, but my headaches were just beginning. The response rate was too low. (None of the mail questionnaire surveys we had done at the Stanford Survey Research Facility had achieved less than a 76 percent response rate.) The questionnaire was too long and complicated. Too many persons were off the island at the time. The personal data section was so complete that some potential respondents feared that in such a small island society their identity would be known. Many of the civil servants thought it would be improper for them to answer. A local columnist wrote a parody of the questionnaire in the major daily paper. Finally, postal clerks went on strike twice at crucial periods during the follow-up mailings. I reluctantly had to accept a final response rate of 29.6 percent, but, considering the difficulties that I had, I felt fortunate to have even that.

I see that I have painted the picture grimmer than it actually was. On the other side of the coin, I was learning a lot about doing social research and about Jamaica—being involved in the issues that the mail questionnaires had raised, including more than I have mentioned here, I learned a great deal about Jamaican leaders, political change, and Jamaican society. Then, there was the bonus of an occasional fine dinner party where I suspect I was good-naturedly invited only because I was that "peculiar American chap who was sending 'round all those silly questionnaires, you know." And, most importantly, there was the warmth, friendship, moral support, and intellectual guidance of the Institute staff in the presence of H. D. Huggins, Lloyd Braithwaite, George E. Cumper, David T. Edwards—with whom I roomed for awhile, and M. G. Smith; of Teddy and Hyacinth Cummins, Hugh W. Springer, and Philip M. Sherlock; and of Lambros Comitas, who, like J. Mayone Stycos and his wife Mary two years earlier, was a fellow American on a research trip of his own.

The response rate was disheartening, but there was little else to do but make the best of it. I returned to UCLA, and with the help of my wife and UCLA graduate students James A. Mau, Charles C. Moskos, Jr., Andrew P. Philips, and Harry E. Ransford began the job of coding the data, punching them on IBM cards, running marginal frequencies and cross-tabulations, and preparing tables. The usual drill. Although I was able to pull out a few articles (Bell 1960a, 1960b; and Mau et al., 1961), I had no sense whatsoever of what the data, taken together, added up to by way of an integrated theme. These were trying days, and they were to continue until after another, longer field trip to Jamaica in 1961-62, during which time, and with the help of others, I found the story that could be teased from the data. It was only then that I could write *Jamaican Leaders* (1964).

The Democratic Revolution in the West Indies

From the fall of 1958 until the fall of 1961, I plugged away at the Jamaican data, while doing a number of other things as well. Naturally, I continued my interest in my past work in urban sociology and in working with graduate students. Nason E. Hall (1962) and Dorothy L. Meier (1962)—who collected her data as part of the Metropolitan Dayton Survey with Walter C. Kaufman—both worked on dissertations under my direction. Jim Mau and Charlie Moskos, among others, completed their master's theses. I was teaching political sociology and a seminar in leadership and social structure, gradually building up my background in these areas, and with Richard J. Hill and Charles R. Wright, two dedicated professionals who were colleagues at UCLA, I did a review of the literature on *Public Leadership* (1961).

Still disappointed about the Jamaican survey and not finding the key to the mysteries locked in the data, I decided to do the whole thing over again, armed with my past Jamaican field experience and the help of some graduate students. Thus, in the fall of 1961 I returned to Jamaica, under a grant from the Carnegie Corporation of New York and with additional assistance from the Social Science Research Council, to study elites and nationalism not just in Jamaica, but also in Antigua, Barbados, British Guiana, Dominica, Grenada, and Trinidad and Tobago. With me were James T. Duke, James A. Mau, Charles C. Moskos, Jr., Andrew P. Phillips, and Ivar Oxaal.

Each of these wrote a doctoral dissertation from his West Indian field work, and the results of our work have been published. Ivar Oxaal and I prepared a summary monograph, *Decisions of Nationhood* (1964); I edited a collective effort, *The Democratic Revolution in the West Indies* (1967); Jim Duke completed *Equalitarianism Among Emergent Elites in a New Nation* (1963); Charlie Moskos wrote *The Sociology of Political Independence* (1967); Jim Mau portrays the pursuit of progress in Jamaica in *Social Change and Images of the Future* (1968); Pete Phillips finished his report on *The Development of a Modern Labor Force in Antigua* (1964); and Ivar Oxaal, in a superbly written book, describes the rise of the nationalist movement in Trinidad and Tobago in *Black Intellectuals Come to Power* (1968).[4] We would encounter severe local critics, especially among some West Indian radicals and authoritarians—the extremes at each end of the political spectrum—but we succeeded according to our own lights in doing a good job. This time, I felt that the thing had been done correctly.

Our arrival in the fall of 1961 was propitious. Independence hung over the British West Indies like a bright rising sun—or a dark cloud, depending on one's political persuasion—but it hung there. It dominated conversations nearly everywhere. We had thought that there was to be a West Indian nation comprising the ten island territories, but the West Indies Federation was near collapse. In September, 1961 a referendum held in Jamaica sealed its fate. Jamaica was to "go it alone" and was to become politically independent of the United Kingdom on August 6, 1962. Trinidad and Tobago became independent on August 31 of the same year, Guyana on May 26, 1966, and Barbados on November 30, 1966. The smaller islands were to receive not full independence but more internal autonomy. History was being made, and in the microcosm of the English-speaking Caribbean, global trends of the dismantlement of the European empires and the rise of third-world nationalism were being worked out, trends that were altering the face of Asia and Africa. With the exception of a few backwaters and cul-de-sacs, the transition from colonies to nation-states is now complete. The "age of nationalism" has been ushered in during the second half of the twentieth century, and today, on every continent, the characteristic and dominant form of political organization is the nation-state. We were indeed addressing ourselves to events of great moment. Could our sociology be made to raise questions equal to some part of their meaning? Could our methodology be made to answer questions of sufficient scope, depth, and consequence?

Our work in the British Caribbean represents our attempt to find answers in a series of case studies in the sociology of nationhood. Two key concepts will serve to briefly summarize our work: the democratic revolution and the decisions of nationhood.

THE DEMOCRATIC REVOLUTION

Our underlying thesis is that the rise of the new nations is part of the spread and development of the democratic revolution through time and space from the eighteenth-century Atlantic com-

[237]

munity to the twentieth-century global society. In his excellent two-volume (1959, 1964) work on *The Age of the Democratic Revolution,* R. R. Palmer attempts to summarize "what happened in the world of Western Civilization in the forty years from 1760 to 1800" and explores the meaning of these years for the subsequent history of mankind. His thesis is that the events of the eighteenth century should be seen:

> ... as a single movement, revolutionary in character, for which the word 'democratic' is appropriate and enlightening; a movement which, however different in different countries, was everywhere aimed against closed elites, self-selecting power groups, hereditary castes, and forms of special advantage or discrimination that no longer served any useful purpose. These were summed up in such terms as feudalism, aristocracy, and privilege, against which the idea of common citizenship in a more centralized state, or of common membership in a free political nation was offered as a more satisfactory basis for the human community [1964: 572].

Palmer uses the term "democratic" to refer to this movement because it was the last decade of the eighteenth century "that brought the word out of the study and into actual politics" (1959: 20). He points out that then the words "liberal," "radical," and "progressive" did not exist, and that when "moderates or conservatives wished to indicate the dangerous drift of the times, or when the more advanced spirits spoke of themselves, they might very well use the words 'democrat' or 'democracy' " (1959: 13-14).

Although the term included the political notion that "the possession of government, or any public power, by any established, privileged, closed, or self-recruiting groups of men" was wrong and that "the delegation of authority and the removability of officials" was right, it also "signified a new feeling for a new kind of equality, or at least a discomfort with older forms of social stratification and formal rank..." (1959: 4-5). In fact, the democratic movement had as an overriding central theme "the assertion of 'equality' as a prime social desideratum" (1964: 572). And the ideal of equality came to take on a variety of related meanings and to apply in many different situations, including that existing between colonials and residents of a mother country.

The word "revolution" he uses because the movement posed a conflict between incompatible images of the future, opposing views of what the community ought to be and what it was, because it included serious political protest, and because it involved a series of rapid changes that resulted in the reconstitution of government and society. Violence and destruction need not necessarily accompany a movement or situation for it to be called a "revolution," although, of course, brute force, civil war, and terror sometimes dominate the scene.

With very few exceptions, Palmer restricts his discussion to what is now called the Atlantic community, Europe and America (mostly Anglo-America) of the last forty years of the eighteenth century. In his last paragraph of his final volume, however, he suggests a wider application to all revolutions since 1800 in Europe, Latin America, Asia, and Africa. Our detailed studies of the new nations of the Caribbean should be seen in this broad framework. With the West Indies as a laboratory, we have tried to test the proposition that much of the political, economic, and social change going on throughout the world in the last half of the twentieth century can be understood as a continuation of the democratic revolution—especially as an extension of the drive toward equality—to which Europe and America of the latter part of the eighteenth century gave birth as a realizable human aspiration.

THE DECISIONS OF NATIONHOOD

Although we drew on concepts and theories from many sources, we formulated a conceptual framework which we call "the decisions of nationhood" within which all of our studies of leadership, nationalism, and the belief in progress can be placed. The framework derived from our research task of understanding the recruitment, socialization, and performance of new national leaders during the time of political transition from colony to nation-state. Despite the rapid and possibly confusing changes which occur during this period of "modernization," it is actually an excellent time in which to analyze and clarify just what, from a sociological standpoint, a nation-state is. The reason for this is simple: nation-states do not just happen, they are *made* to happen by men who must, if they are to be successful, at least implicitly pay heed to the organizational principles—the functional requisites and strains—inherent in this form of social organization. By the logic of the situation in which they find themselves, they are forced to cope, often simultaneously, with all of the issues which we have termed "the decisions of nationhood."

Our list of the decisions of nationhood, which we propose as a preliminary but widely applicable scheme with considerable analytic utility for the study of all new nations, is given below:

(1) *Should we become a politically independent nation?* This decision may have priority over all others in time, since the other decisions of nationhood may never arise if this one doesn't, and in importance, since the purpose and objectives behind the desire to create a politically independent state have implications for particular preferences with respect to the alternative outcomes of the other decisions.

(2) *How much national sovereignty should the new nation have?*

(3) *What should the geographical boundaries of the new nation be?*

(4) *Should the state and the nation be coterminous?* This question pertains to the degree of cultural homogeneity that the new state should strive to attain. Here, we use the term "state" in its legal and political sense in order to distinguish it from the cultural, linguistic, religious, or communal connotations often intended by the term "nation."

(5) *What form of government should the new nation have?* For the new nations of the twentieth century, the most important aspect of this question has been how much political democracy to have.

(6) *What role should the government play in the affairs of the society and of the economy?*

(7) *What should the new nation's external affairs be?*

(8) *What type of social structure should the new nation have?* The issue here usually resulted in a conflict between those persons who favored more egalitarian and socially inclusive social institutions and those who did not.

(9) *What should the new nation's cultural traditions be?*

(10) *What should the national character of the nation's people be?*

The distinctive feature of this approach is that it takes certain aspects of social reality that are usually accepted by sociologists as given and makes them problematic. The approach invites the study of the process of *becoming* and, as we shall see, of the emerging future. In the last three questions, for example, we have in a sense reversed the usual formulation of sociological, anthropological, and social-psychological research problems. That is, in fact, the whole point. Of course, we are well aware that the facts of the past leave any society in the present with a particular social structure, set of cultural traditions, and distinctive psychological types. New national leaders, no matter how divergent their aspirations for the future are from the actualities of the present, cannot create a new social order, a new culture, or a new basic personality structure among themselves and their people very quickly. Yet most of the new national leaders have set about the tasks of just so transforming their new states. It may take decades, more probably generations, but the effects of their policies can already be observed in many countries. Most of the new nationalist movements promised just such transformations.

We called these questions the "decisions of nationhood" because it was the transition to nationhood that raised the underlying questions, that molded the new elites who were to act as leaders in the decision-making process, and that altered the nature of the political community within which they were to be decided. The decisions are not such that once made they cannot be altered. The questions can be raised again and again in the life of a nation and different decisions reached. Nevertheless, the way the questions are resolved in the early life of a nation often sets the course for subsequent developments and in some cases may close the issue for generations.

Each of our studies was oriented toward finding the answers to one or more of the decisions of nationhood as they were being decided in the British Caribbean. Our most persistent focus was on the value contexts and conflicts surrounding the decisions. (There were, of course, as everywhere, opportunists as well as opponents and proponents to the democratic revolution in the West Indies.) The studies were thus related and interconnected, though they embraced a variety of data—questionnaires filled out by secondary school and university students, interviews with leaders of various sorts, interviews with sugar factory workers, participant-observation, a sample survey of urban slum dwellers, and intellectual histories of top nationalist leaders. The results are too numerous and complex to review here, but the reader may be referred to the published reports that are now available.[5]

An Experiment in Graduate Education

In 1966, after I had made a trip to the Caribbean that included visiting Ivar Oxaal who was then Professor and Head of the new Department of Sociology at the University of Guyana, a former student of mine took me aside at a publisher's party in Miami

Beach at the annual meetings of the American Sociological Association. Amidst smoke and alcohol and surrounded by herds of sweating, clacking sociologists, I got his simple, but detailed and well-documented message: I had failed him and others as a graduate teacher. He didn't have to tell me. Seven years earlier when my wife and I were planning the West Indies Study Program, I had reflected on my work with graduate students at Stanford and Northwestern. Some successes, a few losses, some indifferent results. It didn't seem good enough. Thus, I proposed to William Marvel, then of the Carnegie Corporation, not just another research project in the Caribbean, but one that would also include an experiment in graduate education. It was to be an experiment, however, in which there were no controls. We were simply going to try out a few things which on the basis of our experience seemed better than what was usually being done in graduate programs. My conclusion is that what we did worked pretty well, but there may be no single best way to arrange a graduate program. Each generation of students seems to come forward with its own special strengths and its own particular needs. Perhaps programs need to be flexible enough to permit each student in some respects to have a program tailor-made for him.

We established a series of workshops, one for the entire summer of 1960, that ran periodically throughout the life of the project quite in addition to other courses or seminars the five graduate student Fellows took. We brought a few West Indian leaders and scholars such as Vernon L. Arnett, Hugh W. Springer, and M. G. Smith to Los Angeles for intensive joint-interviewing sessions. We sought advice from American social scientists, such as George I. Blanksten, David A. Wilson, Russell Fitzgibbon, political scientist James S. Coleman, Karl W. Deutsch, and Reinhard Bendix. Before leaving Los Angeles we wrote lengthy workshop papers on the political, economic, and social structures and changes in each of the West Indian territories we were to study; we wrote summaries of the literature in the fields of social change, leadership, social stratification, and political modernization that were relevant to our

[243]

studies; and finally, among other things, we wrote preliminary proposals for our specific research projects to serve as flexible guides upon our arrival in the West Indies. And each of the Fellows agreed to spend a year or two more than it would have otherwise taken him to do his dissertation.

One of the distinctive educational features of our procedures was a more than routine attempt to integrate the total graduate school experience of the Fellows. The purpose behind this integration was to construct an individualized Ph.D. program for each of the Fellows that would be more purposive, more meaningful, more directed (allowing for less floundering around), and perhaps somewhat more ambitious than the usual Ph.D. program. Such an integration, of course, would not have been possible without the cooperation of many persons at UCLA, including the faculty of the Department of Anthropology and Sociology and to a lesser extent of the Department of Political Science as well. It was also made easier since I occupied the dual roles of Director of the West Indies Study Program and Chairman of each of the Fellows' doctoral committees. The procedure was as follows:

First, the attempt to create a sense of group purpose and unity through frequent formal and informal association.

Second, at an early stage of the graduate students' careers, the selection of the general subject matter of the dissertations they would later write.

Third, from available seminars and courses in the regular program, the selection of those that represented the most advantageous background in theory and method from the viewpoint of the projected dissertation topic.

Fourth, the deliberate exploitation of every course and seminar taken by the Fellows so as to squeeze everything possible from them relevant to the Fellows' proposed dissertations. We held regular discussions in our workshops in which the Fellows reviewed their work in courses and seminars as it related to the general theoretical and methodological problems of studying leadership and political change in emergent nations.

[244]

Fifth, some integration of the Fellows' thinking during their preliminary written and oral examinations for the Ph.D., which was accomplished by giving each Fellow, about a month before the written examination, a theme that would be woven into all the examinations and that related to the general theory underlying the ideas behind his proposed dissertation topic.

Sixth, a further integration of the Fellows' knowledge of the theory and method of sociology as the Fellows prepared their formal, written dissertation proposals prior to going to the field. These were discussed not only in our workshops but also with other faculty members, especially other members of the Fellows' doctoral committees.

Seventh, consultation with me and others in the field as the Fellows started collecting their data, during which time their prior proposals more or less changed as they learned about the actual situation that confronted them. Very flexible use was made both of commitment to their own prior research goals and sometimes to easily forgotten reference groups of doctoral committee members waiting back at UCLA. At one point we held a three-day workshop in Jamaica when Raymond W. Mack and Richard C. Snyder from Northwestern University joined us, evaluated our progress, and advised us regarding revisions in our conceptions and data collections.

Eighth, after field work was completed, a year of workshops and seminars back at UCLA that included from time to time participation by UCLA faculty members—such as Eshref Shevky and Anthony Oberschall, Caribbean scholars, graduate students from the West Indies, and a West Indian leader, in addition to the Fellows and myself. These discussions focused on the particular interpretations the Fellows were making of their data and on the unifying themes underlying all the studies, and they occurred while the Fellows were analyzing their data and doing the preliminary writing of their dissertations.

Ninth, although we were engaged upon a collective enterprise, we organized our research tasks so that each graduate student did a complete research project from beginning to end himself. Thus, unlike the San Francisco neighborhood studies where many persons contributed parts to a single overall whole, our strategy in the Caribbean research was to have a solo dimension to it and we tried to have a series of single wholes distributed to particular persons, but to have them add up to something. This procedure had the advantage of dividing responsibility in such a way that each person in the last analysis did not have to rely on anyone else for what was to be each person's own research report.

We did the above, and more, in a conscious effort to make every task or requirement a Fellow entered into as a graduate student relevant not simply to his obtaining the Ph.D. degree (in. fact we deliberately opposed the instrumental careerism increasingly characteristic of many graduate schools in the United States), but also to his own perception of the nature of the specific research contribution he was hoping to make as well as to his more basic values as a human being. I tried to put into practice all that I believed that I had learned about graduate teaching before. We strove for value relevance in our research as well as scientific excellence. I sought to convince the Fellows to live in the present and not to think of the dissertation as a time to get over with quickly so that they could "begin to live" afterwards. I asked them not to lift their hand to do anything in connection with our program that they did not believe was worthy. No expedient research decisions were to be made. As soon as we started that, I feared that cynicism and poor work would follow. I stressed the importance of cumulative research and the apprenticeship role. I did what I could to help them in the transition to professional status, especially during out-of-the-office situations trying to reveal what the total life experiences of sociologists were like. My wife and I gave endlessly of our time and much individual attention. Finally, I tried to be an exemplar. This, of course, was the most difficult principle of all. Each of us becomes cynical, depressed, or disillusioned upon occasion. I tried to keep such feelings to myself.

I don't really know how successful all of this was, since we didn't do a proper experiment. Perhaps the secret of graduate education is simply to be lucky, have good graduate students, and spend time with them.

Before leaving discussion of the West Indies Study Program, I should say three other things about it. First, I learned as much or more than the graduate students involved. I would never have been able to write *Jamaican Leaders* without their help. We may not need a scorecard to tell the teachers from the students, but certainly the flow of ideas runs both ways. Although I learned much from each of the Fellows, there are still talents they possess that I can only respect, not duplicate in my own behavior—for example, Charles Moskos' ability to establish instant rapport whether with West Indians or, as he was to do later in another study, American soldiers in the bunkers of Vietnam.

Second, we were all greatly influenced by the four West Indians who came to UCLA under our program to do graduate work: Trinidadian Andrew G. J. Comacho, now on the faculty of the University of the West Indies in Trinidad; Guyanese Neville W. Layne, who would be associated with Ivar Oxaal in the Department at the University of Guyana; Trinidadian Anthony Maingot, who is now Assistant Professor of Sociology and History at Yale and who with Kai T. Erikson is part of our effort to link sociology and history; and Barbadian Dudley E. Parris, who is coming to Yale to help establish a curriculum in Afro-American studies.

Third, the exploitation of the former colonial world by the industrially advanced nations goes on. We went to study the West Indies and West Indian leaders, we stayed to be taught by both, especially by Jamaican Vernon L. Arnett. My present and future sociological efforts cannot help reflecting my West Indian research experiences.

Images of the Future

In 1964, after spending a year as a Fellow at the Center for

[247]

Advanced Study in the Behavioral Sciences, where I continued working with by-then-Dr. Charles C. Moskos, Jr., I moved to Yale. I was attracted to Yale for a variety of reasons, despite the fact that there may have been differences between some aspects of my style, personality, and temperament—and possibly political persuasion—and the senior Yale sociologists at the time. I was a Westerner unfamiliar with the ways of the East and the Ivy League. But the first course in sociology taught anywhere in the world had been given by William Graham Sumner at Yale in 1875 (see Kennedy, 1961). There was a great tradition, and in my talk with then-Provost Kingman Brewster, Jr., I was led to believe that Yale sociology was in line for strengthening, and I was challenged by the opportunity to work with the Yale sociologists in expanding the department, which we are now in the process of doing. Part of the tradition was a concern with both historical and cross-cultural and comparative studies. My West Indian research experience had convinced me that American sociology was parochial and needed more both historical and comparative perspectives. Today, under my chairmanship, Yale sociology is trying to bring about closer ties with the humanities, especially history, and to add to our already established programs distinction in area and comparative studies.

Yale sociology for some time (from the days of Maurice R. Davie) had been characterized by a combination of rigorous scientific method and a concentration upon practical, value-relevant problems. Although Davie had retired, the most established part of the department when I came, Medical Sociology, under the direction of A. B. Hollingshead and Jerome K. Myers, was continuing this tradition. Such a combination fit my own convictions.

Based upon his research in New Haven, Davie had written one of the original critiques of the Burgess concentric zone theory of urban growth and other aspects of the Chicago school of human ecology. Thus, although I had never known Davie personally, there was a congeniality in perspective in the department with my own uneasiness with some of the theoretical assumptions of the Chicago school and with my own work in social area analysis. Furthermore,

Jerry Myers had earlier worked with some of the same problems on census tract statistics, and Lee L. Bean had contributed two interesting studies to the social area literature. Finally, I still held my aspirations to become a political sociologist, and Yale had the top department of political science in the country.

By a year, Jim Mau preceded me to Yale, where he is now an associate professor as well as Assistant Dean of the Graduate School, and we have continued our collaboration. In addition to the democratic revolution and the decisions of nationhood, there was a third organizing principle in our West Indian studies: the concept of images of the future, for which we are indebted to Dutch sociologist Frederik L. Polak (1961), economist Kenneth E. Boulding (1956), and political scientist Harold D. Lasswell (Eulau, 1958), who is now our co-participant in the new Yale Collegium on the Future. Mau and I are trying to state at an abstract and general level a theory of social change and a set of strategies for the scientific study of the future. Primarily, we are generalizing what we learned from our particular studies of decision-makers, images of the future, and the social contexts of decision-making in the West Indies, so that the theories and strategies may be applied to other sociological problems and different institutional settings.[6] The principles of nation-building can be applied with profit to understanding the processes—no! the *acts*—of creating, maintaining, changing, or destroying social institutions and organizations of any kind. Thus, at the most abstract level we seek the answers to questions such as: How does society, including its institutions and organizations, come to be what it is? How can it become something else? How and why do structuring, restructuring, and destructuring occur? What are the alternative future possibilities for society? What choices do people have and how do they go about making them? How can society and social changes be brought under greater control and made to serve better the needs and hopes of man? Building on our own earlier work and the prior work of others—especially that of Wilbert E. Moore—we are now beginning to sketch a broad framework of concepts and theory

[249]

that may help in the search for the answers.

A few Yale graduate students are extending our work. Arvin W. Murch (1967), now a postdoctoral fellow in France, has done an excellent study of the French Antilles, comparing his results to those reported by Charlie Moskos on the British West Indies. Menno Boldt and Bettina Huber have contributed chapters to *The Study of the Future*, and Boldt is now in Canada planning a study of French Canadian nationalism while Huber is studying images of the future among 800 white South African elites. Joseph Landis is nearly finished with a book on the sociopolitical history of Guyana that invites comparison with Ivar Oxaal's earlier work in Trinidad. Steve Alger has studied images of the future among scientists and humanists at three American universities and Janet Merrill (Alger) is completing her comparative, sociohistorical study of the American revolutionary war and the decisions of nationhood on which the United States was founded.

Charles Moskos is now an Associate Professor of Sociology at Northwestern University with Scott Greer, John Kitsuse, and Ray Mack. Ivar Oxaal—after putting our forthcoming research strategies for studying the future and our directives for social science responsibility into action as head of a team investigating wildcat strikes at a bauxite company sixty-five miles up the Demerara River in Guyana—is, at the time of writing (1968), at the Russell Sage Foundation writing a book on Negro executives in a white world, and next year will be at the Institute for Advanced Study at Princeton.

Reviewing the past twenty-five years of my life, as I've had to do to write this, I realize that I have had, like most people, many lives. In my late teens and early twenties I was a naval aviator and aide to a Task Unit Commander in the Philippines. Right after World War II, I was a flight instructor, charter pilot, and stunt flyer; then, ironically, a life insurance underwriter. I've been an urban sociologist, and a political sociologist. I've been a student, a teacher, and a departmental chairman. And if I may indulge myself, I've been a horseman, riding over the heaths and downs of

England, the sugarcane fields of Barbados, and the countryside of the United States wherever a willing mount, a flat saddle, open land, and something to jump can be found. This is, of course, not to mention the many odd jobs, and the roles of son, husband, and father.

I hope there will be more. The wise thing for me to do next would be to move toward synthesis and general theory, if I have it in me. Certainly, there is need for both, especially in the face of the tremendous increase in information that now threatens to engulf us. Yet I confess, even today, to having something of that old restless itch and a slight yearning to live a bit dangerously again. Friends are appalled; enemies chortle. But with a bit of luck, perhaps my next decade of research will be with Eduardo Mondlane's guerrillas in the bush of Mozambique,[7] with Charlie Moskos studying the withdrawal of American troops from Vietnam, with Ivar Oxaal heading up the Demerara River, or on the streets of American cities with Scott Greer. That is, with a bit of luck.

NOTES

1. For example, see: Bell (1955a), Bell and Greer (1962), Bell and Moskos (1964), Duncan (1955a, 1955b), Hawley and Duncan (1957), Schnore (1962), Tiebout (1958), and Van Arsdol et al. (1961, 1962).

2. There is insufficient space here to review the findings of the San Francisco surveys. However, such a review with a fairly complete bibliography of the published reports may be found in Bell (1965).

3. Bell and Willis (1957) applied the index to the 1950 census data for all tracted American cities. In an excellent methodological appendix, the Taeubers (1965) compare my index in its normalized form with other indexes that have been proposed to measure residential segregation.

4. Additionally, a number of articles have been published which are cited in the books just listed.

5. In this discussion I have followed Bell and Oxaal (1967a, 1967b).

6. A brief summary of this work will soon be available. See Bell and Mau (forthcoming).

7. Since this was written, the head of Frelimo was assassinated in Dar es Salaam.

REFERENCES

BELL, W. (1968) "The city, the suburb, and a theory of social choice." Pp. 132-68 in S. Greer et al., The New Urbanization. New York: St. Martin's Press.

——— (1965) "Urban neighborhoods and individual behavior." Pp. 235-64 in M. and C. Sherif (eds.) Problems of Youth. Chicago: Aldine.

——— (1964) Jamaican Leaders: Political Attitudes in a New Nation. Berkeley: University of California Press.

——— (1960a) "Attitudes of Jamaican elites toward the West Indies Federation." Annals of the New York Academy of Science 3 (January): 862-79.

——— (1960b) "Images of the United States and the Soviet Union held by Jamaican elite groups." World Politics 12 (January): 225-48.

——— (1959) "Social areas: typology of urban neighborhoods." Pp. 61-92 in M. B. Sussman (ed.) Community Structure and Analysis. New York: Thomas Y. Crowell.

——— (1958) "Social choice, life styles, and suburban residence." Pp. 225-45 in W. Dobriner (ed.) The Suburban Community. New York: G. P. Putnam.

——— (1956) "Familism and suburbanization: one test of the social choice hypothesis." Rural Sociology 21 (September-December): 276-83.

——— (1955a) "Comment on Duncan's review of 'Social Area Analysis.' " American Journal of Sociology 61 (November): 260-61.

——— (1955b) "Economic, family, and ethnic status: an empirical test." American Sociological Review 20 (February): 45-52.

——— (1954) "A probability model for the measurement of ecological segregation." Social Forces 32 (May): 357-64.

——— (1953) "The social areas of the San Francisco Bay region." American Sociological Review 18 (February): 39-47.

——— (1952) A Comparative Study in the Methodology of Urban Analysis. Ph.D. dissertation, University of California at Los Angeles.

——— [ed.] (1967) The Democratic Revolution in the West Indies: Studies in Nationalism, Leadership, and the Belief in Progress. Cambridge, Mass.: Schenkman.

BELL, W. and S. GREER (1962) " 'Social Area Analysis' and its critics." Pacific Sociological Review 5 (Spring): 3-9.

BELL, W. and J. MAU (forthcoming) "Images of the future: theory and research strategies." In J. McKinney and E. Tiryakian (eds.) Theoretical Sociology: Perspectives and Developments. New York: Appleton-Century-Crofts.

BELL, W. and C. MOSKOS, JR. (1964) "A comment on Udry's 'Increasing scale and spatial differentiation.' " Social Forces 42 (May): 414-17.

BELL, W. and I. OXAAL (1967a) "Introduction." Pp. 1-19 in W. Bell (ed.) The Democratic Revolution in the West Indies. Cambridge, Mass.: Schenkman.

——— (1967b) "The nation-state as a unit in the comparative study of social change." Pp. 169-81 in W. E. Moore and R. M. Cook (eds.) Readings in Social Change. Englewood Cliffs, N.J.: Prentice-Hall.

——— (1964) Decisions on Nationhood: Political and Social Development in the British Caribbean. Denver: Social Science Foundation, University of Denver.

BELL, W. and E. M. WILLIS (1957) "The segregation of Negroes in American cities: a comparative analysis." Social and Economic Studies 6 (March): 39-75.

BELL, W. et al. (1961) Public Leadership. San Francisco: Chandler.

BOULDING, K. (1956) The Image: Knowledge in Life and Society. Ann Arbor: University of Michigan Press.

BROOM, L. et al. (1955) "Characteristics of 1,107 petitioners for change of name." American Sociological Review 20 (February): 33-39.

DUKE, J. T. (1963) Equalitarianism Among Emergent Elites in a New Nation. Ph.D. dissertation, University of California at Los Angeles.

DUNCAN, O. D. (1955a) "Reply to Bell." American Journal of Sociology 61 (November): 261-62.

——— (1955b) "A review of 'Social Area Analysis.' " American Journal of Sociology 61 (July): 84-85.

EULAU, H. (1958) "H. D. Lasswell's developmental analysis." Western Political Quarterly 11 (June): 229-42.

GREER, S. et al. (1968) The New Urbanization. New York: St. Martin's Press.

HALL, N. (1962) Similarity of Social Characteristics and Neighboring Behavior: A Study of Four Metropolitan Neighborhoods." Ph.D. dissertation, University of California at Los Angeles.

HAWLEY, A. and O. D. DUNCAN (1957) " 'Social Area Analysis': a critical appraisal." Land Economics 33 (November): 337-45.

HYNEMAN, C. (1959) The Study of Politics: The Present State of American Political Science. Urbana: University of Illinois Press.

KAUFMAN, W. C. (1961) A Factor-Analytic Test of Revisions in the Shevky-Bell Typology for Chicago and San Francisco, 1950. Ph.D. dissertation, Northwestern University.

KENNEDY, R. J. [ed.] (1961) "The nature and scope of sociology as conceived at Yale." Pp. 3-12 in The Papers of Maurice R. Davie. New Haven: Yale University Press.

MAU, J. (1968) Social Change and Images of the Future: A Study of the Pursuit of Progress in Jamaica. Cambridge, Mass.: Schenkman.

――― et al. (1961) "Scale analyses of status perception and status attitude in Jamaica and the United States." Pacific Sociological Review 4 (Spring): 33-40.

MEIER, D. L. (1962) Anomie, Life Chances, Perceived Achievement, and Modes of Adaptation. Ph.D. dissertation, University of California at Los Angeles.

――― (1957) Anomie and Structural Accessibility to Achievement. M.A. thesis, Northwestern University.

――― and W. BELL (1959) "Anomie and differential access to the achievement of life goals." American Sociological Review 24 (April): 189-202.

MOSKOS, C. C., JR. (1967) The Sociology of Political Independence. Cambridge, Mass.: Schenkman.

MURCH, A. W. (1967) Political Integration as an Alternative to Independence in the French Antilles. Ph.D. dissertation, Yale University.

OXAAL, I. (1968) Black Intellectuals Come to Power: The Rise of Creole Nationalism in Trinidad and Tobago. Cambridge, Mass.: Schenkman.

PALMER, R. R. (1964) The Age of the Democratic Revolution: A Political History of Europe and America, 1760-1800; The Struggle. Princeton: Princeton University Press.

――― (1959) The Age of the Democratic Revolution: A Political History of Europe and America, 1760-1800; The Challenge. Princeton: Princeton University Press.

PHILLIPS, A. P. (1964) The Development of a Modern Labor Force in Antigua. Ph.D. dissertation, University of California at Los Angeles.

POLAK, F. L. (1961) The Image of the Future: Enlightening the Past, Orienting the Present, Forecasting the Future. New York: Oceana.

POLK, K. (1957) The Social Areas of San Diego. M.A. thesis, Northwestern University.

RIESMAN, D. (1958) "The suburban sadness." Pp. 375-408 in W. Dobriner (ed.) The Suburban Community. New York: G. P. Putnam.

SCHNORE, L. F. (1962) "Another comment on 'Social Area Analysis.' "
Pacific Sociological Review 5 (Spring): 13-15.

SHEVKY, E. and W. BELL (1955) Social Area Analysis. Stanford: Stanford
University Press.

SHEVKY, E. and M. WILLIAMS (1949) The Social Areas of Los Angeles:
Analysis and Typology. Berkeley: University of California Press.

SMITH, E. R. (1957) "Self-Government and the Political Elite in Jamaica,
1939 and 1954." M.A. thesis, Northwestern University.

TAEUBER, K. and A. TAEUBER (1965) Negroes in Cities. Chicago: Aldine.

TIEBOUT, D. M. (1958) "Hawley and Duncan on 'Social Area Analysis': a
comment." Land Economics 34 (May): 182-84.

TRYON, R. C. (1955) Identification of Social Areas by Cluster Analysis.
Berkeley: University of California Press.

VAN ARSDOL, M. D., JR., et al. (1962) "Further comments on the utility of
urban typology." Pacific Sociological Review 5 (Spring): 9-13.

——— (1961) "An investigation of the utility of urban typology." Pacific
Sociological Review 4 (Spring): 26-32.

WILLIS, E. M. (1956) "A Comparative Study of Negro Segregation in American Cities." M.A. thesis, Northwestern University.